Midnight in Tehran

Midnight in Tehran

*Operation Long Jump,
the Nazi Plot to Assassinate
Roosevelt, Churchill and Stalin*

CHRISTOPHER SANDFORD

McFarland & Company, Inc., Publishers
Jefferson, North Carolina

LIBRARY OF CONGRESS CATALOGUING-IN-PUBLICATION DATA

Names: Sandford, Christopher, 1956– author.
Title: Midnight in Tehran : Operation Long Jump, the Nazi plot to assassinate Roosevelt, Churchill and Stalin / Christopher Sandford.
Other titles: Operation Long Jump, the Nazi plot to assassinate Roosevelt, Churchill and Stalin
Description: Jefferson, North Carolina : McFarland & Company Publishers, Inc., 2023. | Includes bibliographical references and index.
Identifiers: LCCN 2023022510 | ISBN 9781476687568 (paperback : acid free paper) ∞ ISBN 9781476649511 (ebook)
Subjects: LCSH: Operation Long Jump, 1943. | World War, 1939-1945—Secret service—Germany. | Conspiracies—Iran—Tehran—History—20th century. | Conspiracies—Germany—History—20th century. | Teheran Conference (1943 : Tehran, Iran) | Roosevelt, Franklin D. (Franklin Delano), 1882-1945. | Stalin, Joseph, 1878-1953. | Churchill, Winston, 1874-1965.
Classification: LCC D810.S7 S2395 2023 | DDC 940.53/141—dc23/eng/20230517
LC record available at https://lccn.loc.gov/2023022510

BRITISH LIBRARY CATALOGUING DATA ARE AVAILABLE

ISBN (print) 978-1-4766-8756-8
ISBN (ebook) 978-1-4766-4951-1

© 2023 Christopher Sandford. All rights reserved

No part of this book may be reproduced or transmitted in any form or by any means, electronic or mechanical, including photocopying or recording, or by any information storage and retrieval system, without permission in writing from the publisher.

Front cover image: Tehran Conference, November-December 1943, the strategy meeting of Premier Joseph Stalin, President Franklin D. Roosevelt, and Prime Minister Winston Churchill at the Russian Embassy at Tehran, Iran. U.S. Army photograph from the collection of the Office of War Information. Courtesy of the Library of Congress, Naval History and Heritage Command, National Museum of the U.S. Navy.

Printed in the United States of America

McFarland & Company, Inc., Publishers
  Box 611, Jefferson, North Carolina 28640
    www.mcfarlandpub.com

To Pete Barnes

For gluttony and drunkenness, hunger and thirst, wenching and dicing and playing, riot and roaring, murdering and being murdered, torturing and being tortured: in a word, hurting and harming, and in turn being hurt and harmed—this was their whole life.
—Hans Jakob von Grimmelshausen,
Simplicius Simplicissimus (1668)

Those enemy chiefs who [can] see reason, will see reason. Those who can't will receive the logical treatment.
—Heinrich Himmler (1942)

Acknowledgments

It's a pleasure to thank Governor Jay Inslee and other high officials of Washington, where I mostly live, whose accordion-style cycle of lockdowns and other restraints at least afforded the opportunity to write a third or fourth successive book since the pandemic first struck. If nothing else, it's interesting to note the comparison between the priorities of the state authorities and others depicted in the pages that follow and those of our current national and local rulers, transformed as the latter have been since 2020 into a sort of sanitary dictatorship devoted to the religion of health. Nonetheless, it goes without saying that neither our political masters, nor any of the names listed below, can be blamed for the shortcomings of the text. They are mine alone.

For archive material, input, or advice, I should thank, professionally, AbeBooks; Acton Institute; Alibris; *America*; the Bodleian Library, Oxford; Bookfinder; the *Brazen Head*; the British Library; British Newspaper Library; Central Lutheran; Common Ground; the Cricket Society; the *Daily Mail*; Dwight D. Eisenhower Presidential Library, Abilene, Kansas; Emerald Downs; the FBI Freedom of Information Division; Franklin D. Roosevelt Presidential Library and Museum, Hyde Park, New York; the General Register Office, London; *Hedgehog Review*; the History Press; Imran Khan; Barbara Levy; Library of Congress; Dylan Lightfoot; the Mitchell Library, Glasgow; *Modern Age*; National Security Archives; *The Oldie*; Charlie Perdue; the Radleian Society; Renton Public Library; Seaside Library, Oregon; the Seeley Library, Cambridge; HM King Simeon of Bulgaria; *The Spectator*; UK National Archives; University of Washington; U.S. National Archives and Records Administration; U.S. State Department, Office of the Historian; Vital Records; and the late Aaron Wolf.

And personally, the Rev. Maynard Atik; Pete Barnes; Rob Boddie; Robert and Hilary Bruce; Don Carson; Monty Dennison; the Dowdall family; Barbara and the late John Dungee; Steve Fossen; Malcolm Galfe; Steve and Jo Hackett; Duncan Hamilton; Alastair Hignell; Alex Holmes; Jo Jacobius; Jo Johnson; Lincoln Kamell; Terry Lambert; Belinda

Lawson; Todd Linse; the Lorimer family; Les McBride, Dan McCarthy; the late Charles McIntosh; the Macris; Lee Mattson; Jerry Miller; the Morgans; Colleen and the late John Murray; Greg Nowak; the late Chuck Ogmund; Robin and Lucinda Parish; Owen Paterson; Roman Polanski; the Prins family; the late Malcolm Robinson; Ailsa Rushbrooke; Rupert Rushbrooke; the late Sefton Sandford; Peter Scaramanga; Fred and Cindy Smith; the Smith family; David Starkey; Jack Surendranath; Matt Thacker; the late Ben and Mary Tyvand; Diana Villar; the late Charlie Watts; Rogena and the late Alan White; Debbie Wild; the Willis Fleming family; Heng and Lang Woon; the Zombies.

The book's index was kindly prepared by Robin B. James, and my deepest thanks, as always, to Karen and Nicholas Sandford.

Contents

Acknowledgments   vii

1. Unconditional Surrender   1
2. The Peacock Realm   32
3. "One Wonders about the Wrestlers"   57
4. Agent Cicero   82
5. Gathering Shadows   116
6. "The Greatest Surfeit and Concentration of Power Ever Seen"   135
7. Zero Time   160

Chapter Notes   199
Bibliography   209
Index   211

1

Unconditional Surrender

President Franklin D. Roosevelt's comparatively rare press conferences often had a quixotic charm, and you could never quite tell how much he was laughing at himself. So it was, anyway, on the sunny afternoon of Friday, December 17, 1943, when the 61-year-old head of state summoned half a dozen favored reporters to the Oval Office to brief them on the recent high-level Allied conferences in Cairo and Tehran. The polio-stricken president sat in a wheelchair discreetly tucked behind his heavy walnut-veneered desk, which was flanked by a furled American flag on a brass pole with a plastic eagle on top. Gazing around the room, Roosevelt's visitors would have seen solid, confidence-inspiring furniture in dark mahogany, a faux marble fireplace, several framed nautical prints on the walls, and shelves full of biblical texts, classical poetry anthologies, and bound government manuals whose dark leather spines and gold lettering also signaled a certain gravitas. Roosevelt still projected the strong, indomitable good cheer of his public image, the familiar cigarette holder clenched jauntily in his teeth, although the more observant of his guests would have noticed that he had lost weight and seemed to have trouble focusing on the prepared statement on the desk in front of him, instead ad-libbing, to the obvious consternation of his staff, as he struggled to read the closely typed text. The president had once told Orson Welles that they were the two hardest-working actors in America.

Under the arresting headline "STALIN BARED PLOT AGAINST PRESIDENT," the next day's *New York Times* conveyed Roosevelt's remarks as follows:

WASHINGTON, Dec. 17—President Roosevelt disclosed today what the Russians said was a plot endangering his life at Tehran, the knowledge of which caused him to move his residence from the American Legation to the Soviet Embassy.

Mr. Roosevelt, mentioning the matter during his press conference in discussing the need for security, did not say specifically whether the plot was aimed at all three Allied leaders meeting in Tehran, although he implied as much.

> While the President was at the American Legation on his first night at Tehran, Premier Stalin sent word to him of a plot and urged him to move over to the Soviet Mission, adjoining the British, which housed Prime Minister Winston Churchill, in the same compound.
>
> The President observed that in a place like Tehran there probably were hundreds of German spies around, and it would have been a pretty good haul for the Germans if they could have gotten all three of the conferees while they were going through the streets.[1]

And that was all the paper had to say on the subject. There had been some muffled laughter in the room when Roosevelt made these last remarks, as though the great showman was treating his audience to one of his characteristic quips. According to the official transcript, the president had "chuckled" as he reflected on his recent adventures in the Iranian capital. There had been no follow-up questions from the members of the press, and in short order they had been ushered out to resume their rich and exemplary private lives in Friday night Washington. Roosevelt's veteran news secretary Stephen Early personally escorted the group off the premises and down to the Northeast Gate on Pennsylvania Avenue. The *Times* correspondent later remarked that their host had been "extremely genial," displaying "many of his own chief's skills as a communicator" before waving them goodbye. Perhaps Early had simply been relieved that the whole exercise ended as it did. Back then, before the days when government press officers came to resemble celebrity publicists, spoon-feeding narratives to compliant scribes, there was always at least the chance that the commander-in-chief would go spectacularly off-message.

Had Roosevelt meant merely to gently kid his guests on that unseasonably mild December afternoon, some wondered, when, after all the hardship and sacrifice of the early war years, it seemed that what the president had called the "gloomy thunder" of events was finally lifting, and the tide turning in the Allies' favor? After all, Roosevelt knew, even if the journalists didn't, that plans were already afoot for the climactic invasion of Europe, then scheduled for the early spring of 1944, and that according to the timetable a million Allied troops would be on the ground in northern France within a month of the initial landing, thus beginning the decisive battle in the West. Possibly, too, a hint of oriental intrigue of the sort conjured by the image of scores of Nazi agents swarming the narrow alleys and chaotic, aromatic bazaars of wartime Tehran was almost to inspire a sense of nostalgia in the president, particularly now that he was back in the comparative safety of the White House. Or, equally likely, perhaps Roosevelt simply hadn't appreciated the true extent of the danger, nor of the ease with which German intelligence continued to intercept high-level Allied traffic, such as the supposedly secure phone call between the president's closest adviser Harry Hopkins and Winston Churchill (using the codename John Martin) on October 9, 1943, in order to confirm Roosevelt's attendance at the Tehran conference. The call ended at 8:00 p.m., central European time, and at 9:15 that same night Walter Schellenberg of the Sicherheitsdienst (SD), the principal security agency of the SS, handed his führer a pink slip, which stated simply: "American and English heads will meet. Possibility of liquidation."

The full transcript Adolf Hitler read that night was both almost comically banal, as though merely reporting on two old friends finalizing some social arrangements, and yet momentous in its implications for the future direction of the war.

> **CHURCHILL:** John here.
> **HOPKINS:** Yes.
> **CHURCHILL:** Can you give me any hopeful answer?
> **HOPKINS:** Yes.
> **CHURCHILL:** Good.

After that there appears to have been some static on the line because Churchill could be heard to say only that something could be "free, open, and…" and the other party to reply "Yes" several times before the conversation resumed:

> **HOPKINS:** The note has not yet gone, but it will be sent.
> **CHURCHILL:** I see, good.
> **HOPKINS:** Is that all right?
> **CHURCHILL:** Yes.
> **HOPKINS:** All right. Goodbye.
> **CHURCHILL:** Goodbye.[2]

The boyish-looking, black-uniformed Walter Schellenberg was then just 33, but already commanded much of Germany's espionage network, both in the Reich and throughout the conquered territories. He worked eighteen hours a day, primarily out of an anonymous brick-and-concrete building in south Berlin. Schellenberg's office was on the fourth floor, and furnished by a colonnade of four mock Grecian pillars and two elaborately lit portraits of Hitler, one in a brown uniform and one in black, on either side of a framed swastika ensign. The spy chief sometimes entertained visitors by pressing a button under his desk, which caused the panel on the wall behind him to slide open. It revealed a steel-helmeted soldier sitting on a campstool at the controls of an MG 34 light machine gun mounted on a tripod. The barrel of the gun was pointed directly at the visitor's head. "One cannot conduct a war without making enemies," Schellenberg liked to remark.

Schellenberg's principal colleague and frequent rival was Admiral

Wilhelm Canaris, the silver-haired chief of the Abwehr, or German military intelligence. Though initially committed to the Nazi cause, the latter would increasingly come to doubt the soundness of their führer's judgment. On July 23, 1944, three days after the failure of the officers' plot to assassinate Hitler and assume control, Schellenberg would personally arrest Canaris, who perished in a concentration camp shortly before the end of the war. His final words on walking to the gallows were "I die for my Fatherland. I have a clean conscience. I only did my duty for my country when I tried to oppose the criminal folly of Hitler leading Germany to destruction."³ Canaris was 58 at the time of his execution. Schellenberg survived the hostilities, but was later arrested by the British and testified against the Nazi leadership at the postwar Nuremberg trials. He served two years in prison and later moved to Italy, where he died in 1952, either of liver cancer, or, as some believed, the effects of poison administered by one or more of his numerous enemies. He was 42.

The principal architect of Operation Long Jump, Walter Schellenberg.

* * *

It would be wrong to suggest that the summit under discussion by Churchill and Hopkins in October 1943 was seen merely as a sort of technical forum intended to consolidate the remorseless Allied successes on the battlefield. The overall war situation was fluid, to euphemistically describe the daily carnage in both the European and Pacific theaters, and significant differences remained among the Big Three leaders. The conference held between Churchill and Roosevelt at Casablanca the previous January had only added to their absent colleague Stalin's impatience to launch a second front and thus relieve the pressure on his severely taxed

1. Unconditional Surrender

Soviet forces. He was not impressed to be told that the long-awaited invasion might be further postponed until as late as the spring of 1944, nor entirely convinced by the progress of Anglo-American operations elsewhere. In a terse exchange of cables with Roosevelt in March 1943, Stalin claimed that while the Allied advance in North Africa was at "a standstill," the Germans had taken the opportunity to move 36 further divisions into the Russian heartland. He insisted that a planned Anglo-American attack on Sicily could not replace a full-scale campaign to liberate northern France, that further delay would be "a serious danger," and that "the vagueness of your [Roosevelt's] statement about the opening of a second front in Europe provokes alarm which I cannot suppress."4

Of course, pessimism among the Allied heads of government, extending to anguished doubts about their collective military and civilian resources, and general ability to stay the course, was nothing new. Flying back and forth across the English Channel in the frenzied atmosphere of June 1940, at a time when the French still fleetingly held their shoulders against a front line being battered by the invading Germans, Churchill had begged Roosevelt to issue a public statement of support—and more pertinently, a supply of arms—to the beleaguered Allies. Roosevelt refused. Churchill in turn felt moved to offer a note of reproach to his "strangely fickle friend" in the White House. "I understand all your difficulties with American public opinion and Congress, but events are moving downward at a pace where they will pass beyond the control of public opinion when at last it is ripened.... This moment is supremely critical for the world. A declaration that the United States will if necessary enter the war might save the

Wilhelm Canaris, the obfuscating Abwehr chief who went defiantly to his death in April 1945.

day. Failing that, in a few days French resistance may have crumbled, and we shall be left alone."⁵

Which is what happened.

Churchill was understandably distressed at what he called "the threat to Christian civilization.... If [Britain] fails, then the whole world, including the United States, and all that we have known and cared for, will sink into the abyss of a new dark age made more sinister, and perhaps more prolonged, by the lights of a perverted science."

There were perhaps less eloquent but equally profound expressions of the undoubted pressure of world events elsewhere in the 65-year-old prime minister's household. After retiring to bed later that same night with a large box of official documents, Churchill was "furious," his secretary Jock Colville wrote, at the Americans' equivocation. "In his emotion, he upset his whisky and soda over all his papers."⁶

While the Atlantic alliance would happily recover much of its old luster in the months following the catastrophic shock of the Japanese attack on Pearl Harbor, and the subsequent American declaration of war against the Axis, Churchill and Roosevelt continued to regularly disparage each other's strategic vision. A further coup for Nazi interests came in the fissure between the Western Powers and Russia, enough in mid-1943 to encourage Hitler's belief that, if he held out, his enemies' conflicting ends would lead to a diplomatic crisis in the Alliance. For once his hopes were not entirely delusional. In the same week Stalin and Roosevelt exchanged their ill-tempered cables about the prospect of a second front, the Germans announced that their occupying forces in Russia had come across huge mass graves in the Katyn Forest near Smolensk. They found more than 4,000 bodies, which were identified as those of the Polish army officers listed as "missing" since the outbreak of war. The subsequent discovery of two further sites brought the number of dead to 27,500. All of the deceased had been shot through the back of the head. The officers had been swiftly arrested or captured following the Soviet invasion of Poland in September 1939, in which the Russians had acted as Hitler's confederates, tried in absentia, and found guilty of being "counter-revolutionary landowners ... spies and saboteurs ... hardened ... enemies of Soviet power." The men had been individually murdered in a hut with padded, soundproofed walls, at a Stakhanovite quota of 275 "erasures" a night, by Stalin's favorite executioner Vasily Blokhin. The Russian dictator was not known for his cordiality toward many ethnic groups, foreign or domestic, but he had an almost preternatural loathing of Poles, dating back to the post–Revolutionary war between the two states of 1919–21.

On discovering the killing fields at Katyn, the Germans blamed the Russians. The Russians blamed the Germans, and, on a note of near-farcical indignation, announced that they were severing diplomatic relations with the rump Polish government in London, which had had the temerity to protest. Churchill could offer the Poles—for whose national integrity Britain had gone to war in the first place—no support. As he drily remarked, he would "sup with the devil" if it helped to secure ultimate victory. Roosevelt's own reaction to Katyn was a masterclass in the art of appeasing a criminal psychopath. "I am inclined to think that Prime Minister Churchill will find a way of prevailing upon the Polish government in London to act with more common sense," the president wrote in an emollient cable to the man he called "Uncle Joe" Stalin in May 1943, at a time when the bodies were still being exhumed at Katyn.

It would be wrong, then, to describe the inter–Allied relations of this period as uniformly distinguished by their spirit of communal goodwill, or even by their commonly agreed strategy. The English-speaking union of which Churchill often spoke, aligned in its basic values and shared history, never quite became the bedrock of the world order. The nearest the two Western powers came to a formal alliance was the Atlantic Charter of August 1941, and even that provided merely a broad statement of principle insisting that the United States and Great Britain would "jointly support the security of the world." Similarly, the 45-word bilateral Anglo-Soviet agreement that same summer signified only that the two governments would "render each other assistance in the present war against Hitlerite Germany." There was no pretense of ideological rapport beyond that. The war did not bring about any noticeably wider alignment of interest between its principal victors, as the history of Europe from 1945 to 1989, and arguably beyond, attests. Sometimes mutual wariness within the Alliance spilled out into open contempt. Stalin was singularly unimpressed, in fact satirically amused, by Churchill's boasts about General Bernard Montgomery's victory over the Axis forces at El Alamein, which the British saw as the turning point of the war. As their stubborn resistance continued at Stalingrad over the winter of 1942–43, Red Army generals archly compared Montgomery's "little clash" to the experience of commanders like Georgy Zhukov and Ivan Konev "who had won a whole series of brilliant victories that were several times as important as El Alamein, in both their results and their scope."[7]

Nor were such Allied squabbles confined to a few barrack-room gibes reflecting the profound and sustained Soviet military disdain for Western counterparts with only a fraction of both their combat experience and battlefield losses. The discord went right to the top. As late as February 1945, returning from what proved to be their final meeting at Yalta, Roosevelt remarked to his speechwriter Sam Rosenman that "dear old Winston" was over-loquacious at these affairs, and, what was more, "the president was beginning to feel uneasily that the traditions of British imperialism were playing too heavy a part in Churchill's thinking."[8]

Nonetheless, there was evidence even by the time the Allies found themselves debating the correct response to the Katyn horrors that the tide of the war was turning gradually but perceptibly in their favor. The reality was that by the spring of 1943, the Axis was caught in a situation where nothing added up anymore. The German army was divided against itself, with Hitler wanting every available man for the desperate attempt to shore up the fast-crumbling Eastern front, a campaign that reached its final crisis that July at Kursk, while the commander-in-chief of the Replacement Army, General Friedrich Fromm, needed a minimum of twelve reserve divisions merely to maintain order at home and perform basic occupation duties in Italy. The ensuing tension in the two men's relationship would become such that Fromm saw fit not to actively oppose the July 1944 assassination attempt against Hitler, an oversight for which he paid first with his job and then his life. Like Canaris, Fromm was imprisoned and executed shortly before the end of the war. His final words also echoed those of his Abwehr colleague. "I die because it is ordered. I have always wanted only the best for Germany."[9]

Italy would "contribute more sparingly to the German cause," in the measured words of the Italian King Victor Emmanuel III, following the events of July 25, 1943, the date on which Mussolini was dismissed as prime minister and his successor in office, Marshal Pietro Badoglio, entered into secret armistice negotiations with the Allies. Italy from that point on was effectively open to the highest bidder. Hitler was not pleased to learn of these developments. In fact, he threw a fit. It took the form of a furious tirade that left everyone who witnessed it, or even heard about it later, shaken and exhausted. The führer denounced his primary ally's defeatism, shouting that "we'll get ready to grab the whole mess, all that rabble.... I'll send a man down to Rome tomorrow with orders to arrest the whole government, the so-called king and that scum. I'll grab all that riffraff, particularly Badoglio and the entire gang," he noted, bringing his fist down on the desk for emphasis. No one had ever before seen him lose control so completely.

The entire Italian nation was a laughingstock, Hitler continued. He would raze it to the ground. Someone present in the room rashly mentioned the matter of the Vatican. "That doesn't matter," screamed Hitler. "I'll go right into the Vatican. Do you think I care about that? We'll destroy that right off. All the diplomatic corps will be hiding in there.... I don't give a damn if the entire crew's in there, we'll get the whole lot of swine out. We can easily do that." Hitler normally refrained from outright vulgarity, but he allowed himself an exception in this case. "We've got a

1. Unconditional Surrender

fucking war on!" he reminded his audience, lest they had forgotten. In the midst of his raging, Hitler's body was racked by a violent spasm, and one of the führer's secretaries unlucky enough to have been present later insisted that she had seen actual foam at her chief's mouth. Long after the war, journalists and historians would marvel at the various survivors' accounts of the scene, passing it down through the ages like old salts recalling a historic hurricane.[10]

The Reich's already fragile pact with her Japanese allies was showing similar signs of strain by the early months of 1943. That Hitler might have ambivalent feelings about his principal accomplices in the east was apparent even in February 1942, with the news of the fall of Singapore. Winston Churchill regarded the event as the single worst disaster in British military history. Even so, Hitler expressed only guarded pleasure at the announcement, even admitting to sorrow that the British were losing their empire in this way when they could have just as easily accepted his hand of friendship in 1939. "This is good, though perhaps also sad news," he told the visiting Rumanian dictator Ion Antonescu (yet another Nazi vassal to later be executed) during the latter's visit to Berlin. Hitler went on to order his foreign ministry not to overdo the pronouncements on the fall of Singapore. "We've got to think in centuries," he remarked. "One day the showdown with the yellow race will come." At best, Hitler took a strictly pragmatic view of the need to integrate his national interests with those of the Japanese. "I'm accused of sympathizing with the orientals," he told his secretary Christa Schroeder. "What does that mean? The Japanese are yellow-skinned and slit-eyed. But they are fighting against the Americans and the English, and so are useful to Germany."[11] An element of paranoia underwrote Hitler's entire career, but by the middle of 1943, with his armies in disarray on the Russian front, and his principal alliances under political and military strain almost everywhere else, the 54-year-old führer was close to a state of madness—not, perhaps, in the clinical sense, but in his high-risk and increasingly desperate bid for continental and ultimately world dominance.

In addition to these strategic challenges, there were also certain technical developments in the summer of 1943 that seemed to ultimately promise to decisively alter the course of the war. These were what the British euphemistically called "Tube Alloys," or the effort to build the world's first atomic bomb.

In June 1942, Prime Minister Churchill met President Roosevelt in the latter's birthplace and lifelong family home at Hyde Park, New York. Settling in after an extended lunch for a conversation in the president's small, book-lined downstairs office, Churchill had suggested that the two principal Western allies join forces in assembling this "at once retrograde and almost fantastical" weapon. "What if the enemy should develop the Tubes before we do?" he asked. "However skeptical one might feel about the assertions of the scientists, much disputed among themselves and expressed in jargon incomprehensible to the layman, we could not run the risk of being outstripped in this mortal sphere." It was an unusual setting, with the early afternoon sun filtering in the president's oak-paneled study, and the two old friends seemingly sitting relaxed over their coffee and cigars, in which to be discussing the means to potentially annihilate the world. Churchill later recalled, "I strongly urged that we should at once pool all our information, work together on equal terms, and share the results, if any, equally between us."[12] Thus the Manhattan Project was born. Like so much of the Anglo-American alliance, both then and later, it became increasingly a case of Washington operating as a strategic headquarters and London functioning as a sort of subsidiary branch office, but the essential course of events agreed that early summer afternoon by the two allies, speaking in a tone almost as if they were drawing up a few items on a shopping list, would eventually come to determine the events at Hiroshima and Nagasaki, and all that ensued.

The two heads of government met again in the same informal surroundings a year later. A small group of senior scientists had recently been arguing that the Allies should tell the international community about the unprecedented force of the new weapon, in the hope that its mere existence would be enough to encourage the Axis powers to lay down their arms. Roosevelt and Churchill were not persuaded. Their secret memorandum on the subject read, "The suggestion that the world should be informed regarding Tube Alloys, with a view to international agreement regarding their control and use, is rejected ... but when a weapon is finally available, it might, perhaps, after mature consideration, be used against the enemy, who should be warned that this bombardment will be repeated until they surrender."[13]

Set amidst this rising momentum on the Allied side was Roosevelt's seemingly almost casual announcement of Sunday, January 24, 1943, while seated in the garden of a whitewashed villa in Casablanca, his pearl cigarette holder set at an even more than usually rakish angle: "The elimination of German, Japanese and Italian war power means the unconditional surrender by Germany, Italy and Japan. It does not mean the destruction of the population of those countries, but it does mean the destruction of those philosophies which are based on conquest and the subjugation of other people."

Roosevelt's words, spoken at the end of the latest conference intended to coordinate Allied strategy, apparently came as a rude shock to the "dear friend" seated in a hard chair immediately at his elbow. Churchill later privately insisted that he had offered "no direct or tacit endorsement of the president's effusion," which he feared would only encourage the "Nazi dictator's resolve to go down in flames." The prime minister was right. As Hitler told his regional party leaders in early February, he felt "liberated" as a result of Roosevelt's speech from any lingering obligation to seek a negotiated peace.[14] The war, for him, had become a matter of survival or total destruction. On February 18, the Nazi propaganda minister Joseph Goebbels amplified the theme when he asked his audience during a speech at the Berlin Sportpalast whether they believed in total war, "more total and radical than we can even imagine today?" The roar of assent from the crowd was truly deafening; the speaker had clearly struck the most responsive possible chord.

Encouraged, Goebbels's voice rose as he announced, "The history of our party and our state has proven that a danger recognized is a danger defeated. Our coming hard battles will be under the sign of this heroic struggle. They will require previously undreamed-of efforts by our soldiers and our weapons. A merciless war is raging. The führer was right when he said that in the end there will not be winners and losers, but only the living and the dead."

Another tumultuous roar of approval erupted. "In this hour of national reflection and contemplation, we believe firmly and unshakably in victory. We see it before us, we need only reach for it. We must resolve to subordinate everything to it. This is the duty of the hour. Let the slogan be: 'Now, people, arise, let the storm break!'" Goebbels shouted. After that, "there were scenes of true pandemonium in the hall," it was reported. Greater German Radio remained on the air for twenty minutes, broadcasting the sound of the frenzied ovation to its audience. This was perhaps the moment at which it became clear that the war would not end in a compromise solution.

* * *

To Hitler, war was an intensely personal affair. As late as July 1940, following the fall of France, he told the German Reichstag that while he felt obligated "by conscience to appeal once more to reason on the part of England.... I see no compelling grounds for continuing this conflict," he nonetheless retained his fundamental doubts about Britain's newly appointed prime minister. In fact, Winston Churchill was a "voracious beast," an "immoral and repulsive individual" and "crude drunkard," who was "drenched indelibly in blood." Hitler seemed to have been genuinely perplexed when the categorical British rejection of his peace overture followed within the hour. Even Joseph Goebbels found his führer's calculus toward Britain difficult to understand. Two days later, the propaganda chief explained to his staff the need to "maintain the hatred for the English leader at the previous level, but to avoid the danger of our people beginning to demand action instead of accusations and threats. So we must tread water, for we mustn't anticipate the führer's actions."[15]

Hitler saw himself as the state. He believed that the individual had a decisive role to play in history, and that the physical elimination of his enemies' high command was a legitimate part of any reasonably prudent national policy. The war, for him, was really all about a few "criminally stubborn" personalities. A week after his Reichstag speech, Hitler went, for what was to prove the final time, to Bayreuth to attend a performance of Wagner's *Gotterdammerung*. While there he saw the friend of his starving-artist youth, August Kubizek, also for what proved the last time. Hitler told Kubizek that it was Churchill, backed by the "Jewish plutocracy," who was the real warmonger. "I did not become chancellor of the great German Reich in order to fight," he announced. Kubizek believed him.

In time, Hitler took an equally dim view of his latest adversary, Franklin Roosevelt. Like Churchill, it seemed he, too, was an "agent of international Jewry." Among other unappreciative terms, Hitler called the president a "hypocrite," "soft-headed," and an "inveterate Freemason," whom he despised. Formally declaring war on the United States on December 11, 1941, he described the stricken Roosevelt as "a cripple" who was sustained in office only by the "entire satanic insidiousness" of the Jews, maliciously set upon the destruction of the peace-loving German state.[16]

Bolshevism, Goebbels similarly informed the readers of that week's *Das Reich* newspaper, was the "work of Jewish party doctrinaires" and "sly Jewish capitalists," primarily Churchill and Roosevelt, "principals in the great world conspiracy against Germany." In another speech to the Reichstag soon afterward, Hitler blamed Roosevelt for provoking war to cover up the failures of the New Deal. The escalating conflict was all down to "the gimp," he remarked. Fanatical applause repeatedly interrupted his speech. Hitler then took the opportunity of a sentimental return to the Löwenbräukeller beerhall in Munich to blurt out, "I will outlast the Jew Roosevelt [he did, by eighteen days] … I can afford to wait and take my time to win this war in my own ways." After a moment in which he seemed to fall into a sort of reverie, his hands folded behind his back, eyes downcast, he then suddenly announced, as if the thought were just occurring to him, "I am Führer of a Reich that will last for a thousand years to come." In contrast to his own "mission … willed by divine providence," he added, Churchill and Roosevelt were "criminal types, sit[ting] over there in their plutocratic little world, surrounded and enslaved by the moneybags and the Jews." After a few more generic remarks about the inevitability of German victory, Hitler returned to the issue clearly foremost in his mind. "Ja, Herr Roosevelt—and his Jews!" he exclaimed. "He wants to run the world and rob us all of a place in the sun. He says he wants to save England, but he means he wants to be ruler and heir of the British Empire."[17]

Hitler's attitude to Joseph Stalin, meanwhile, came to reach the level of a pure and honest personal hatred rarely seen outside marriage. The relationship had gotten off to a rocky start even during the honeymoon period of August 1939, when the German foreign minister Joachim von Ribbentrop flew to Moscow to conclude the Reich's notorious non-aggression pact with the Soviet Union. In the days following the signing ceremony, Hitler spent less time celebrating this historic new concurrence of interest between the world's leading fascist and socialist states than in poring over the press photographs taken of the treaty's subsequent champagne reception in the Kremlin. In particular, he requested a close-up of Stalin, which he studied at length through a magnifying glass, to see if the Soviet leader's earlobes were "ingrown and Jewish, or separate and Aryan." The results were apparently reassuring. The führer's new comrade, according to the earlobe test, was no Jew.

But this was only a brief respite from Hitler's prevailing low opinion of all three of his current or future Allied opponents. In his November 1941 speech to the Old Guard of veterans of the 1923 putsch, he returned, like a dog to its vomit, to the theme of Jewish guilt for the war. Evidently it now struck him as inevitable that the Soviet Vozhd (or "führer" equivalent)—"the world's greatest servant of Judaism"—would seek to confront the peace-loving Reich. Stalin, to whom Hitler had plighted his state's troth barely two years earlier, was no more than "an instrument in the hand of almighty Jewry." Behind him stood "all those Jews who in thousandfold ramification lead the Russian empire." Even this was mild compared to Hitler's tirade in July 1942 while at his summer headquarters nicknamed Werewolf, near Vinnitsa in the Ukraine, as the eastern campaign entered its second and decisive year. Stalin was no better than a "common gangster," a "thug" and "latter-day Genghis Khan" who needed to be "erased" from the scene without further delay, Hitler informed his audience, while further haranguing them on subjects ranging from the evils of smoking to the future construction of an autobahn system throughout the soon-to-be conquered Soviet territories, and, with a certain grim inevitability, the need to remove the last Jews from German soil. As early as June 6, 1941, a special *Führererlass* (führer edict) had promised immunity from prosecution to German soldiers who committed atrocities in the coming war with Russia, whose ethnic minorities were to be "dealt with promptly and with the utmost severity."

The ever-constant Goebbels soon took up the theme. The Russian people had to be brought to the realization that Hitler's coming victory over the "beast Stalin" and the "bestiality of the Bolshevist government" lay in their best interests, he announced. Later in August, Hitler repeated at a conference of his generals that "the vital thing now [was] to concentrate every available man and capture as quickly as possible the whole of Stalingrad and the banks of the Volga"—the "decisive blow" that would remove the "Red Czar" from power.

Hitler's profound lack of empathy for his fellow head of state and former ally was fully reciprocated on Stalin's part. At Tehran in November 1943, the Vozhd informed his Allied guests at dinner that following the war, "the German leadership must be liquidated." Hitler and at least 50,000 others, Stalin added, should be "rounded up and shot." Winston Churchill was present and temporarily excused himself from the room in protest at these remarks. After a few moments of standing alone in a darkened hallway, Churchill felt a hand suddenly clap him on the shoulder, and turned to see Stalin, grinning malevolently in the half-light, assuring him that he had merely been joking. Churchill agreed to return to the table but was never wholly persuaded that the Soviet leader's words had all been a bit of innocuous fun. "I was not then, and am not now, fully convinced that it was mere chaff, and that there was no serious intent lurking behind," he wrote in 1951. "However, I consented to return, and the rest of the evening passed pleasantly."[18]

In later years, Churchill's lingering suspicion that the Vozhd's remarks at Tehran had not been entirely in jest prompted this acute exchange with Andrei Gromyko, Russia's 1950s ambassador to the United Kingdom and later his nation's long-serving foreign minister.

> GROMYKO: "His Lordship [sic] is mistaken in the matter. There was never any proposal on the part of the People's Commissar of Defense [Stalin] such as the one you relate."
> CHURCHILL: "I know what I heard."
> GROMYKO: "Neither the People's Commissar nor the Council of People's Ministers would consent to such a formula."
> CHURCHILL: "What I say is a fact."
> GROMYKO: "What I say is also a fact."
> CHURCHILL: "I was present at the dinner."
> GROMYKO (displaying that talent for rhetorical bombast that was a strong source of his political advancement in the USSR): "I too attended the partaking of the comestibles in the circumstances His Lordship describes and absented myself from the People's Commissar's side on only one necessary occasion."
> CHURCHILL: "Perhaps Your Excellency ate something that disagreed with him?"[19]

1. Unconditional Surrender

The Soviet Central Repository of Social Movements—or state archive—later removed any reference to Stalin's alleged wish to purge the defeated Nazi high command or any other such conquered entity. Churchill remained adamant—"after all, this was the same benevolent People's Commissar who had ordered the slaying of the poor Polish soldiers at [Katyn]," he argued. But if the Soviet dictator in fact embraced the widespread liquidation of his nation's adversaries as a legitimate if undeclared function of policy, so did those same foes when it came to advancing their war interests. Murder was part of every belligerent state's course of action, regardless of personal morality or political ideology.

Following the events of June 1940, French general Maxime Weygand, one of the few of his nation's senior military staff to distinguish himself that spring, continued to make difficulties for his country's occupiers. In September, Weygand was appointed to a training role in North Africa. But instead of instilling an appreciation for Nazism in his subordinates, he did the opposite. In June 1941, Weygand went so far as to openly criticize the so-called Paris Protocols that granted the Germans military facilities in France's African colonies. It has to be said that the general's principal objection to the Franco-German accommodation ran on tactical rather than narrowly moral grounds. He applied the required laws against Algerian Jews without apparent compunction but was not happy to see French colonial assets shared in this way with another European power. "It was intolerable to become a mere launching-pad for German ambitions."

In time, Hitler summoned one Colonel Erwin Lahousen-Viremont, an aristocratic former Austrian cavalry officer, complete with spurs and monocle, who had since gone on to join Canaris's staff in military intelligence. The führer had a special mission in mind for him. Lahousen was to take a small band of trained operatives from Abwehr headquarters and sail with them to Algiers, where he would assassinate Weygand. The colonel was to liaise further in the matter with Field Marshal Wilhelm Keitel, Chief of the German High Command, as Hitler "did not care to be seen as dabbling in murder" (a vain hope, perhaps, in light of the subsequent verdict of history), or to "enter into concrete discussions of that kind." But difficulties seem to have arisen at the operational, or possibly even moral, level. "I told Keitel," Lahousen informed the judges at Nuremberg, "that my men had been trained to fight. We were not thugs and assassins." In any event, the plan obviously did not prosper because Maxime Weygand died only in January 1965, in his home in Paris, at the age of 98.

In a similar vein, there was the case of Weygand's colleague General Henri Giraud, who was arrested by the advancing Germans in May 1940, but later escaped by using a ladder made out of torn bedsheets to lower himself down the sheer wall of the Bavarian mountain fortress where he was imprisoned. Giraud made his way back to France, where he tried to persuade the collaborationist Vichy government that they should resist the German occupation. Hitler was not pleased with this turn of events. He gave orders to Canaris to have Giraud tracked down and eliminated. Locating the target should not have been an insuperable problem, as the Frenchman was 6'4" tall and had only one arm, but, again, the plan was seemingly allowed to wither on the vine. The Gestapo rounded up seventeen members of Giraud's extended family, but the general eluded the dragnet and lived long enough to be elected to the postwar French constituent assembly.

There was later a curious footnote to the Giraud affair involving the general's sometime brother-in-arms Admiral François Darlan. Darlan had performed a delicate ideological balancing act following France's surrender to the Nazis, railing at the British for their action in sinking the ships of the French fleet while they lay at anchor off the coast of Algeria in July 1940 but also proving reluctant when called upon to supply French conscript labor to the Germans, or to enforce anti–Semitic laws among what remained of his navy. He continued on friendly terms with Giraud, seemingly united by their distaste for any foreign interference, of whatever stripe, in French national policy making. On Christmas Eve 1942, a young French Resistance activist named Fernand Bonnier de la Chapelle shot Admiral Darlan in his headquarters; Darlan died later that evening. The assassin was swiftly tried and convicted and executed by firing squad less than 48 hours later. It remains unclear to this day if Darlan's killer was operating on instructions from a foreign power, and, if so, which one. A letter discovered years later among the effects of Alexander Cadogan, Anthony Eden's principal assistant at the British foreign office, provides a clue, although it's not known whether this was a call for direct action or merely wishful thinking on the writer's part. "We shall do no good until we have killed Darlan," the note read.[20]

* * *

Clearly Hitler had one of those minds that alternated between long periods of inactivity and sudden, apparently inexhaustible enthusiasm for a given course of action. In any case he soon dropped the attempted conspiracies against Weygand and Giraud just as abruptly as he embraced them in the first place. But up to the end of the war he never wholly renounced the assassination or kidnapping of his enemies as a legitimate extension of state policy. At various times, he directed Canaris's attention to the head of the occupied French state, Philippe Petain, as well as the Allied generals Eisenhower and Montgomery, all of whom were to prove a greater or lesser thorn in the flesh of German interests. Many of the attempted hits were as callous in design as those out of the pages of *The Godfather*, if not as ruthlessly efficient in their logistical execution.

In March 1944, Hitler ordered Canaris to liquidate Josip Broz, alias Tito, who was proving tiresome as the leader of a Yugoslav partisan resistance movement in occupied central Europe. The proposal got as far as being dignified by the codename Operation Rosselsprung (or "knight's move"), along with a plan of action that might have later served as an episode from a luridly melodramatic James Bond film script as interpreted by Woody Allen. The deed was to take place on May 7, 1944, which was Tito's 52nd birthday. Canaris believed that the occasion would be marked by a Bacchic orgy in partisan headquarters and that in the prevailing confusion a hit squad comprised of a few crack SS agents supported by an irregular force of 200 "criminals, foreigners and dogs" armed with axes and scythes could seize their man and bundle him onto a Luftwaffe plane waiting on the tarmac at Zagreb to fly him into captivity in Germany. Cooperation between the elite Nazi extraction team and its ragtag auxiliary crew broke down, however, and they never made it to the scene of the birthday revelries. As Walter Schellenberg was left to ruefully admit, "In lieu of victory, we had to content ourselves with entering Tito's residence and seizing one of his second-best uniforms."

Earlier in the war there had been an equally picaresque scheme to "detain" Edward, Duke of Windsor, the former King Edward VIII, as he and his wife fled their home in France to avoid the oncoming Wehrmacht forces. On June 23, 1940, the German ambassador in Madrid telegraphed his foreign minister Joachim von Ribbentrop to say that "the Spanish Foreign Office requests advice with regard to the treatment of the Duke and Duchess of Windsor, who are due to arrive in Madrid today, apparently in order to return to England by way of Lisbon.... They gather that we might perhaps be interested in apprehending the Duke and establishing contact with him."

According to Ribbentrop's assistant Erich Kordt, his boss was "electrified" by this proposal, shouting, "We must get hold of him! Franco must arrest him!"[21] Ribbentrop's plan was evidently to kidnap the Windsors, and then in time to have the duke resume the throne of England under a benign German occupation. The scheme got as far as an exchange of telegrams in which Hitler remarked that Germany was about to attack Great Britain, that peace depended on the removal of the "Churchill clique" in London, and that Germany was willing to restore the "rightful English king" to his people. The duke in turn expressed his appreciation of "the Führer's desire for peace" but regretted that he was about to take up a position as governor of the Bahamas, omitting to add that he had been threatened by Churchill with a court-martial if he failed to immediately sail for

Nassau. That seems to have put an end to the Windsor affair but not to the Germans' interest in liquidating or neutralizing high-value targets throughout the war.

Joseph Schnabel, a graduate of the Abwehr special operations school at Quenzgut, on Lake Quenz, some fifty miles west of Berlin, later had this to say of the curriculum:

> In the first place, they taught us to hate. We had to know the personal history of the enemy leaders. Thus, when asked who Roosevelt's advisers were, we had to enumerate a dozen names, adding before each, "the Jew..." During this phase of our schooling we also had to know every aspect of the damage done by Allied air raids to German towns.... The instructor would ask the question, "What would you do if you could lay your hands on the person who ordered that raid?" In our answer, we had to deal not with the military leader, but always with the head of the enemy state.[22]

The Abwehr school bonded its pupils in blood. All passing students took part in mass executions called "marriages." The primary victims were sacrificial groups of Jews, gypsies, homosexuals, blacks, the physically or mentally infirm, dissenting clergy, prisoners of war, and even individual members of the artistic community whose works Hitler disliked. A few of these same graduates preferred to take a clerical role on passing out into the ranks of the SS. Many others found writing up statements more tedious than physically beating their prisoners into signing them. In time a few elite recruits from the Quenzgut academy were given more ambitious career goals. It was decided, in Himmler's words, that those enemy leaders "who could see reason, will see reason; those who can't will receive the logical treatment; that is, they [would be] liquidated."

By January 1942, Himmler's malign bailiwick included the German clandestine services, with the SS acting as an umbrella organization for a sprawling network embracing the Geheime Reichssicherheitshauptamt (Reich Main Security Office) and Staatspolizei (Gestapo). Within the latter were three sub-divisions dealing with regular, criminal, and security policing and known colloquially as ORPO, KRIPO, and SIPO. The more you study the Nazi intelligence hierarchy, the more you find its distinguishing features (apart from the silly acronyms) to have been the sheer scale of its operations and breadth of its interests, ranging from the re-education of dissident poets to the termination of uncongenial foreign heads of state. As noted, there was also a sub-unit initially for law enforcement but increasingly devoted to overseas duty, the SD, commanded until May 1942 by the blond, cold-eyed Reinhard Heydrich. A standout Nazi monster in a crowded field, Heydrich was the epitome of the jackbooted, Nordic type who so prospered at that time and whom even Hitler addressed fondly as "the man with the iron heart."

1. *Unconditional Surrender*

In November 1941, the SD hatched a plan to use a Luftwaffe Arado cargo plane to land a twelve-man hit squad in a remote part of the Valdai Hills northwest of Moscow. From there they were to make their way on foot, along the banks of the Volga River, to a safe house on the outskirts of Kalinin (today's Tver), some eighty miles from the state capital. Their mission was to travel from there by night and infiltrate Stalin's suburban dacha at Kuntsevo, where they believed not only the Soviet ruler but much of his personal staff were to be found "habitually stupefied by vodka [and] carnal excess" in the early hours of each morning, and thus uniquely vulnerable to a surprise attack. This was the moment when the German

The mutually unlamented Heinrich Himmler and Reinhard Heydrich, seen in Vienna at the time of the Nazi Anschluss of March 1938.

force would strike from both the front and rear. Four men would storm the inner office, each armed with a Sten gun and a supply of hand grenades, while their colleagues swiftly cut the building's communications, demolished the nearby guard house, and summarily dealt with any remaining opposition. A third unit would be posted on the main access road to the dacha to warn of any oncoming civilian or military traffic and, in the emotive words of Heydrich's written brief, "deter this with a bang."

It had all the ingredients both of a possibly first-rate, state-sponsored assassination coup or, alternatively, of a spectacular debacle. But at the last moment, displaying one of those sudden reversals of policy that constitute the fabric of his personal leadership style, Hitler scrubbed the mission. He apparently believed that Stalin's nerve had given way following the recent fall of Kiev, prompting the Vozhd to remark in private that "Lenin [had] created the Soviet Union, and now we've fucked it up." For public consumption, Stalin mounted the reviewing stand in Red Square that same week and urged his countrymen to resist the German invader. Back in Berlin, Hitler watched a captured newsreel film of the speech. He was astute enough to notice that Stalin's address, supposedly delivered from "atop Comrade Lenin's Mausoleum," was in fact recorded in a heated Kremlin studio. On film, the fact that the Vozhd's breath did not steam as it left his mouth was a giveaway. Stalin was desperate, Hitler reasoned, and would soon plead to come to the negotiating table. Germany would be better served by dealing with a defeated adversary than "needlessly stirring up a hornets' nest" by killing him. If so, it was not the least of the führer's strategic miscalculations, as no record can be found of any diplomatic approach, or peace overtures, however tentative or indirect, by the Soviet Union either at this time or later.

In a renewed attempt to eliminate Stalin before the tide of the war turned for Germany, Walter Schellenberg commissioned another wet job in April 1942. "Our experts produced a strange mechanism for this," he recalled in his posthumously published memoir *The Labyrinth*. "The explosive was fist-sized and resembled a handful of mud. It was to be affixed to Stalin's automobile…. The radio transmitter, intended to activate the bomb, was no larger than a cigarette box and could automatically explode the device from a distance of ten kilometers. The blast was so powerful that almost nothing remained of the car on which we tried it."[23]

It seems Schellenberg got as far as dropping two men by parachute into the woods near Moscow, from where they made their way to an abandoned farmhouse. According to the plan, the SD team was due to link up later that night with members of an anti–Stalin resistance cell. Shortly before midnight, one of the men took a torch and swung it out of an upstairs window to attract the attention of their local contacts. But something had gone seriously wrong with the arrangements. At the signal several men dressed in military camouflage uniforms and brandishing Tokarev PPD submachine guns burst into the hideout and swiftly detained the two enemy operatives, who were never heard from again. Not for the last time, the People's Commissariat of Internal Affairs (NKVD) had infiltrated a plot against the Soviet state. The next time Schellenberg brought him a proposal to eliminate Stalin, Hitler vetoed it on the grounds that, successful or not, it would be "asking for trouble from Providence."[24]

* * *

Between the Windsor affair of June 1940 and the last-ditch bid to eradicate the senior Allied service chiefs following the Normandy landings four years later, Hitler's intelligence services operated with maniacal energy and calculated purpose, if only fitful success. Their efforts were significantly boosted by the news delivered by Wilhelm Ohnesorge, nominally the Reich postal minister, but whose brief extended to developing new radio and wireless technology, on March 6, 1942. With an annual budget of RM 240m ($96m), Ohnesorge had scraped up 110 technicians, installing most of them in an imposing, tree-lined compound on the banks of Lake Muggelsee in the eastern suburbs of Berlin. Together they had succeeded in unscrambling the high-level signals between the enemy chancelleries in London, Washington, and, more sporadically, Moscow. As a result, the Germans would learn of various Allied strategic decisions almost as soon as they were made, as well as listening in on conversations between enemy ministers. Heydrich quietly established a liaison committee to coordinate the information gathered between the SD, the Armed Forces High Command (OKW), and the Reich Chancellery.

Intelligence operations against the United States, which Hitler had initially doubted would prove effective because of the distances involved, were soon stepped up as a result of the intercepted traffic. During the spring of 1942, Abwehr agents began to materialize all over the American heartland. Perhaps the best-known infiltration plan was Operation Pastorius, in which eight English-speaking Nazis were to launch a series of sabotage attacks on U.S. economic targets, including the hydroelectric plant at Niagara Falls, the Penn Salt factory in Bensalem, Pennsylvania, and the National Aluminum Company works in Illinois, Tennessee, and New York. The agents were also instructed to spread a wave of terror by planting explosives under bridges, in railway stations, and at selected department stores and schools. The Pastorius team came ashore on the moonless night of June 12, 1942, by U-boat, landing on a deserted beach at Amagansett, New York, on the south shore of Long Island. They carried counterfeit birth certificates, Social Security cards, and nearly $175,000 (around

$3.15m today) in cash. The whole enterprise was thoroughly planned and funded and might have succeeded but for a critical flaw. One of the saboteurs, George Dasch, having had second thoughts about the mission, walked into the Washington office of the FBI and told agents the locations of the other members of the crew. All eight enemy agents were subsequently tried by a military tribunal. Dasch and a fellow penitent named Ernst Burger were handed lengthy jail sentences; the other six were given the electric chair.

Meanwhile, thanks to the bravery of a few dedicated men in London and Prague, Heydrich, now combining his SD-Gestapo duties with a role as so-called Reich Protector of Bohemia and Moravia, had been struck down. The Czech government-in-exile trained nine volunteers for the mission, of whom two, Josef Gabcik and Jan Kubis, were selected. On the morning of May 27, 1942, Heydrich set off by chauffeur-driven Mercedes for the nine-mile drive from his home to his headquarters at Prague Castle. Later in the day he planned to fly to Berlin, where he was due to meet Hitler. Captured German documents suggest that he was about to be transferred to occupied France to deal with the Resistance movement.

In view of what we know today (and was widely known at the time) about the draconian penalties Hitler imposed on his opponents, the fact that Gabcik and Kubis acted as they did speaks eloquently. The two Czech irregulars were duly waiting to ambush Heydrich's car as it slowed down to negotiate a hairpin bend on a cobbled street in Liben, on the eastern bank of the Vltava River, about midway to its destination. But the plot, like all the best plots, nearly came to grief. As the Mercedes drove past him, Gabcik took aim with a submachine gun, but it jammed and failed to fire. At that point Kubis tossed a grenade against the side of the car. There was an explosion. Heydrich, seriously injured by shrapnel but still barking orders at his driver, vaulted out of his seat, firing at the assassins as they fled between two stalled trams, before collapsing to the ground. He was taken to Prague's Bulovka hospital, where he lingered until June 4, after apparently remarking as his epitaph, "The world is just a barrel-organ which the Lord turns. We all have to dance to the tune which is already on the drum." Heydrich's assassins later shot themselves rather than be captured.

Hitler's revenge was characteristically severe, even by his exacting standards. In the week following the attack on Heydrich, 100 Czech civilians were rounded up and shot each evening. Himmler then determined that the killers had been parachuted by the British into the village of Lidice, a dozen miles northwest of Prague. All 307 adult male citizens of the area were murdered, small children were thrown into cattle troughs to drown, and any pregnant women were sent to Bulovka hospital, where

Heydrich (front center) and Schellenberg (far right) with SS colleagues in Oslo, September 1941.

their babies were forcibly aborted before the mothers were shipped to Berlin to be experimented on by "racial experts." Lidice was wiped off the map by a combination of bombs and flamethrowers. Heydrich was 38 at the time of his death and, save in senior Nazi circles, not widely mourned.

* * *

The Allies' ambitions to decisively turn the course of the war by targeting high-value enemy combatants did not stop at the odious Reich Protector. Only luck saved Heydrich's ultimate chief from repeated assassination attempts, some the fruits of deliberate planning, others more of opportunity and improvisation. On February 15, 1943, Hitler flew to the captured Ukrainian city of Zaporozhe, only thirty miles from the front line, to meet with his commander Erich von Manstein. Manstein convinced the führer that offensive action was needed in the area to regain the initiative and prevent encirclement by the Red Army. The German counterattack was duly launched, capturing 615 tanks and killing some 23,000 Soviet troops. Crass as it is to use the term "too few" in relation to battlefield casualties, it could be reasonably applied here. By the time the Wehrmacht launched its full-scale assault around Kursk later that spring, the Soviet forces had outnumbered them by nearly three to one. The German push was called off on July 13, 1943, thus effecting a complete and irrevocable reversal of fortune on the Eastern front and, by extension, in the war.

Hitler lingered in the Zaporozhe region for some days following his initial winter conference with Manstein, with only a few anti-aircraft units and his traveling six-man protection squad standing between him and the outriders of the Russian 5th Shock Army. It showed either blind faith or impressive nerve on the führer's part to then travel back to the local airfield in a convoy of just three cars and a token entourage of fifteen men. As the wheels of Hitler's camouflaged Focke-Wulf Condor monoplane left the ground, a column of Russian T-34 tanks, fully visible to the Condor's passengers, approached to within gun range, only to then pause, ignorant of the unique significance of the plane, due to fuel shortages. Back in Berlin, the führer's narrow escape lent wings to Goebbels's fantasies of final victory. "Our stock has risen enormously, not only with our people, but also the rest of humanity." He added, "Providence [had] placed the Führer in a very special position for conveying guidance and leadership to a world which needs it so badly."

A whimsical plan then took shape in April 1943, involving the impressively titled Friedrich-Werner Graf von der Schulenburg, a German diplomat who served as his country's last ambassador to the Soviet Union before the rupture brought about by Operation Barbarossa, and the renegade General Andrey Vlasov, late of the Red Army, to launch a concerted attempt on Hitler's life. The two self-styled statesmen seem to have believed that such an initiative would usher in a golden new age of Russo-German friendship, with themselves at the heart of the resumed alliance. Instead, both men were seized, summarily tried, and hanged by their respective governments. In 2010, Anatoly Kulikov, Russia's minister of Internal Affairs under Boris Yeltsin, released papers suggesting that Stalin had prepared a detailed assassination plan of his own to eliminate the entire German senior political hierarchy in July 1943, but had suddenly canceled this due to fears that after Hitler's death any of his surviving associates would conclude a separate peace treaty with the West.[25] The führer's security could be oddly lax. Seemingly enjoying divine protection, or so he fondly believed, much of his daily routine was dull and monotonous, and attended not by a praetorian guard of jackbooted sentries but a few bored household staff and lucky—or unlucky—court insiders. "Since the daily party always consists of the same people, there is no stimulation from outside, and nobody experiences anything on a personal level," Christa Schroeder wrote to a friend in February 1942.

Stalin's original thinking in such circumstances had been to consider inserting a mole onto the surprisingly lightly vetted kitchen staff of the Reich chancellery in Berlin, from where he or she would take the

1. Unconditional Surrender

The NKVD's Lavrentiy Beria clutches Stalin's five-year-old daughter Svetlana at the dictator's resort on the Black Sea, with Stalin and the Old Bolshevik Nestor Lakoba, with headphones, in the background. Lakoba later died of what was described as a heart attack after having dinner with Beria.

opportunity to lace Hitler's favorite teatime pastries with cyanide and, as the order put it, "await the inevitable." The whole scheme got as far as the desk of the ruthless Lavrentiy Beria—the Soviet Robespierre—deputy premier and the NKVD's chief exterminator who spent his evenings cruising the streets of Moscow in his car with two bodyguards, picking up adolescent girls. ("Scream or not, it doesn't matter," he informed his young victims once back in the soundproofed cellar of his home.) Beria would draft a characteristically fussily detailed plan outlining the arrangements for "our warrior comrade to insert himself into the enemy fastness as you describe," but by then Stalin had again changed his mind. The paper came back to Beria with a one-word official stamp, "Refused."

A more decisive Allied operation went into effect on April 18, 1943, when Japanese Admiral Isoroku Yamamoto, the planner of the Pearl Harbor attack, was shot down and killed when flying between military bases on the Solomon Islands. Four days earlier, U.S. Naval Intelligence had intercepted and decrypted a message with details of Yamamoto's tour and forwarded this to the attention of U.S. Navy secretary Frank Knox. There is no record of any communication passing between Knox and President Roosevelt in the period April 14–18, although the commander-in-chief seems to have been familiar with at least the broad outline of the plan. A dispatch to the White House on April 19 from a Colonel Boone of the U.S. Army Air Corps 339 Squadron indicated that his pilots had destroyed three Japanese aircraft the day before, and according to the Department of Defense log, "Material suggests that Adm. Yamamoto may have been one of those downed." The president "received the report without comment," the file concludes.

The Yamamoto incident serves as a sort of prequel to the extraordinary events of June 1, 1943, when the Luftwaffe shot down a civilian BOAC Douglas DC-3 airliner flying from Lisbon to Bristol on the southwest coast of England. Among the seventeen fatalities was the 50-year-old British actor Leslie Howard, perhaps best remembered for his role as Ashley Wilkes in *Gone with the Wind*. One persistent theory about the attack is that freelance German agents lurking about the Portuguese capital had noticed a thickset man smoking a cigar board the plane that morning, had somehow leaped to the conclusion that this individual was no less than Winston Churchill, and hurriedly relayed the news to Berlin. Though fanciful, this wasn't quite as far-fetched as it sounds. The British premier had been only some 300 miles away in Gibraltar that week before prudently flying home in a military aircraft escorted by a wing of RAF fighters.

The cigar-smoking individual seen boarding the BOAC plane that morning was in fact Howard's friend and financial adviser Alfred Chenhalis. Chenhalis was then 43, and Churchill was 68, but to the part-time spies hanging around the Lisbon airfield, one portly Englishman in a double-breasted suit may have looked fatally like another. Informed of the tragedy two days later, Churchill observed, "The brutality of the Germans is only matched

The mastermind of the Pearl Harbor attack, Admiral Isoroku Yamamoto, who perished in a state-sponsored assassination in April 1943.

by the stupidity of their agents." For whatever reason, Hitler was in a particularly irritable mood that weekend while staying at his Bavarian retreat the Berghof. After dinner on Saturday night, one of his female guests grouped around the fire in the home's reception hall had impetuously questioned her host on his current war aims. "What concern is it to you?" Hitler snapped. There was a lengthy, uncomfortable silence. The logs could be heard crackling in the fireplace. After a few moments, an aide materialized to silently usher the woman and her husband out of the room.[26]

The Nazi special operations initiative did not stop with merely murdering a popular film star and his accountant. According to SS General Karl Wolff, and corroborated by witness testimony at Nuremberg, in September of that year Wolff was ordered to kidnap Pope Pius XII and bring him to Hitler's field headquarters at Rastenburg, in today's northern Poland. Two thousand German troops promptly surrounded the Vatican and systematically cut all access routes linking the miniature state to the Italian capital. It has to be said that the pope had not hitherto been entirely inimical to the Nazi cause. "Every word We address on the subject [of the extermination of the Jews] and all Our public utterances, have to be carefully weighed and measured by Us in the interests of the victims themselves," he had remarked in June 1943. His Holiness did not add that another reason for his caution was that he regarded Bolshevism as a far greater threat to world stability than Nazism. In the end, Hitler seems to have had another of his familiar changes of heart on the matter, apparently in the belief that an unfettered pope might prove useful in an eventually negotiated peace.

It's a moot point whether any of these various schemes, if ever successfully carried out, would have significantly altered the fortunes of war in one direction or another. But it's certain that both sides kept up the attempt until very nearly the end. In August 1944, the British Special Operations Executive (SOE) put up a plan that was tabled at the cabinet level. Codenamed FOXLEY, it gave as its object "the elimination of HITLER and any high-ranking Nazis who may be present." Its tactics aimed for breadth. "FOXLEY will be undertaken by Sniper's rifle, Piat gun or Bazooka, H.E. and splinter grenades; derailment and destruction of the Fuhrerzug [train] by explosives; and other clandestine means."[27] The SOE proposals were discussed as late as January 1945 but were never authorized, due to a division between Churchill and members of his coalition government as to whether the removal of Hitler from executive control of the Third Reich was in fact sound policy to expedite German defeat. The consensus seems to have been that he was by then such an incompetent military commander that almost any other viable candidate to replace him would present more of a challenge to the Allied cause.

Leslie Howard and his costar Rosamund John in the film *Spitfire*, released in the same year a plane carrying Howard and 16 other passengers was shot down by the Luftwaffe; there were no survivors.

There were also those within the Reich sufficiently alarmed about the direction their country was taking to seek to replace Hitler by direct means. These internal plotters were a mixed bag. Some were principled dissidents, and some were the human jetsam that tends to float toward the unlicensed-assassination world: opportunists, criminals, and a handful of fantasists. In time they were joined by an increasing number of men who harbored more narrowly tactical reservations about their führer's military judgment. On March 13, 1943, Hitler arrived at the Smolensk headquarters of 42-year-old General Henning von Tresckow, a high-born Prussian career officer who had come to have doubts about his commander-in-chief's sanity. Under the initial plan, a group of like-minded officers was to shoot Hitler collectively as he sat with them at lunch, but in the end this proposal was abandoned as impractical. Tresckow, however, had a backup. He decided to use one of his subordinate officers to plant a device on the führer's plane that would explode on the return flight to Berlin. The officer duly handed over a parcel supposedly containing two bottles of brandy to a member of Hitler's entourage. It was in fact a bomb made from British plastic explosives. The plane took off but somehow landed safely, leaving one of Tresckow's co-conspirators to hurriedly retrieve the erratic bomb before it exploded or was discovered. It was later found that the device's firing pin had been correctly released, but the detonator was a dud.

A few days later, Tresckow and his confederates tried again. This time Colonel Rudolf von Gerstdorff, another Prussian nobleman, was to approach the führer at the Heroes' Memorial Day celebration at the Zeughaus in Berlin and blow himself and Hitler to bits. Moments after Hitler entered the hall, Gerstdorff snapped off two ten-minute delayed fuses on explosive devices hidden in his coat pockets. He had no trouble insinuating himself into the VIP party. But, contrary to expectations, Hitler rushed through the tour in less than five minutes. Gerstdorff could only hurriedly find the nearest men's room, remove the fuses from his pocket, and—seconds before they were due to explode—flush them down the toilet. Undeterred by these successive failures, the army plotters made four more known attempts on Hitler's life at intervals over the winter of 1943–44, culminating in the famous Valkyrie affair of July 1944. The subsequent investigation and reprisals were brutal even by prevailing Nazi standards. The Gestapo swept up more than 7,000 people, of whom they murdered 4,980. Claus von Stauffenberg, the officer who had carried the Valkyrie bomb, was summarily shot, as in time was the man who had ordered his execution, General Fromm. Henning von Tresckow committed suicide by holding a hand grenade under his chin and detonating it. Rudolf von Gerstdorff died in his own bed in 1980, at the age of 74.

Just to finally establish that both sides in the conflict regularly took the opportunity to target their individual adversaries, there was the strange tale of King Boris III of Bulgaria. In 1943, Boris, whose nation was officially aligned with Germany, refused Hitler's direct order to deport Bulgaria's sizeable Jewish minority back to the Reich for forced labor or extermination. Instead, the king urged his Jews to move to the countryside and blend in with the general population. On August 14, 1943, Boris was summoned to a stormy meeting at the Rastenburg lair. He told Hitler that while his country had indeed declared a "symbolic" war on the United States and Britain, he wanted nothing to do with it. At that, Boris returned to Sofia, where he died at the age of 49, just thirteen days later. The official cause was given as heart failure. Both doctors who attended the king believed that he had in fact been a victim of the same poison found two years earlier in the postmortem examination of the Greek prime minister, Ioannis Metaxas, another similarly equivocal recruit to the Axis cause, a slow toxin that took a week or more to do its work. Six years old at the time, the new King Simeon II was deposed by the Communists after the war; he eventually returned to become Bulgaria's prime minister and is still alive today.[28]

Even this paled next to the tragicomic saga of the ruling Horthy dynasty in Hungary. In August 1944, the Budapest government withdrew its support from the Axis and turned against Germany and her allies. Soon Hungary's head of state, Admiral Miklos Horthy, a 76-year-old career naval officer, was negotiating a treaty with the Soviet Union. Hitler initiated Operation Panzerfaust, sending his Vienna-born commando Otto Skorzeny, whom we'll meet again, to Budapest with instructions to remove Horthy and his circle from office. He took his brief literally. Horthy's 37-year-old son and assistant Miklos Jr. was in a meeting with Soviet diplomats when Skorzeny and his crew burst in, rolled up the Hungarian in a rug, and carried him down to a truck waiting in front of the building. Skorzeny then led a column of four Tiger II tanks down the main street of Budapest to capture the palace where Horthy Sr. lived and ruled with only a token parachute battalion for protection. A total of seven soldiers died during the ensuing 30-minute skirmish. The head of the Hungarian state was swiftly persuaded to abdicate to save his son's life. Both Horthys were taken into captivity, the younger of the two at Dachau, but survived their mutual ordeal and lived to be 88 and 86, respectively.

When Skorzeny reported back to Berlin, Hitler, greatly amused by the tale of the rug, shook his fellow Austrian by the hand and informed him, "I am now going to give you the most important job of your life."[29] He explained that he was about to launch a surprise attack in the Ardennes, the so-called Battle of the Bulge, and that Skorzeny's role would be to direct Operation Greif, a dirty-tricks campaign designed to wreak havoc behind enemy lines. He and his men would disguise themselves in American uniforms, sabotage key military installations, seize bridges, issue fake orders and "neutralize" senior enemy leaders up to and including the Supreme Allied Commander Dwight D. Eisenhower. "The target will be brought to [Berlin], but in the event of sufficient resistance or hesitancy lethal force may be applied."

It remains debatable whether Skorzeny ever came close to a viable plot against the man who went on to become America's 34th president. But in the early hours of December 17 of that year the U.S. Army captured four German saboteurs operating near the Belgian town of Liege and found papers on them suggesting that their mission was to snatch a Pyrrhic victory to feed Hitler's fantasies by eliminating "the Jew Eizenhour [sic]" and his staff in pursuance of Operation Greif. As a result, Eisenhower spent Christmas 1944 isolated for security reasons. So great was the paranoia caused by Skorzeny and his men that the Allies saw spies and fifth columnists everywhere. One of the rumors doing the rounds was that the Germans had parachuted a double for the now–Field Marshal Montgomery into the sector, and that this individual, dressed in British uniform, was even now busily issuing treacherous orders to misdirect Allied troops. When U.S. guards halted his car at a checkpoint, the real Montgomery—not known for his easygoing charm at the best of times—told them that he would not put up with such nonsense and ordered the driver to keep going. The guards then shot out his tires and dragged the hero of El Alamein to a nearby barn, where he was detained for several hours.[30] Taken as a whole, the incident did not conspicuously advance the cause of Anglo-American relations. A total of sixteen German irregulars were eventually arrested and executed by Allied firing squads, although Skorzeny survived to die of natural causes in 1975 at the age of 67.

* * *

Clearly there is no way of knowing with any degree of certainty how the premature death or deaths of any one or more nation's key leaders might have affected the outcome of the war. Possibly it would have come as a more profound shock in Germany or the USSR than in the Western states, where there was at least an established chain of political command. When Franklin Roosevelt succumbed to a stroke in April 1945, the new U.S. president, Harry Truman, pursued the same policies as his predecessor. But clearly all sides in the conflict continued to see the removal of their opponents' principal civilian or military authorities as a legitimate means to eventual victory. Throughout the war, Allied and Axis powers were to prove equally tireless in attempting to drive on their plans for a host of covert operations, not excluding assassinations, whether designed to inflict a decisive or merely symbolic blow against the enemy. We may think today that if the moment ever came to choose between our duty and our conscience, or between committing or not committing a state-sanctioned murder, we might take the more human and less atavistic path. Everyone likes to believe that their better selves would emerge in a moral crisis, such as being offered the chance to kill even a small number of uncongenial individuals to save the lives of many others, but few of us will ever find ourselves in the situation where such a choice might arise. In November 1943, in Tehran, a small group of German assassins did.

2

The Peacock Realm

To say that the Tehran of the early 1940s was a melting pot does not quite do justice to the sheer chaotic tribalism of the place. Under its modern-day founding father Reza Pahlavi, who ruled as shah from 1925 to 1941, both the Imperial Kingdom of Iran and its capital city were in the throes of a seemingly perpetual cultural revolution. Uneasily suspended between the ancient and modern, rich in natural resources and of major strategic value to both sides in Hitler's war, the place prefigured some of the role Berlin would play in the 1950s and beyond, the crisis zone of world affairs where foreign agents would jostle for influence and the powder-keg of factional rivalries and distrust was liable at any time to erupt into bloodshed. Police informers, political and religious dissidents, Bolsheviks, Nazis, and the ideologically flexible, circling one another in a miasma of sweat, sewage, and garlic, cripples with stumps for arms and legs, children with festering wounds, all to some extent or another were players in the region's game. Tehran was alive with spies of all shapes and sizes and every political color. There were armed soldiers patrolling at the front doors of some of the city's best restaurants, and beggars with hairless, scab-encrusted heads reclining at the rear. Writing of the visual patisserie of medieval towers and fairytale minarets squeezed alongside the squat, Soviet-style apartment blocks that had come to characterize the Tehran of Reza Pahlavi's rule, an embedded Abwehr agent named Julius Schulze-Holthus recalled,

> An old town with a network of narrow alleys and the covered-in passages of the bazaars in whose magical twilight the riches of the land seem to be piled, as in an Aladdin's cave—barbaric carpets, miniature paintings, wonderful tarsia work of precious woods and the sparkling splendor of the silversmith's craft. The blood flows faster here than in the smart paved streets of the government quarter, with the palaces of the shah and the ministers, more actively, too, than in the broad avenues of the new city, with their two-storied houses set back from the road and shady alleys reminiscent of a Russian provincial town.[1]

2. The Peacock Realm

Here, then, was an oasis of civilization that predated biblical times, where modern refinements had taken only a tenuous hold. The dense forests on all sides of Tehran rang with the loud grief of jackals and coyotes, and camels disappeared from the city streets only after successive government fiats in the 1930s. A tax Reza imposed on tea and sugar financed the Trans-Iranian Railway, while the same revenue source paved new roads

Hitler's signed photograph for the Shah of Iran; two men linked by their belief both in Aryan supremacy and the benefits of an unfettered oil supply.

between all Iran's major cities, opening the country for the first time to travel by car, a development many of the more traditionally-minded clerics and their followers deplored. But it would take more than post-industrial dislocation to trigger the seemingly permanent cycle of sectarian insurrection and the simmering conflict between the forces of modernization and those of archaic religious piety that still characterizes the Iranian state today. Something altogether more material was needed. As so often in that schizophrenic part of the world, at once so richly endowed and so riven by factional strife, the fate of the geographic entity known successively as the Parthian Kingdom, the Umayyad Caliphate, the Safavid Empire, the Persianate State, and Eran (or land of the Aryans) was determined by oil.[2]

The British had been the first to capitalize when a wealthy London socialite named William Knox D'Arcy somewhat whimsically ventured into the Iranian desert in 1901 to search for what he called "native assets." For seven years he contended with hostile terrain, an uncertain political situation and rising costs. But the venture paid off with a strike at Shiraz in the southwest part of the country. By the time Reza took the throne, the Anglo-Persian Oil Company, the predecessor to today's BP, was the third largest petroleum producer in the world. The huge refinery built at Abadan, 600 miles south of Tehran, came on line in 1916, and in the young Winston Churchill's account, "blasted away day and night, [with] an infernal roar of furnaces and the clanging of iron plates that made a thought-annihilating thunder." A flourishing export traffic put Iran on the strategic map and allowed Reza to push through a series of civil reforms intended to force the nation's "prehistoric Mohammadian orthodoxy," as he put it, into the twentieth century, if not at the expense of his semi-divine power. In time the shah moved into an impregnable new fortress, a 12-story granite palace with gold-faucated bathtubs and a master bedroom where a ball of multi-faceted colored mirror glass could be made

North-central Tehran, seen with the Elburz mountains in the background.

to spin slowly, drenching the walls and molded cornices, and whatever figures lay below, in specks of eerie, wiggling light, thus anticipating the disco era by some fifty years.

Oil revenues and the consequent upgrade to Iran's physical infrastructure and military capabilities soon attracted the attention of all the major foreign intelligence services. As "Wild Bill" Donovan, the founding father of America's Office of Strategic Services, the precursor of the CIA, noted, "Persia, where East meets West, was the biggest show we had, and Tehran was probably the most important base for the Service until Berlin replaced it." The Abwehr's Major Schulze-Holthus had been planted in the region in 1941, in a mission made even more delicate than normal by the fact that the Russians then occupied the northern part of Iran and the British the south. One of the major's earliest briefs was to rendezvous with a six-man German Signal Commando team who had been dropped by parachute into the foothills of the Elburz mountains north of Tehran. The original plan was to make their way, disguised as native herdsmen, into the city center and ambush a bus carrying Soviet technicians working on the region's main oil pipeline. But the operation had to be abandoned because the bus, typical of Iranian buses, failed to turn up. The team was forced to return to the hills and make its way home to Berlin by a combination of camel and truck. That got them as far as the port town of Bandar Abbas, where they were taken on board a U-boat waiting for them off the moonlit coast of the Persian Gulf.

It sometimes seemed Iran was the perennial supporting character in the annals of wartime spycraft. Neither as obviously central to strategic decision-making as the chancelleries of London, Moscow or Berlin, nor as ideologically fickle as the likes of Spain, Turkey or Rumania, the so-called Peacock Realm was nonetheless strongly positioned as a bulwark against the thrust of the Axis toward the southeast. To the SD's Walter Schellenberg, reciprocally, Tehran was at "the heart of veiled activities," somewhere to "discommode" the occupying Allied forces, with the goal of turning Iran and its neighboring states into a sort of client partnership capable of servicing the Reich with massive supplies of arms, oil, and other materiel. Balked from late 1942 of all opportunity to expand in North Africa, the Germans instead looked acquisitively at the new shah's forbidding kingdom. Sometimes their incursions consisted of comic-opera affairs such as that of the aborted bus hijacking, or a broadly similar caper to send a dynamite-packed riderless camel train into the local British garrison, which failed when the animals strayed off course and wandered back to their natural habitat, to explode harmlessly on the fringes of the Salt Desert. But there were also more serious initiatives. In 1943, Hitler's War Directive No. 32 gave Schellenberg at least tacit approval for his operations at the highest executive level.³ "The struggle against the British positions in the Mediterranean and in western Asia will be continued by converging attacks launched through Iran," he wrote. Unlike many such orders, the führer's decree on Iran remained in force until the end of the war.

It might fairly be said that the actual execution of Hitler's grand geopolitical ambitions in the sphere remained a largely improvised, faintly ramshackle affair, but in time Schellenberg was at least able to successfully insert two trained agents in the area. Their brief was not to cause short-term havoc with hijacked buses or booby-trapped camels but to go undercover, posing as commercial travelers, establish local contacts, and await further instructions. Coming ashore at the port city of Pahlavi (today's Bandar-e Anzali) on the southern end of the Caspian, wearing identical sweat-stained tropical suits and carrying Abwehr-issued black leather briefcases (for deception purposes, prominently stamped on the inside "MADE IN HONG KONG"), they went by the faintly vaudeville-sounding aliases of Max and Moritz. In reality they were a young Quenzgut graduate named Franz Mayr and a former Hitler Youth organizer-turned-SS Sturmführer, Roman Gamotha.

As a pair, the new arrivals made an unlikely team to be at the forefront of a major international espionage ring with the aim of assassinating three enemy heads of government and decisively turning the course of the war. Mayr was described as "short with thinning hair, black eyes, and a clipped Hitler mustache," and Gamotha as "dark and rugged, with the features of a Hollywood ruffian," with a rather unglamorous habit of loudly sniffing a menthol inhaler while holding the other nostril before loudly clearing his sinuses with a noise like that of an unclogging drain. Inevitably the two operatives suffered a culture shock when adjusting to their surroundings. Their first apartment on the outskirts of Tehran smelled of the sacrificial sheep regularly roasted in the block's central courtyard, and the building's plumbing had a distinct touch of the haphazard to it. They had walked down the gangway of their ship with the modern equivalent of $20,000 in carefully forged Iranian and British banknotes, but money worries soon gnawed away. Both men were dedicated Nazis. It took time before the reality of living hand-to-mouth in a putrid Tehran suburb burned some of the romance out of their situation, leaving a residue of stoic resignation. Gamotha noted in his diary that it was "necessary to overcome one's disappointment, for the work assigned to us represents things that mean a great deal to me personally, to which I will therefore dedicate myself with all zeal and a deep inner sense of contentment." It was almost as though he was writing for himself and posterity.

Mayr, who, unlike his colleague, at least spoke passable Farsi, appears to have been the more proactive of the two SD men in assimilating the local culture. As if to illustrate his brief to go underground, he took a job first as a municipal sanitation worker and then as a gravedigger in the vast complex of the Mesgarabad cemetery, 20 miles from the city center. Gamotha in turn began to spend much of his time around the German enclave of Igdir across the border in eastern Turkey, where he posed as a commercial traveler dealing chiefly in carpets and semi-precious metals. Schellenberg wrote of the two men in his postwar memoir, "Over time, they organized their own network in the Near East. Normally they communicated with me through a cover firm in Berlin, but in case of emergencies sent wireless messages which I received independently from the SD."[4] Gamotha continued to commute in and out of Tehran from his Turkish outpost to set up a network of safe houses for his fellow SD agents arriving in the town in advance of the Allies' conference in late November 1943.

After Gamotha and Mayr came men such as Erwin Ettel, a small, blunt-faced 47-year-old Cologne preacher's son who had worked his way through the upper ranks of Lufthansa to join the foreign service and ultimately become German ambassador to Iran. The abrupt deposition of Reza Pahlavi by the occupying Soviet and British forces in favor of the Allies' sock-puppet candidate, Reza's 21-year-old son Mohammad—the last shah of Iran—brought significant changes to the nation's diplomatic status quo. As a result, Ettel hurriedly decided that he and his mistress should relocate to Afghanistan in his official Mercedes. The traffic proved impossible, however, and in the end he simply changed his name and took up residence in an abandoned gamekeeper's shed on the banks of Lake Namak, south of Tehran. From there the one-time ambassador would pursue his cloak-and-dagger activities as best he could. "I am only a cog in the wheel," he wrote disarmingly in December 1942, which was perhaps to downplay his role in the accelerating campaign of German dark arts in the region.

Alongside Ettel was a displaced Armenian rug merchant named Ahmad Asadi, who made contact with Mayr and Gamotha in January 1943. Apparently motivated by a burning dislike of the British, Asadi remarked of his nation's latest Western occupier, "The English! Have you ever seen how they strut about here.... The sahibs, the white landlords who look upon us as colonials and treat us like filth." He, too, was ready to act, not only to stand right in the center of the particle storm of political turmoil raging in Tehran but to use it as the impetus to take direct action "and efface that imperialist swine Churchill." The Reich Security Administration (RSHA) parachuted money for its agents in Iran onto desert fields marked by flickering red flares. There was a typically rigid German system for this: individual drops of up to RM 3,000 (roughly $1,500 at the time) could be approved merely on a radio signal from Ettel or another agent, and payments up to RM 15,000 ($7,500) by two signals in an agreed sequence, sent at suitable intervals. Amounts above that went to the RSHA, where the section chief reviewed them and passed the forms up to Schellenberg for his signature. Payments above RM 50,000 ($25,000) could be authorized only by Canaris.

It was an unusual career move for a former accredited state envoy, but soon the middle-aged Ettel personally joined the reception committee, regularly marching into the desert or climbing high into the rocky foothills dressed in shepherd's robes, to help retrieve the packages and containers that fluttered and drifted to earth from the nighttime sky. Sometimes the collection team found themselves surrounded by a herd of mountain goats or wild boar as the curious animals wandered up to get a closer look. Once while waiting for a drop, Ettel saw other human figures approaching on the hillside. Creeping up behind them, he found himself facing a man with a black-painted face carrying a distinctive spear-tipped dagger which he could see was inlaid with a silver Imperial eagle on the handle. "We looked at our respective weapons and said, 'I think we must be on the same side,'" Ettel recalled. They agreed to split up the night's cache before separately making their way back from the mountain.

Ettel was not a young man, and the road down the escarpment was no more than a gravel track, which was neither straight nor lit. He stumbled and fell several times before he reached a copse of thorny shrubs and ferns, which marked the point where a winding dirt path led the former diplomat south toward Namak. He and his three companions covered the next twenty miles by camel, a five-hour progress, which eventually took them down a second rocky trail with barbed wire strung up on either side amid ominous signs of a newly laid minefield. No one was blown up, but to look inconspicuous the bedraggled party decided to abandon their mounts just as the sun was coming up on the edge of the lake and cover the last three miles on foot. Ettel did so in some discomfort. It was later discovered that he had fractured his ankle in one of his earlier falls on the descent. Finally collapsing into the rustic mud-and-straw hovel that served as his base, Ettel was almost ridiculously nonchalant about his injury. "There's nothing much wrong with me. I shall sleep well tonight," he assured his companions before repeatedly dunking his chapped face in the rusted cattle trough that acted as his washbasin. Ettel's share of the night's spoils came to RM 8,000 ($4,000), part of which he used to plant anti–British rhetoric in Tehran's daily *Ettelaat* (no relation) newspaper and part on purchasing a secondhand American jeep for use on any future parachute-drop sorties. There was also a small side supply of Mauser M712 machine pistols and ammunition, "which may provide us some sport in the future." Ettel's ankle took six weeks to mend. By the time he was fully fit again, he had a new mission in mind, and the romance of struggling up and down the Elburz foothills in the moonlight seemed suddenly less important.

* * *

When words like "Nazi" and "spy" are mentioned, we perhaps think of a ruthlessly efficient organization staffed by sinister, leather-clad Gestapo operatives on terms of some familiarity with a wide range of the most indescribable tools of horror. Those things were all part of the wartime German intelligence and espionage effort, but in that world it's easy to forget the most important factor—bureaucracy. That brief demarcation dispute between Erwin Ettel and his fellow Axis agent on the darkened Iranian hillside mirrored the broader confusion that dogged the two principal Reich ministries involved in the planning of the state's covert operations, the Abwehr and SD Ausland. The retention of the two side by side inevitably duplicated efforts and muddled responsibility. Sometimes the twin organs of the state even threatened to neutralize each other. It seemed that even Hitler's Greater Germany was too small to hold them both.

As the war situation darkened for Germany in 1943, the SD made less pretense of enthusiasm for many of the state's more flamboyant espionage activities. A report in January read, "The news of [covert operations] in North Africa has evoked no applause from the population.... There is no real taste for such fatuities." Several Nazi party functionaries began to refer to the SD, in turn, almost as if it were the propaganda arm of a foreign power. Hans Frank, the brutal governor-general of Poland, told his postwar trial (where he was summarily convicted and hanged) that he had voiced "most serious misgivings concerning the so-called confidential information reports about Poland which the SD continually brandished about the Reich."[5] These had been "simply low-level spy stories," he added. Similarly, in early 1943 Gauleiter Albert Florian wrote to Martin Bormann, chief of the Party Chancellery and by then arguably the second most powerful man in the Reich, to complain, "My suspicion, hitherto unfortunately lacking evidence, that the SD was meddling in Party matters is now fully substantiated. I therefore propose to forbid any political director or member of my staff to undertake any duty on behalf of the SD."[6] Sometimes there was even a quaintly libertarian objection to the sheer scope of Walter Schellenberg's activities. On January 22, 1943, Gauleiter Carl Weinrich wrote for the record to the Party Chancellery: "I refuse once and for all to allow the SD to poke its nose into my affairs. After all we are not in Russia, and do not need to be shadowed by an OGPU."[7]

Inevitably, Schellenberg's relations with his Abwehr counterpart Wilhelm Canaris were ambivalent, at best, often competitive, and sometimes positively hostile. Independent-minded espionage chiefs are not always natural sharers. As early as November 1939, the so-called Venlo Incident had served as a powerful reminder, if Canaris needed it, that the SD was encroaching on traditional Abwehr turf. Like many such special-operations affairs, this one combined drama with a generous degree of slapstick. Taken as a whole, Venlo was a victory for the German intelligence services but hardly a unifying one.

Representing himself as a Major Schammel and claiming to be a member of an anti–Hitler cabal that wanted to make peace with Britain, Schellenberg had managed to personally befriend two MI6 Secret Service officers, Major Richard Stevens and Captain Sigismund Best. After a brief courtship, he was able to lure the two agents to a meeting at the Café Backus near the Dutch frontier town of Venlo. As the British officers pulled up in their shiny new American Packard, not exactly a model of circumspection, they spotted "Schammel" standing on the second-floor terrace of the café. He gave them a cheery sweep of his arm. They interpreted this as an invitation for them to join him for a drink upstairs. In reality it was a signal for an SD heavy named Alfred Naujocks to suddenly crash through the border in his car, firing his Luger wildly over the heads of the surprised British visitors, and killing a nearby Dutch army officer, Lieutenant Dirk Klop, in the process. At that point, Best and Stevens promptly surrendered and were driven back over the frontier into Germany. After interrogation at Gestapo headquarters in Berlin, the men were sent to the notorious Sachsenhausen concentration camp but survived that and subsequent confinement at Dachau to be liberated by Allied troops in May 1945.

In due course, Hitler took the Venlo incident not as an opportunity to apologize to the neutral Dutch government for violating their national sovereignty and shooting dead one of their citizens but helping justify Germany's invasion of the Netherlands in May 1940. Canaris for his part was not pleased by the overall course of events. The SD had gatecrashed a long-running Abwehr surveillance operation, he complained, settling for "one cheap success" instead of the prospect of any long-term infiltration of British intelligence. "He left us in no doubt that Schellenberg was a person we should be wary of having any contact with," one of Canaris's secretaries noted.[8] The Abwehr chief was on ground well beyond this elsewhere, remarking that his rival spymaster was a "schweinhund" and "shitkopf," among other unappreciative terms. The censure did not unduly trouble Schellenberg, whom Hitler personally invested with the Iron Cross, first class, for his services.

Adding a further layer of complexity to the byzantine world of German wartime intelligence operations was the Reich postal minister Wilhelm Ohnesorge, whose duties, as we've seen, extended far beyond merely overseeing the smooth running of the nation's daily mail service. Ohnesorge was the first Nazi official to warn Hitler, in a note of September 8, 1942, that "at this hour America is assembling all her professors of chemistry and physics to obtain from them extraordinary achievements."[9] Schellenberg puffed this up in a covering letter to the Chancellery. "Of extreme importance for future tactical consideration," he wrote, while Canaris argued exactly the reverse. "There has been nothing found in the foreign press, especially the American, on any unusual production or use of uranium for blasting purposes," he noted, and thus reports of any Allied doomsday weapon were either "entirely fanciful or non-existent." It would be hard to imagine how a head of state intelligence could be any more mistaken.

Below this level no fewer than six separate branches of the Abwehr operated their own intelligence-gathering units. Sections 1, 2, and 3 were respectively concerned with obtaining information through sabotage, codebreaking, and counterespionage. The service's Brandenburg Division, the preserve of Major General Alexander von Pfuhlstein, dealt in subversion and psych-ops, which primarily involved activities behind enemy lines. In May 1940, von Pfuhlstein's unit supplied tactical support to reinforce important traffic points during the invasion of Holland, and in June 1941, the commandos of Brandenburg Division managed to cross and capture the main bridges over the Duna River on commandeered Soviet trucks in the early stages of Operation Barbarossa. The following spring, a special command of the Brandenburgers was deployed as part of Operation Salaam in the North African desert. They had some success

The Nazi postal minister Wilhelm Ohnesorge, whose duties went well beyond ensuring the safe delivery of the Reich's daily mail.

in pinpointing Allied troop movements, but an attempt to infiltrate paratroopers to sabotage enemy oil depots around Tripoli ended in failure due to a faulty dropping point. Von Pfuhlstein was one of those career officers who came to question the strategic direction of the German war effort and was arrested for high treason following the Valkyrie plot of July 1944. Pfuhlstein's file was duly passed to the dreaded People's Court, effectively a death sentence for the accused, but in this case Himmler did not consider execution to be helpful. The defendant was a Knight's Cross, wounded three times, and something of a folk hero in the German press. Pfuhlstein survived the war, as well as a subsequent period in Allied detention, and died peacefully in 1976.[10]

The Abwehr also maintained a foreign bureau, which monitored the overseas press, preparing a daily summary for Hitler's attention, and, when called upon, taking appropriate action to either "support or undermine the activities of individual persons," as their terms of reference delicately put it. Their chief from the summer of 1938 to the end of the war was Captain (later Vice Admiral) Leopold Burkner. Under Burkner's watch, the international department sometimes strayed from the clerical to the more actively operational side of the Abwehr spectrum; for instance, when it came to financing a somewhat loosely defined network of Arabs in Palestine to engage in sabotage and sporadic armed uprising against the occupying British and Free French forces. Burkner also survived the Gestapo dragnet that descended in July 1944 and briefly took command of the Abwehr after Canaris's fall. He subsequently spent two years as an Allied prisoner and went on to become the director of the German office of the Dutch national air carrier KLM. He died in 1975 at the age of 81.

Rounding off the Abwehr hierarchy was the sinister-sounding Section Z, under the control of Major General Hans Oster. Despite its name, it was a largely administrative body concerned with personnel, finances, and the numerous other petty details of any twentieth-century government agency. One of the largest rooms in Oster's Berlin headquarters housed the central Abwehr files, dozens of metal tubs in the shape of a giant beer barrel whose covers opened at the top. Each agent was assigned a card or, if sufficiently prominent, a bulky manila envelope. Canaris seems to have taken a certain sadistic glee in tormenting the head of this final tentacle of his far-flung Abwehr empire. According to the historian David Kahn,

> During tennis matches, Canaris loved to place Oster, who was fastidious in his dress, in a damp corner of the clay court behind his house and then keep after him until he finally got Oster to slip and stain the seat of his freshly pressed long white trousers. When he received an oral report from Oster, Canaris typically probed into it with persistent exactitude, and stopped only when his subordinate admitted doubts.[11]

Oster was yet another of those highly placed officers who grew skeptical about the direction Germany's war effort was taking. He was dismissed from his post in April 1943 after being accused of helping a group of Jewish refugees escape to Switzerland disguised as Wehrmacht soldiers. He at least survived until April 1945, when Canaris's secret diaries were discovered and, in a rage upon reading them, Hitler ordered that all current and past Abwehr conspirators be executed. In the pre-dawn hours of April 9, Oster was forced to strip naked before being led to the gallows in the courtyard at Bavaria's Flossenburg concentration camp. He was 57 at the time of his death. Canaris and the dissident Lutheran theologian Dietrich Bonhoeffer were hanged at the same time. A fourth prisoner, Canaris's one-time Vatican emissary Josef Mueller, was also scheduled to die that morning but was reprieved at the last moment, apparently in the hope that he might help Germany negotiate more favorable terms with the advancing Allies. He later remembered that as he had waited in his cell the air had begun to fill with the charred fragments of the bodies executed that day, "the ashes float[ing] down through the iron bars looking over the crematoria, settling all around me."

The fastidious Hans Oster, Canaris's deputy and sometime rival in the Abwehr hierarchy, who went with him to death in April 1945.

In all, then, the world of German intelligence operations in 1939–45 was far from the callously efficient Teutonic ideal. "Kafkaesque" might be going too far, but not, perhaps, heading entirely in the wrong direction, to describe the various overlapping functions and inbuilt contradictions of the Abwehr-SD network. In this jungle of a governmental system, as incalculable as any oriental sultanate, it often fell to small cells of fanatically motivated individual agents to accomplish those missions otherwise doomed to remain in the eternal bureaucratic purgatory of a ministerial drawing board.

* * *

In its way as arcane as the looking-glass world of Nazi espionage, the relationship between the Big Three wartime commanders-in-chief seemed to worsen even as their nations' strategic fortunes improved. Reflecting on her father and President Roosevelt, Mary Soames, Winston Churchill's youngest and last surviving child, captured the human face of the Atlantic alliance by quoting a French proverb. "In love, there is always one who kisses, and one who offers the cheek." Churchill was the suitor, Roosevelt his coquettish quarry. Sometimes it seemed less of a truly concerted effort to rid the civilized world of the Nazi menace, and more of a messy ménage à trois with the Soviet despot as the object of the Westerners' mutual desire.

On May 4, 1943, Roosevelt wrote to Stalin to suggest a meeting.

"The simplest and most practical method that I can think of would be an informal and completely simple visit for a few days between you and me," he proposed before turning to the matter of logistics.

> Africa is almost out of the question in summer, and Khartoum is in British territory. Iceland I do not like because for both you and me it involves rather difficult flights, and, in addition, it would make it, quite frankly, difficult not to invite Prime Minister Churchill at the same time.[12]

It almost touches the level of a classic French bedroom farce to note that Churchill was staying under Roosevelt's roof at Maryland's Camp David (then called Shangri-La) at the very moment the president wrote his billet-doux. The British premier was still blissfully unaware of his host's duplicity when on May 19, he addressed a joint session of Congress on the theme of the "completely unified" Allied plans for a tripartite conference:

> We, both of us, earnestly hope that at no distant date we may be able to achieve what we have so long sought—namely a meeting with Marshal Stalin. But how, when, and where this is to be accomplished is not a matter upon which I am able to shed any clear ray of light at the present time, and, if I were, I should certainly not shed it.[13]

Churchill was not pleased to only subsequently learn of Roosevelt's plans for a meeting à deux and said as much in an indignant cable. "[U.S. ambassador] Averell Harriman told me last night of your wish for a meeting with Uncle Joe alone," he wrote, insisting—perhaps more accurately, pleading—that he be included.[14] Roosevelt wired back, falsely protesting his innocence. "I did not suggest to UJ that we meet alone," he wrote, in a blatant fiction. "But he told [me] that he assumed (a) that we would speak alone and (b) that he agreed that we should not bring our staffs." Now that he thought of it, however, Roosevelt continued, perhaps there was something to be said for the idea. Stalin, he told Churchill, might very well "be more frank" if he, Churchill, was absent. Still spinning his ally a line, the president added, "Of course, you and I are completely frank in matters of this kind...."

Stalin soon rendered the discussion moot. He could not possibly leave his country, he informed his squabbling allies at that moment in the Soviet Union's destiny, failing to mention the more mundane fact that he was terrified of flying. No safe overseas land routes were available to him in 1943. Then the Vozhd climbed back on his old hobbyhorse and asked the two Western chiefs when the long-awaited second front would be opened.

There are many diligent and exhaustively researched accounts that dwell upon the highly strategic decisions taken by President Roosevelt and Prime Minister Churchill and their staffs, and the consequences these had for many millions of people, combatants and civilians alike, around the world. What such studies lack, perhaps, is the all-important human factor. The essence of history is surely to seek to re-create the way of life and habits of thought and feeling of a past age convincingly, while at the same time realizing and letting the reader see that people who lived then were not the abstractions they may be presented as by academics but made of flesh and blood like us, and with comparable feelings of love and hatred, fear and resolution, sometimes obsessing like us, too, even if what occasioned those concerns was different. In the case of Roosevelt and Churchill, for at least part of the time, one such preoccupation was the matter of their personal safety, or more accurately, their wildly divergent perspectives on it.

When Churchill traveled to Washington over the Christmas season of 1941 to meet Roosevelt for the first time since America entered the fray, he crossed the Atlantic on the Royal Navy battleship *Duke of York*, sailing unescorted through seas infested by German U-boats hunting just off the Irish coast. He brought with him three political assistants and an equal number of military aides, two secretaries, a doctor, and a mobile version of his Downing Street War Room, complete with maps, charts and miniature colored models of planes and ships, which, with the glee of his always readily available inner twelve-year-old, he later set up for his host's amusement in the White House. Churchill's sole security man on the tour was Inspector Walter Thompson, a career police officer who had just celebrated his 51st birthday.

Gruff, keen-eyed, and slightly ferret-faced, typically dressed in a pinstripe suit and a trilby, Thompson was one of those men then prominent in the upper echelons of British life who combined a touch of amateurism with impressive reserves of personal fortitude. Certainly Churchill had ample reason to be grateful to him over the years. On one occasion, the pro–Nazi French countess Hélène de Portes lunged at the prime minister's throat while brandishing a knife but was thwarted by Thompson. ("I regretted being so bold with a lady," he later remarked in his memoirs.) On another, Churchill insisted on standing on the roof of Downing Street to witness the Blitz, and it was only by throwing himself on top of the premier that Thompson saved him from shrapnel. These were not entirely isolated incidents. As a rule, Churchill's disdain for his own safety was a bodyguard's nightmare. With no formal reporting structure or supervision, and little advice in the matter from Churchill, Thompson was not so much opposed to his duties as left to his own devices.

Surely one of the most poignant scenes in the Churchill-Thompson relationship came when the two middle-aged men found themselves motoring alone in the remote Scottish Highlands. Their car stalled as it navigated a steep hill, sliding backward before coming to rest on the muddy banks of a large lake. At that point both passengers removed their jackets, rolled up their sleeves, and attempted to push the vehicle back on the road. This went on for some time. Eventually the driver of a passing post office delivery van stopped, assessed the situation, and seemingly not particularly moved by the spectacle of a world-famous statesman and his aide standing alone in their shirtsleeves by the side of a Scottish loch, agreed to go to the next village to send for a replacement car.[15] Churchill was due at a formal event in only an hour or so, and while he awaited alternative transport, he unselfconsciously stripped down to his underwear by the side of the road and changed into his evening suit, which became liberally spattered with mud in the process. "Good sport," Britain's wartime savior remarked, fortifying himself from a hip flask to pass the time until at length a notably dilapidated farm vehicle hove into view to conduct him to his destination. Aside from the central fact of his disability, it is hard to imagine President Roosevelt in the same straits.[16]

In the same spirit of extreme informality, while on a private visit following his May 1943 address to Congress, Churchill decided that he might care to go skinny-dipping in the sea off Palm Beach, Florida. Thompson felt duty-bound to get his chief into a pair of swimming trunks but failed. "Nobody knows I am staying here, and I have only to step out of the back door into the water," Churchill observed.

"You could be seen through glasses, sir," said Thompson.

"If they are that much interested, it is their own fault what they see," Churchill replied.

Told that a large shark had been seen basking in the water close to

Winston Churchill's friend and bodyguard Walter Thompson, wearing his usual pinstripe suit, watches as Churchill tries out a tommy gun.

where he swam, Churchill retained his composure. "Just keep an eye out, would you?" he inquired of Thompson as the latter sat in his habitual pinstripe suit in a deckchair set well back from the water's edge. Half an hour later, Churchill emerged from the surf to humorously take credit for the shark's non-appearance. "My bulk must have frightened it away," he remarked before again lighting the inevitable cigar.[17]

During the Allied meeting at Quebec that August, Roosevelt's naval aide Admiral Wilson Brown remembered more than once having to resort to subterfuge to keep "Winston hours"—which as a rule extended to two or three o'clock in the morning—from further draining the physically infirm president. "To break up a night talk, I several times invented a fictitious telephone call from Washington when I could tell by [Roosevelt's] face that he had had enough."[18] After one such session adjourned, a 24-year-old Canadian army clerk named Emile Couture found a large leather folder by Churchill's seat at the table stamped with the inscription "WSC-FDR, Quebec Conference 1943" on the cover and kept it as a souvenir, not realizing that it contained nearly complete early plans for the D-Day invasion. After reading the contents, the young clerk hid the file under his barrack-room mattress until he could safely return it to Walter Thompson in the morning. Couture was later awarded the British Empire Medal for "services rendered."

After Quebec, Churchill took an ordinary public train back for further talks in Washington. "Winston enjoyed himself hugely, making V-signs from his carriage window at all the engine drivers on the line and at all the passers-by," the diplomat Alexander Cadogan noted disapprovingly in his diary. "He quite unnecessarily rushes out on to the rear deck of the car, in a flowered silk dressing-gown, to attract and chat with anyone he can find on the platform at stopping-places."[19] Churchill was less enthusiastic about his latest visit to Roosevelt's home at Hyde Park. "There was no peace there, security men all around in the grounds, and at night a vast searchlight overhead." Thompson later reflected on the experience, "The heat was oppressive, and I couldn't sleep. Nor could Winston; one night he got up to watch the sun rise." As the prime minister and his unarmed minder stepped out onto the lawn in the pre-dawn light, Churchill turned to Thompson and said, perhaps only half in jest, "You had better go ahead, Walter. I don't want a Secret Service bullet through my head." There was something a bit ostentatious and un–English about the president's security apparatus, both visitors agreed. In general, the British looked down, at least privately, on such matters, regarding them as mildly vulgar and not becoming the head of a great democratic power.

Joseph Stalin had no such petty-bourgeois inhibitions, and by the mid–1930s his personal security detail resembled an army. For many years his principal bodyguard was a former Hungarian theatrical hairdresser named Karl Pauker, born in Budapest in 1893, who had deserted to the Russians in the First World War. Academics debate to this day the chicken-and-egg dilemma of which came first, Stalin's mental disintegration or his inner circle's descent into psychotic barbarism. The answer may be that there was a degree of osmosis involved; neither party found anything pathological about the other's madness, suggesting each shared the condition. The USSR under Stalin is the only state in recorded history to have declared the mutual experience of its founding fathers a capital crime.

In August 1936, the Vozhd unleashed the full fury of his psychosis on his one-time revolutionary comrades Lev Kamenev, Grigori Zinoviev, and fourteen other Old Bolsheviks who were put on trial, if it could be called that, for conspiring in a terrorist campaign to "wipe out the Great Guide and the rest of the People's leadership." The accused men's defense consisted of a lengthy self-condemnation. It would have been surprising had they done otherwise since they had all been repeatedly assured that their lives would be spared if they confessed their treachery. All sixteen were nonetheless summarily convicted, taken down to the cellars, and shot.[20] As a special treat, Pauker was allowed to witness the scene and later entertained Stalin and his surviving presidium colleagues with an impression of Zinoviev in his death struggle, falling on his knees and whimpering pitifully, "Please, comrade, for God's sake call Joseph Vissarionovich." Stalin laughed "uncontrollably and loudest."

He also laughed last. Pauker, too, was part of the original Bolshevik party created by Lenin. Sooner or later the old guard would all have to be eliminated for good, victims of the criminal derangement which made it possible for Stalin to satisfy his political and psychological whims at the same time, each reinforcing the other. Barely a year later, Pauker would be taken down and shot, just like Zinoviev, and just like Zinoviev, he would beg his murderers for mercy.

Stalin's paranoia was an engine that never stopped running. It operated on professional and personal levels: the more power he accumulated, the more he felt threatened. By the time he came to host a wartime conference with his two principal allies, the security arrangements catered to the demands of a mind which was not so much morbidly mistrustful as in the grip of a clinical psychosis. According to the author Michael Dobbs,

> No effort was spared on the safety front. The soldiers stationed along the road were merely the visible tip of a vast operation stretching twelve miles on either side of the highway. Stalin's palace was surrounded by three concentric security zones.... Lavrentiy Beria's men had also occupied local villages and ordered everybody out of their homes. "The noise and the shouting were indescribable," remembered one eyewitness. "All you could hear throughout the village was crying. People lost their daughters, their sons, their husbands." Roughly 180,000 men, women, and children were rounded up, forced into freight cars, and transported to the deserts of Uzbekistan on the same railway system that Stalin had used to reach the conference.[21]

In policy terms, it would be fair to say that by about the middle of 1943, the bane of Stalin's life wasn't so much Hitler as his chronic worry about opposition from within and without to his vision of the Soviet state of his dreams—a vast military camp in which he assumed total control over every administrative agency, from foreign policy to culture to the distribution of provincial wheat harvests, with the Party machine and the goons of the NKVD on hand to ensure unanimity and subservience to the top. Compared to their Soviet ally, both Roosevelt and Churchill were almost ludicrously amenable to their real or imagined enemies.

The long-time Soviet commissar Lazar Kaganovich, one of the few of the original Bolshevik guard to survive to see old age, later recalled that he had known five or six different Stalins and that a new personality had begun to emerge around 1932. "He now felt vulnerable to attack." In March of that year, a 200-page pamphlet written by the senior party functionary Martemyan Ryutin openly criticized the regime's economic policy, which it argued had brought about a massive fall in the income of the working class, high taxation, and a near-collapse in the value of the currency. Stalin interpreted the document as a direct call for his assassination and had Ryutin arrested; sentenced to a seemingly lenient ten years' imprisonment, he would later be caught up in the genocidal purges of the middle part of the decade. Now charged with high treason, Ryutin had the nerve to write a defiant last letter to his sometime colleagues on the presidium. "I am not afraid of death, if that is what the investigative apparatus of the NKVD has in mind for me. I declare in advance that I will not plead for a pardon, since I cannot confess to things which I have not done.... I am completely innocent." Ryutin was casually tortured by his captors on and off for a further two months, but they got nothing out of him. He was shot in January 1937 at age 46.

The burden of Stalin's surpassing mental state was not borne just by his perceived political opponents. In Minsk, the Soviet Union's leading Jewish theatrical figure Solomon Mikhoels was killed by an NKVD hit team acting on Kremlin orders. The 57-year-old was crushed under a tractor, his body dumped in a side street, and his death attributed to a hit-and-run accident. Mikhoels was buried with full state honors. Stalin's already pronounced persecution mania soon reached new heights when, on holiday at Sochi on the Black Sea, his motorboat came under fire from the shore: a high-stakes charade, it later emerged, orchestrated by Lavrentiy Beria to impress on his boss that he, Beria, was indispensable to his personal welfare and should thus remain at his side most of the day, ready to jot down and execute his slightest whim. The strategy worked, at least up until Stalin's death from an apparent stroke in March 1953. Nine months later, Beria was tried for treason, convicted, and promptly shot. Some say that at the end he faced his executioners with courage and tried to speak but had his mouth stuffed shut with a towel; other reports have him clinging to the boots of his guards and begging for mercy in a way even Karl Pauker might have found distasteful.

Scholars today believe that between 900,000 and 1.2 million Soviet citizens, among them 23,000 members of the NKVD, lost their lives in the central two years of the Stalinist terror. How many in all perished or were sent to the camps remains a question that may never be satisfactorily answered. An estimate by the historian Robert Conquest suggests a total of 18 million deaths in 1930–39. At the last Party congress before the war,

Stalin drily remarked that he had recently found it necessary to promote a number of the younger generation, adding with a touch of dark humor: "Alas, there are now fewer old cadres than are ideal, and their ranks are continuing to thin out."[22]

Stalin's formidable protection apparatus did not deter the efforts of the Reich Security Office to remove him. We've touched on Walter Schellenberg's scheme of the remotely controlled car bomb and the various attempts to breach security around the Vozhd's dacha. On another occasion, in early 1943, SD agents successfully parachuted into a remote area outside Riga but then encountered a Soviet troop patrol on their way to Stalin's nearby field headquarters, with disastrous results for their mission and themselves. Most of the Germans were unceremoniously shot and buried in a mass grave where they fell. Schellenberg remembered that prior to execution, one of the men had been set on fire to entertain his captors but had managed to break free long enough to take his own life by biting down on a cyanide tablet sewn under his collar. In retrospect, the Riga operation serves as a kind of vignette of the way the opposing forces were now fighting the war: one of undoubted daring and courage, with sadism never far below the surface.

Following the abrupt exit of Karl Pauker, Stalin acquired a new head of his protection detail: Nikolai Vlasik, born in 1896, the diminutive but psychotically aggressive son of illiterate Belorussian peasants who had left school at eleven, and boasted of never having read a book except for Lenin's 1917 page-turner *The Tasks of the Proletariat in the Present Revolution*. Vlasik's purview, like Pauker's, included supervising Stalin's personal security, meals, domestic life, and children. The bodyguard's ability to seduce "hundreds" of women, and to consume industrial quantities of vodka without becoming drunk, seem to have endeared him to his employer. Vlasik would rarely leave Stalin's side when the latter finally traveled overseas to meet his Western allies. One of his jobs was to periodically "cleanse" the other guards under his command, which he did by removing them in the dead of night to the Sukhanovo prison located on the grounds of an old monastery south of Moscow. The historian Stephen Kotkin writes of the accommodations there.

> Almost no light ever penetrated the darkness of the five-by-seven-foot cells, some of which were located far underground. Inmates were often not permitted to sleep or sit, but instead forced to stand all night, and freezing water was run through constantly. Executions took place in the former cathedral. Altogether, more than 100 of the highest-ranking bodyguards were shot.[23]

With a certain inevitability, Vlasik would eventually fall foul of Stalin's caprices, even if in unusual circumstances. His fatal error was neither

Nikolai Vlasik, the loyal bodyguard who fell afoul of Stalin because of some defective bananas.

strategic nor procedural, but culinary. One night Vlasik proudly presented the boss, as he fondly called him, with a bunch of specially imported bananas, a Babylonian luxury in wartime Russia, to accompany his dinner. Stalin peeled one and found it was not ripe. He tried two more; they, too, were not ripe. At that point Stalin summoned Vlasik.[24]

"Where did you get these bananas?" Vlasik tried to explain, but Stalin cut him off. "These bandits take bribes and sell us inedible food. What was the name of the banana boat?"

"I don't know," Vlasik was forced to admit. "I didn't take an interest...."

These last five words proved critical in sealing Vlasik's fate. He was arrested and in due course given the usual grim charade of a trial. The presiding judge inquired about Vlasik's lifestyle at the time he had been Stalin's chief watchdog.

"Where my duties were concerned I was always in order," Vlasik testified. "My meetings with women were on account of my health and in my spare time. I admit that I had a lot of sex."

"The head of government warned you that such behavior was unacceptable."

"Yes, he once informed me that I was abusing my relations with females."[25]

The transcript continues, "Defendant Vlasik, tell the court what property you obtained illegally, without payment."

2. The Peacock Realm

"As far as I remember, an upright piano, a grand piano, three or four carpets...."

"What about the fourteen cameras? ... And where did you get cut glass vases, wineglasses, and porcelain tableware in such profusion?"

Vlasik was found guilty of corruption and given the usual treatment. "My mind and body were tormented, and I suffered a heart attack. I had months without sleep," he later reported. In the end Stalin's death probably saved his life. Vlasik was released from Sukhanovo and lived another ten years in obscurity until 1967. In his memoirs he wrote, "I was severely hurt by Stalin. For 25 years of doing an irreproachable job, receiving nothing but praise and awards, I was excluded from the Party and flung into prison." From his cell, he had bombarded the boss with letters, begging for mercy for him and his family. "But I heard nothing."

Such were the inner courts of the three principal Allied leaders at the time they came together to coordinate their strategy for finally ending the war at Tehran in 1943.

* * *

On January 12, 1943, the day after the influential Italian American newspaper editor Carlo Tresca was gunned down in New York City—supposedly by the NKVD as retribution for his criticism of Stalin—President Roosevelt's shiny silver Douglas C-54 Skymaster landed at Mediouna airport just south of Casablanca. It was the first ever presidential Atlantic flight and the first time a president had ever left home shores in wartime. The first leg of Roosevelt's journey took him to Bathurst, South Africa, and from there via a series of dusty provincial airstrips to the Moroccan coast. Six weeks earlier, the president had summoned his principal Secret Service agent, 32-year-old Montana native Mike Reilly, while he was eating breakfast in bed and told him with a wide grin, "I have to go to Africa," adding with what his bodyguard called "boyish glee," "Churchill and his chiefs of staff are going, and our chiefs will be there too. Mike, there are many reasons why I must go." Even so, Reilly may have mistaken his boss's mood of resignation for one of active enthusiasm, because Roosevelt hated flying and the dangers it might entail almost as much as Stalin did. His wife Eleanor wrote in her memoir that she had "hoped he would be won over to the marvels of flight in [1943], but instead he disliked it more than ever."[26] Roosevelt's cousin and intimate friend Margaret "Daisy" Suckley made the same point in her diary. "I think F. has mixed feelings about this trip," she wrote. "He is somewhat excited about it—The adventure of it—seeing all he will see, etc. On the other hand it is a long trip, with definite risks—But one *can't* and *mustn't* think of that."[27]

As we've seen, the principal takeaway message from Casablanca came when Roosevelt sat in the sun-bathed garden of his suburban villa, Churchill somewhat incongruously in a hard wicker chair drawn up at his side, and the press sprawled at their feet, to announce that the Allied war objective was now no less than the unconditional surrender of the Axis powers. The conference had its headline. The phrase apparently came as a bolt from the blue to the assembled reporters—who had not even known that the president, the prime minister and their combined military staffs had been amongst them in North Africa for more than a week—and may have been news to Churchill, who was later quoted as saying, "I was startled by the public announcement [of unconditional surrender]. But I tried to hide my surprise. After all, I was Roosevelt's ardent lieutenant."[28]

As anyone familiar with the 1943 film *Casablanca* will know, that city—which lay comfortably within range of German bombers operating from Tunisia—was then a hotbed of Nazi spies, even if the conference seems to have slipped their notice. (For some time, the Germans believed "Casablanca" was the codename for the White House and that the Allied meeting would thus take place in Washington.) The principal security threat to the two Western leaders came from a more conventional source. Just eleven days before Roosevelt's plane bumped down on the asphalt at Mediouna airport the Luftwaffe had dropped a mix of 215 short tons of high explosive and six short tons of incendiaries on Casablanca's docks, starting around 200 fires and killing 64 civilians at worship in a nearby mosque. Taken as a whole, the city seemed to Mike Reilly an almost willfully perverse venue for Roosevelt, Churchill, and their staffs to choose for themselves, whatever the shortcomings of the local Abwehr intelligence effort. "It was the most critical single meeting of the war to that date, and it took place in a Wild West of violence."

One evening during the conference, a local gypsy woman in her twenties was arrested by the civilian police in a darkened field in the Mers-Sultan district on the outskirts of Casablanca. She had apparently been caught laying out a line of flaming torches to act as an improvised landing strip for an aircraft. The gendarmes kept her in an outdoor detention camp for the next two days, where she was visited by American and British interrogators. She contemptuously told them that the Allies would lose the war, although she seems not to have grasped that the two principal Western leaders were even then housed only a few miles away. Following that she and another female suspect were marched out onto the adjoining wasteland by their Moroccan captors. The gypsy woman asked only that a lock of her hair be cut off and returned to her fiancé in the next town. Then both women were shot, and their bodies dumped in the back of a truck which rumbled off into the night. Roosevelt later heard of the incident from his Secret Service detail and was deeply shocked. There is no evidence that Stalin was especially impressed by the West's insistence on the absolute surrender of their mutual enemies. "Europe [is] now a jungle," he wrote to Churchill. "What is needed are not words but deeds." Anything less than the full-scale invasion of France was a diversion, and the Vozhd was "at a complete loss" to make sense of it.[29]

Roosevelt's personal security was significantly upgraded on his return from Morocco. Mike Reilly and the rest of the Secret Service detail now avoided the use of motorcades whenever they could, preferring to convey their boss by a customized train with reinforced armored-steel panels and three-inch-thick bulletproof windows. More than just the president's travel arrangements were modified. In March 1943, workmen installed two separate stainless-steel escape chutes in Roosevelt's bedroom, in theory enabling him to slide unimpeded down to the White House lawn if the situation demanded. At the same time—now at the midway point of the war—construction began on the first presidential bomb shelter, housed in the basement of the nearby U.S. Treasury. By April of that year, Reilly admitted to worrying about "Axis parachutists or an organized heavy fifth-column incursion" of the White House, and the army wheeled out eighteen artillery pieces onto the grounds as a precaution.[30] In addition, a squad of four soldiers in an army reconnaissance car equipped with two 50-caliber machine guns constantly patrolled the building's perimeter. An antiaircraft battery was set up on the White House roof, and members of the Chemical Warfare Service established an office in the building in the event of a biological weapons attack. The senior local embedded SD agent, codenamed Rose, transmitted a laconic but realistic assessment back to Berlin. "No chance to do successful business here. Citadel now presents too many obstacles."

In any case, the Germans had no need to attack Roosevelt on his home ground. They knew they could always do so when he left the "citadel" for another overseas conference.

Overnight on January 30, 1943, the shattered remnants of the German Sixth Army finally collapsed at Stalingrad, marking the strategic turning point on the Eastern front. It happened to be the tenth anniversary of Hitler's rise to power, and it also spelled the start of the slow but inexorable slide down the razor's edge to Germany's final defeat. Hitler had no illusions about the gravity of the occasion. "Our generals have surrendered formally and absolutely," he noted, in surprisingly contained tones, at a situation conference in Berlin on February 1. "They'll be brought straight to Moscow and put into the hands of the GPU and they'll blurt out orders for other forces to surrender too."[31] After that he rambled on about the Sixth Army's commander-in-chief Friedrich Paulus, wondering why he hadn't committed suicide instead of prostrating himself before the enemy.

"It's a ridiculous thing. So many men have to die, and then a man like this besmirches the heroism of so many others. He could have got out of this vale of tears and into eternity and been immortalized by the nation, but he'd rather go to Moscow. What kind of choice is that? It just doesn't make any sense."

Then Hitler turned to the Wehrmacht chief Kurt Zeitzler, who had the misfortune to be standing beside him in the conference room.

"Who now poses the gravest threat among our enemies?"

Zeitzler dutifully began a detailed strategic analysis of the current war situation, but his commander-in-chief cut him off with a brusque chop of his hand.

"Which individual foe: Roosevelt, Stalin or Churchill?"

Zeitzler could only reply, "There are presently formidable challenges on all fronts, Mein Führer."

Hitler ordered more schemes to assassinate the three Allied leaders.

3

"One Wonders About the Wrestlers"

Hitler's assets in Iran had not been idle while awaiting their further instructions. The menthol-snorting Roman Gamotha continued to move freely between the Turkish frontier and Tehran, establishing a chain of safe houses for newly arrived SD operatives, while the Farsi-speaking Franz Mayr combined his daytime job as a municipal gravedigger with a variety of ad-hoc paramilitary duties. The repeated sabotage of the main Soviet army barracks just south of the town center was Mayr's primary mission but not his sole objective. He was also to gather and send information on local Allied troop movements, particularly convoys, to note destination labels on railway freight cars, photograph incoming British or Soviet aircraft, and collect evidence of preparations for any possible high-level summit, as well as any other useful military intelligence he could glean. To Mayr, Walter Schellenberg said simply, "Get me as many reports as you can." The goal was a hundred, or roughly two a week, throughout 1943.[1]

On April 1, Schellenberg dispatched a Junkers 290 transport, which crossed over the northern Iranian mountains by the cover of night and landed six SD agents on a deserted airstrip near a salt lake outside Qom. Once their plane took off again the men collected their equipment and began their 70-mile trek to Tehran. Their only accompaniment en route was the steady cry of mountain wolves, and the sickly aroma wafting over them from the nearby Sohan toffee factory. The six arrivals carried a state-of-the-art radio transmitter, two dozen MG 42 rapid-fire light machineguns of the type known as "Hitler's buzzsaw," a large supply of ammunition, plastic explosives, and four thousand £50 British banknotes—worth roughly £5 million, or $7.5m today—for distribution to local contacts. The men had no way of knowing that the money had been printed not by the Royal Mint in London but by a counterfeiting press operated at gunpoint by inmates of the Sachsenhausen camp outside Berlin as part of Operation Bernhard, designed to flood the British currency.

Four days later, the SD team contacted Franz Mayr, whom they found in an ebullient mood. "We have all been selected for work of the highest magnitude. Between us we can significantly shorten the course of the war. In the meantime, make yourselves comfortable here. I'll join you in a bottle of champagne."

When Mayr later left the house to report for his shift at the cemetery, his guests took the opportunity to thoroughly search the premises. They were under orders to look for any evidence that their host might have been turned by the enemy, and now be conspiring against German interests. In the event all they found were several more crates of illicit wine, a well-thumbed copy of Hitler's *Mein Kampf*, and a collection of ladies' underwear. There was nothing in any of this that categorically pointed to Mayr being a line-crosser. Perhaps he had merely succumbed to some of the obvious temptations associated with long-term residence in 1940s Tehran, the men surmised. Their report back to Berlin on April 9 described him as an "absolutely first-class officer in training and outlook." Both Mayr and Gamotha served the Reich with undiminished energy throughout the year.

In the pre-dawn hours a day or two later, Mayr led the SD team back up into the rocky heights west of the city, where after an hour's crouching march they came to a barbed-wire fence that he clipped open, allowing them to pass through the gap "absolutely on our bellies," as he put it. A mile or so farther on, the party suddenly saw a powerful-looking radio tower silhouetted against the moonlit sky, installed there by the British for long-distance communications. "We're going to spoil Mr. Churchill's fun today," Mayr told the group. "Just hand me that knapsack, and be ready to retire on my word."

At that Mayr crunched over the rocks and disappeared into the night, returning five minutes later. "I think we might now take our leave, gentlemen," he announced calmly. At the bottom of a dirt path, the men paused to survey the dim outline of the hill behind them. Through binoculars they saw a flash of orange light, followed by the rumble of an explosion. "I think we can assume our enemy will be suitably inconvenienced," Mayr remarked with a dry chuckle before leading his men back down the winding road toward the faint glow of the city center.

Mayr's team was far from the only German operatives on the ground in Iran that spring and early summer of 1943. In fact, it sometimes seems surprising to learn that there might have been such a thing as a businessman stationed in the region with no known connection to Walter Schellenberg's service. One of the prime embedded assets was named Ernst Merser, a Swiss-born importer of machine parts, or so his elegantly printed calling card said, who operated out of a whitewashed six-bedroom villa on Tehran's fashionable Kakh Street, from where he sent Schellenberg a regular series of reports on matters of mutual interest. In his mid-thirties, compact, muscular, and always exquisitely dressed, Merser was thought handsome, if somewhat demonlike with his pointed chin and dark, quick eyes. Among other things he had a talent for disguise and was known to adopt the uniform of a policeman or customs officer, present himself in that role on an arriving Western-registered ship, and then pretend to carry out a routine inspection for contraband. He would later take the opportunity to wire back any details of troops or other notable passengers he might have noticed on his tour. "We'll welcome you to a party in Berlin one day," Schellenberg cabled Merser in an effusive moment, "and the next morning, we'll pin a medal on you."

For the most part, Merser, at least at this stage, preferred not to put himself directly in harm's way, but he proved an energetic and willing asset to the Axis cause. Colonel Georg Hansen, head of the Abwehr's overseas field bureau, wrote to Canaris on August 13, 1943, with another glowing report. "Merser carries on the most effective work that can be conducted in the given, and extremely difficult, situation, and the activities of his group can act as an example to other, much larger units working under more favorable conditions."[2] Merser had every reason to feel contented and confident. His position was secure. His intelligence haul was regularly landing on the desk of the Abwehr chief and in the Reich Chancellery. He was typically paid a monthly stipend of £150 ($5,400 today) for his services, and like others was ignorant of the fact that this was doled out in forged British banknotes.

Another addition to the burgeoning SD-Abwehr network on the ground in Iran was the sometime Munich lawyer Winifred Oberg, an old-fashioned German patriot, committed to winning the war, but equally happy to line his own pockets in the process. Sent to Tehran in June 1943, his brief was to serve as a spy among spies. Once installed in a safe house, Oberg was to similarly monitor the activities of Mayr and his crew and to send back weekly reports for Schellenberg's attention in Berlin. Short and swarthy, Oberg had no particular skills when it came to intelligence fieldwork, but he, too, proved amenable enough once handed the familiar monthly retainer in impressive-looking British notes. "It was a lovely little job," he said after the war, when enjoying a lucrative position advising several large North American firms doing business in Chile. There was also the fact that Oberg was a homosexual, and that Schellenberg's office safe contained photographs of him in close proximity to the late Ernst Rohm, the SA chief who had been murdered in 1934 after Hitler had come to see him as a threat to his hold on power. No one who had ever fraternized with Rohm, in whatever capacity, could feel entirely safe in the Germany of the early 1940s.

Even these individuals were far from the most exotic of the many Axis operatives active in the Iranian capital at the time the Allied leaders prepared to meet there. We've touched on the activities of Julius Schulze-Holthus, born in 1894, a decorated World War I cavalry officer who had successively practiced as a lawyer in the Weimar Republic and Third Reich. Perhaps his signal achievement in the latter role had been the passage of the Nazis' oddly progressive 1938 Bathing Decree, protecting the rights of naturists to gather on beaches, the beginning of a public-undress culture that can still be glimpsed in Germany today. Schulze-Holthus' postwar interrogation by the Allies described him as one of "a circle of stereotyped, monocle-wearing German officers, who looked on the waging of war as the only reason of their existence."[3] According to MI6, Schulze-Holthus had arrived in Tehran in 1941 and "worked himself in, getting to know his colleagues and his duties, and making contacts among Persian and European circles.... Though he denies that he was working to fulfill any particular Abwehr assignment in this period, he admits that he had his eyes and ears open and lost no opportunity of establishing any contact that might prove useful." A rather curious footnote adds: "Though this individual was wildly profligate in his personal relations with both sexes while [in Iran], today there is no trace of any inversion, and it is clear that he was most active when it came to Persian girls and young women, to an almost pathological degree, in preference to others."

Then there was one Horst Salomon, described by his postwar debriefers as "aged 40 or slightly more, tall, dark, black eyes, limps on right leg, which is short after an 'incident' in the paramilitary in 1923 ... Speaks Frankfurt dialect." Salomon was a flying enthusiast, and his particular brief was to "assess and report on [Allied] air movements in Iran and south-eastern Turkey, [where] possible rendering same inoperative for combat." His army counterpart was the splendidly named Major General Karl-Theodor Franz Heinz von Geldern-Crispendorf, the former German military attaché in Tehran, who stayed on in the region in a civilian capacity and was described by his eventual British handlers in staccato terms, "Slim, tough, tanned face. Ridiculously high-pitched voice. Clever and cautious. Hated Erwin Ettel." Among Crispendorf's local associates was the former Turkish all-in oil wrestling champion Misbah Ebtehaj, a rabid Nazi sympathizer who had moved to Iran and commanded a rough-hewn troupe of *garden koflot*, or cutthroats, about whom there was more than a whiff of Balkan lawlessness, and whose own loyalty to the Axis cause was matched only by their brutality. A ragged contingent of Ebtehaj's followers once presented themselves at the door of Ernst Merser's elegant home in the exclusive Tehran inner suburbs with the request that he take

3. "One Wonders About the Wrestlers"

Pelivani oil wrestlers in action, with Misbah Ebtehaj on the left.

temporary possession of two time bombs they had brought with them in a rucksack, explaining that Field Marshal Montgomery was expected on an inspection tour of the city in the near future, and that they would use the devices to hurl at his car as it passed by them on the road from the airport. Merser was no shrinking violet, as future events would demonstrate, but even he quailed at being handed twenty pounds of volatile high explosive in his living room by a gang of illiterate Turko-Iranian wrestling groupies. He announced with dignity that he would prefer not to act as the group's arsenal; in the end Montgomery did not visit.

Rivaling them all for sheer idiosyncrasy was the opposition's Peter Ferguson of the American OSS, who had gone to Iran in March 1943 with a reputation as a spy catcher, "particularly astute at exposing the liar, since he himself dissimulated at every turn," to again quote the British file. Ferguson was then age 38, tall and athletic, with piercing gray eyes and an immaculately tended Zapata mustache. Before the war he had worked variously as a bartender, movie extra, longshoreman, advertising executive, professional boxer, and deckhand on a Liberian tramp steamer. He also had a weakness for poker, at which he lost prodigious amounts of OSS money while in Tehran. His principal British counterpart in the city was the suavely pinstriped Percy Downward, a slight, blond man in his early thirties who was notionally head of his government's public relations bureau in the region, but who in fact received his orders from the political warfare executive of the foreign office in London. Downward soon established a small but loyal clique of informers by paying out small sums of money (in his case, at least officially coined by the British mint), which he did in the knowledge that "such men would make all the right Rule, Britannia noises [while] exercising their right to entertain other offers."

Downward and Merser were ideological foes but were united by their mutual affection for a 19-year-old Polish émigré to Iran, blonde with mournful gray-green eyes, named Wanda Pollack. Pollack had survived being first raped and then interned by the German troops invading Warsaw in September 1939. The Red Cross had eventually brokered her release, and in time she took a position as Merser's housekeeper and personal companion. The short, early middle-aged German agent and his beautiful if emotionally brittle Polish *jungfer* made a somewhat unlikely pair, although in a city of shadows perhaps such things were bound to occur in a shadowy manner. Adding a further twist to Merser's domestic arrangements was a second sultry young Polish refugee, a Sorbonne graduate and language teacher named Ida Kovalska, who seems to have been of no fixed ideological abode but who soon announced her intention to marry Peter Ferguson. Ferguson in turn revealed that he loved Ida; she was droll and original; yet when he got to know Wanda Pollack—his "broken china doll"—at Merser's house, he loved her, too.

Some of these assets showed more patience, stamina, and application in their attempts to subvert Allied interests in Iran than others. In time one or two of them, such as Horst Salomon and Julius Schulze-Holthus, actively put themselves at the service of the whisky-slugging Nasr Khan, the spiritual head and de facto general of the fiercely bellicose 400,000 Qashqai nomadic tribesmen of southwestern Iran. The dark-eyed Khan, habitually dressed in flowing white robes with a jeweled dagger at his belt, seemed to have stepped directly from the pages of central casting in his role of a charismatic Arab desert chieftain. He was quite possibly the richest man in the country. And he hated the British interlopers on his ancestral land literally with a vengeance. There was a widely circulated story that Khan's father, Ismail, had once been invited to dinner by his rival the shah, who had assured him that they could resolve their differences over a civilized meal in his palace. The history of such gestures in that part of the world would seem to suggest that compliance was almost always fatal, as shown by Ismail's grim demise. Promptly locked up by his host's guards, he had died just a few days later, supposedly after shaving with a razor steeped in a fast-acting poison supplied by the British.

By the summer of 1943, Nasr Khan's ire at his land's principal occupiers had come to assume definite shape. His core army of some 25,000 black tunic–wearing warriors waged a constant guerrilla war against the Western infidels. In London, MI6 estimated that 1,240 British soldiers had so far been killed or wounded in the conflict, 19 RAF Hurricanes had been destroyed on the ground in a single night attack by bomb-wielding Qashqai fighters on horseback, and Khan's desert brigands had made a tangible contribution to the Nazi war effort. "The ruthless forces of native fanatics were [now] clearly aligned on the Axis side," MI6 noted. There was a strange but pervasive belief among the Qashqai that Hitler was the "Shiite Messiah," or Twelfth Imam, who had returned to earth to destroy the Jews and other undesirables.

Nasr Khan's riders also acted as a local reception committee for the Berlin-dispatched agents dropped into the remote Iranian highlands. One such team landed on the lower slopes of the snow-capped Zard-Kuh peak in western Iran on the night of April 22. They were composed of a Quenzgut-trained commander, a German radio officer, and nine previously captured Soviet soldiers who had converted to the Nazi cause. The weather was still freezing, and the men were happy to see the black-clad riders approaching, silhouetted against the dawn sky. An hour later the new arrivals were seated gratefully around a roaring fire in the Qashqais' camp in the nearby Dez River valley. They would set off again the following night to furtively lay charges on the undercarriages of more parked British aircraft, "which we did with some success," in Khan's measured words. On May 22, Walter Schellenberg wrote for the attention of Himmler, "Our lines to Iran deserve special mention.... With their small instruments, each the size of four cigar boxes, the men have been able to send us hundreds of tactically important and highly interesting telegrams ... and to organize operations that have involved small numbers but high returns."[4]

Again, these were not the only covert forces at work in the highly charged atmosphere of Tehran in the middle months of 1943. After their success at Stalingrad, the Soviets now already seemed to be considering their postwar policy. As long as they were collectively fighting the Germans, the three principal Allies had a basis to coordinate their war aims and paper over any differences. But as soon as their common enemy was defeated, and they came into direct contact with each other, their political and strategic interests diverged sharply. The 36-year-old Daniel Komissarov, mustachioed and whey-faced ("as if suffering from a permanent hangover," in Winston Churchill's knowing phrase) notionally served as the Soviet press attaché in Tehran. Unofficially, his duties also included running a network of some 150 agents whose brief was to watch the Western allies as closely as the enemy. Part of this program involved reporting back to NKVD headquarters in Moscow with the details of British or American troop movements. Part involved winning over the hearts and minds of the local population to convince them of their good fortune in having the Russians not only as their co-defenders against Nazi tyranny but also their postwar partners. The author Laslo Havas wrote of the ensuing Red Army goodwill campaign,

> Their soldiers were to act like missionaries rather than occupiers. In case they did not understand what was expected of them, the smallest infringement of the rules, be it brawling, chicken theft, or the molesting of women, would be punished by a bullet in the head.[5]

The British and Americans (of whom there were 12,000 military personnel in Tehran) ran their own, more subdued PR programs in the region, each similarly jockeying for position, and for enhanced access to oil supplies in the years ahead. Each of the three Allies thought that they knew something the other two did not know, but thanks to their sleeper cells, the Germans also knew something that their enemies didn't know they knew. This was how the game was played in the carnival of mirrors of that uniquely deceitful time and turbulent place.

* * *

There was another German parachute drop in the darkened foothills around the salt marshes of Qom on the night of May 25, 1943. Shortly before midnight, a camouflaged Junkers 290 took off from an airfield near Kerch in Nazi-held Crimea for the 900-mile outward journey. The plane carried a payload of seven passengers, a total of eight MG cannons mounted on four turrets, and a cargo of RM 20,000 ($10,000) in a mixture of counterfeit British and American bills and genuine gold coins. There was also a further supply of machine pistols and ammunition. The drop took place at around four in the morning, and on the return leg the pilot was expected to detour over the nearby oil fields so that these could be photographed in the dawn light. Apart from the marathon journey, there were obvious hazards, such as those posed by the Soviet antiaircraft units in northern Iran, involved. Two Junkers had come down during similar incursions just the week before. One crash-landed; the other developed engine trouble and had to descend from 19,000 to 2,000 feet, where Russian fighters destroyed it. Soviet troops on the ground found the remains of both planes, which carried telltale maps of Iran, cameras, and at least one bag of undelivered currency. Hermann Goring, Reich minister for aviation (although he collected offices of state almost at will), was not pleased to be informed of the double loss. It quickly produced one of those scenes, not uncommon in Nazi Germany, that combined terrifying fury and wrenching pathos with a touch of absurdity.

3. "One Wonders About the Wrestlers" 65

Goring read the report of the aborted missions while on board his *Sonderzug* private train, which, among other amenities, boasted two dining cars, a swimming pool, and a special compartment for the Reich minister's pet lion. He, Goring, was visibly distressed at the news. In fact, his staff thought he might be suffering a heart attack as he embarked on a Hitler-like denunciation of his subordinate officers, shouting that he was surrounded by traitors and fools.

"This has destroyed all our plans in Iran," Goring fumed. "If ever I lay hands on that swine"—the surviving pilot, presumably—"I'll have him hanged." Goring had apparently reached the limit of his tolerance for the "cretins" and "Jew lovers" who now constituted the Luftwaffe's front-line flight crews. It went on in this vein for some time. The air force commander Ritter von Greim saw his chief later that night, and even hours after reading the initial report feared that he "might physically blow apart as his face and body swelled with rage, his cheeks a ghastly hue." But in the end the Reich minister did not explode. After his lengthy outburst, Goring sank into a sort of stupor, and for some time after that the entire train was silent but for the muffled sounds of the hungry lion pacing back and forth in the next compartment.

Luckily for its pilot's sake, the May 25 drop over the Iranian hills went as planned. The plane's cargo of money and weapons was pushed out of the rear bay door at the approved altitude of 1,500 feet. There was also a carefully padded final package about the size of an ordinary domestic overnight bag, stamped only with an ominous skull-and-crossbones motif on the side. It contained three two-pound blocks of butter-like "Plastit," a volatile explosive that could be primed with a pencil-shaped detonator. Once that was done, the user needed only to press the button on a remote control, or, alternatively, crush a glass phial containing a thin metal tube of copper chloride that would take about ten minutes to silently eat through the wire holding back the device's firing pin. In the sobering words of the Quenzgut training manual, the resulting explosion would "create a shock wave within any confined space such as a room that [would] compress a human's internal organs."

The middle-aged Erwin Ettel proceeded with some caution, therefore, when again venturing out early on the morning of May 26 to retrieve the latest high-ordnance manna to drop silently over the pink-tinted skies of the central Iran highlands. Earlier that week, the steadily growing German contingent in Tehran had successfully upgraded their hardware to include a full-scale, long-range radio transmitter assembled from smuggled parts and concealed under the floorboards of Julius Schulze-Holthus' suburban home.[6] It was the size of an old-fashioned steamer trunk and proved something of a challenge to operate. Listening through metal headphones, the receiving party would have to tune slowly up and down, sometimes monitoring two frequencies at once, until he locked on to a transmission, hoping that no one would break down the door and shoot him in the process. It was tedious and dangerous work, and in its first few days of operation the radio had brought them little news beyond the local Berlin weather forecast and the various Gauliga professional soccer scores.

On Thursday morning, May 20, however, the Tehran cell at last had news of some genuine significance. Winston Churchill was even then again visiting his friend President Roosevelt in Washington, D.C., and following that, would be traveling to Algiers to confer with General Eisenhower on the forthcoming Allied assault on Italy. From there, the message continued, Churchill would fly home by way of Gibraltar and Lisbon. Taken alongside the report of the local Abwehr spotters, the news would have fatal consequences for the civilian airliner carrying Leslie Howard and sixteen other victims.

There was one other note of particular interest in the Abwehr report of Churchill's movements. According to a source given only as "X," the old fellow "stalks about the world with no more than one or two ill-equipped bodyguards," said to carry only light "indiarubbers" and "matchboxes," as they called truncheons and pistols.

Ettel may have been 47 years old and more used to discussing diplomatic affairs than carrying out wet work against a visiting head of government. Nonetheless, he wrote after carefully storing his explosive cargo that bright May morning, "I could have wept with joy. Here was our rendezvous with destiny."

* * *

The growing momentum of a coherent Iran-based plot against one or more of the Big Three Allied leaders illustrates a particular facet of the German character—a deep-seated reluctance to act against the established authority, an aversion toward sidestepping protocol or appearing to circumvent proper channels, right or wrong. It made for a curious paradox. On the one hand, there was the singular and often mildly comic mishmash of bandit gangs of oil wrestlers and other renegades on the ground in Tehran, ready to act on the matter at a moment's notice. And on the other hand was the callous efficiency of the Nazi party machine, with its strict and inflexibly delineated individual fiefdoms, where unquestioning adherence to the procedure was all, and the component departments' very existence, even their prerogatives of internecine quarreling, lay in the führer's gift.

Nowhere was this jockeying for position under Hitler's aegis more pronounced than in the Reich security services. By mid-1943, the whole edifice had come to more resemble the court of a Renaissance king than the apparatus of modern democracy, as favorites came and went, counselors squabbled over position, and policy decisions were made by a combination, paradoxical as it may sound, of individual whim and a peculiarly Teutonic adherence to the often-sclerotic workings of the central government.

A Cardinal Richelieu in field-gray SS uniform, Walter Schellenberg was at the forefront of this bureaucratic morass. The situation was "fluid," he admitted, if by that term we understand a furiously seething struggle for influence. "I am not exaggerating when I say that the last years of the war were a veritable torture for me," he later ruefully noted in his memoirs.

The spymaster's particular ordeal was not so much one of service on the Eastern front or any of the other singularly uncongenial theaters of war. It consisted, instead, of the daily obligation to eat lunch with the head of the Reich Security Office, the then–39-year-old Ernst Kaltenbrunner. No less a figure than Heinrich Himmler was responsible for this mutually detested fixture, apparently in the belief that it would somehow promote a spirit of fraternal goodwill at the highest level of the state intelligence service. If so, the initiative could be counted only as a mixed success. Here is how Schellenberg described his RSHA colleague in his memoirs.

Kaltenbrunner was a giant, his every movement clumsy, a real lumberman.... His thick neck, which was the straight continuation of the back of his head, underlined one's impression of primitive brutality. With his ugly little brown eyes he stared fixedly, like a viper trying to hypnotize its victim. When asked a question his face would remain completely expressionless, then, after a few seconds of oppressive silence, he would hit the table and begin to speak.... I always felt that a drunken old gorilla was waving its arms in front of me. His hands were too small for his body and his fingers yellow, for Kaltenbrunner smoked at least a hundred cigarettes a day.[7]

The RSHA chief Ernst Kaltenbrunner seen in the dock at the postwar Nuremberg trials; he was hanged in October 1946.

Oddly enough, the daily Schellenberg-Kaltenbrunner meal counted as a warmly convivial affair compared to the former's dealings with the Abwehr chief Wilhelm Canaris. By the fourth year of the war, this particular relationship had become one of near-psychotic mutual antipathy. After one of their infrequent lunches together, Schellenberg noted that Canaris was definitely "not the National Socialist type." Censure hardly came any greater at that level. Canaris, however, had certain potent weapons of his own. He kept detailed files on the unusual relationship between the married Schellenberg and the middle-aged French designer Coco Chanel, for example, and was on grounds well beyond that when it came to Schellenberg's one-time colleague at the Reich Security Office, Reinhard Heydrich, at least prior to the latter's assassination. Canaris knew that Heydrich was, by strict application of the Nazi race laws, partly of Jewish origin, a distinct handicap to career advancement in the current regime. Schellenberg took down the following exchange between his two rival department chiefs at a meeting in Prague.

> "In proposing negotiations to you, admiral," Heydrich began coolly, "I will not conceal from you that after the war the SS will take over everything in the Abwehr's field."
> "After the war, my dear Heydrich?" Canaris replied. "You know very well that nobody will dare touch the Abwehr so long as I am alive."
> "Nobody, Herr admiral? Not even the Führer?"[8]

Amidst the overall atmosphere of medieval intrigue characterizing Germany's wartime intelligence-gathering effort, with Joseph Goebbels molding the führer's stream-of-consciousness pronouncements on the subject into complete sentences, there was at least one recognizably efficient operational canton. This was the elite SS training camp located in a disused girls' boarding school on the shores of Lake Quenz. Its curriculum was poised between the academic and the martial. The place was equipped with laboratories, workshops, and the latest wireless technology. The trainees studied the art of coding and decoding messages and were taught to speak colloquial English. But there was also a more narrowly focused component of the syllabus. Each student was extensively schooled in the arts of knife throwing and rifle shooting, with "young inmates in good condition" selected from the nearby Brandenburg-Gorden prison to serve as human targets. The school's pupils also learned about the properties of nerve gas and how to incapacitate an opponent by scooping his eyes out and forcing them inside the occipital cavity or by crushing his windpipe until the blood vessels burst in the victim's brain. No combat area was left unexplored. Before passing out of the ranks of Quenzgut into the ranks of the SS, a young initiate was made to pull the pin on a live grenade, balance it on his steel helmet, and then remain standing to attention when it exploded.

Some of the roughly 400 staff and students to be found on the premises served only in a support capacity. There were drivers and cooks, for instance, and others destined never to see front-line service. One individual was designated the center's "special recreations" officer, which in practice meant his periodically inviting suitably Aryan adolescent girls to the camp—thus returning it, in a perverse way, to something like its original use—for purposes of "procreational activity," as the order signed by Schellenberg on June 3, 1943, put it, with the all-too-willing young SS apprentices. In this warped view of the world, the need for "ample mammilla," or large breasts, rather than any social skills, was considered the most desirable attribute among the young guests.

While some Quenzgut students found their own loopholes, and so contrived to avoid a future call to SS heroism, those who remained were a curious collection—a smattering of business professionals, doctors, lawyers, and even a trained Munich Opera singer, of those old enough to have practiced a peacetime trade, alongside a hard core of fanatically keen young men who had volunteered for service immediately on leaving school, if not even earlier. When the moment came, Schellenberg would find more than enough candidates at his disposal at Quenzgut to assemble into successive insertion teams for deployment in Iran.[9] By and large, these were men of unusual resilience and fortitude who thought nothing of things such as plunging in for a two-mile swim through the icy waters of wintertime Lake Quenz, and whose training regimen had instructed them in the best means to hack off one of their own limbs should their continued survival depend on it. Surveying the graduating class presented for his inspection on the morning of July 19, 1943, Schellenberg wrote for the record that such men were uniquely well equipped for the "great new tasks" ahead of them.

At first glance, the balding, rather stooped midlife figure of Erwin Ettel was something of a disappointment when set against this superhuman ideal. But no one who met him ever doubted his complete devotion to the Nazi cause. Julius Schulze-Holthus once described the alpine-climbing diplomat as "a small, sinewy man with raw features that spoke of energy and a certain amount of brutality.... In his Foreign Office days, he was looked upon as a hard and dangerous opponent, a sort of fighting cockroach who took on stronger rivals and defeated them by the vehemence of his attacks."[10]

Ettel and his assorted colleagues, including the gravedigger-saboteur Franz Mayr and the other recently dropped SD reinforcements, were not idle during the sweltering Iranian summer months of 1943. Aside from

Recruits to the League of German Girls go through their paces in 1941, some of them to be dispatched for "procreational activity" at the SS training camp in Lake Quenz.

their regular airdrop-collection duties, their specialty was the hit-and-run sortie. Ettel left a summary of their modus operandi.[11] "We [were] to sabotage rail links, ambush convoys, disrupt oil supplies, and above all to gather information on the increasing probability of a 'spectacular,'" by which he meant an especially dramatic strike delivered against Allied interests. The group also made use of their extensive network of local contacts, most of whom proved to be ideologically flexible when presented with handfuls of British or American cash. Some of the Quenzgut-trained professionals considered the auxiliary mishmash of all-in wrestlers like Misbah Ebtehaj and their accompanying retinues a liability more likely to spend the Reich's money on themselves than on any coherent plan to seriously incommode the Allies. Ebtehaj's band of ruffians was not small enough to be easily concealed from British or Russian eyes in Tehran, but not big enough to mount any significant long-term operation to advance Germany's aims as a whole. Roadblocks and machine pistols would not turn the tide of the war in the Middle East, or for that matter anywhere else.[12] "But such men [will] be ready to set the world ablaze when the hour comes," Erwin Ettel wrote.

3. "One Wonders About the Wrestlers" 71

As if to demonstrate the fact, Ettel and some of his confederates now "concluded a little business" together. Using one of the three two-pound chunks of explosive dropped for them, they planned to attack the local headquarters of no less than General Sir Henry Pownall, the commander-in-chief of British forces in the region. Thanks to Ebtehaj and his crew, Ettel knew that the highly regarded Pownall would attend a briefing held in the main British garrison on Englab Square in central Tehran (the Western powers each kept an enclave within the Soviet sector) at some stage in the morning of June 9, 1943. On the night of the 7th, with the help of a local maintenance crew employed by the British but brought into the plot by Nazi cash, three of Ettel's agents reconnoitered the target. The outer gate was wide open to allow the civilian workforce to come and go. The inner gate appeared to be manned by a lone British military policeman, and on the far side of a parade square the watchers could see a small, cinder-block building with blacked-out windows but both a Union Jack and a regimental flag freshly painted on either side of the front door. This latter touch, they concluded, was in honor of the general's visit.

The saboteurs' plan was to return the following night in two teams. One crew was to approach the main gate of the camp in a heavily laden civilian truck, which would then break down, shedding its load of market fruits and vegetables in the process, in a way that distracted any British personnel on guard duty. Amid the confusion, a second unit of three men would climb over a wall on the far side of the compound, clipping the barbed wire on top, and drop down to make their way across the drill square to the small briefing room. They would then plant the explosive charge under one of the wooden floorboards previously loosened by the accomplice work crew and swiftly make their exit. When the moment came, the device would be detonated by a lookout situated on the roof of an apartment block across the street armed with binoculars and a remote-control transmitter. If the attack were successful, it "would completely undermine the British fighting spirit in the area," Ettel wrote. Furthermore, "it might very well show the way for an attack on Very Important targets of opportunity in the future."

Shortly before eight on the already stiflingly hot morning of June 9, the German watcher saw a group of British officers walk smartly up the front steps into the camp's cinder-block staff room. An accomplice standing on the street five floors below flashed him the agreed "go" signal, meaning there were no sudden troop movements to be seen at the main gate. But seconds before the bomber was set to flick off the safety and press the button on his device, at exactly 8:00 a.m., a force of fifteen heavily armed Iranian security police, with a British officer bringing up the rear shouting instructions at them in Farsi, burst onto the roof. They did not pause to negotiate with the Nazi hitman or inform him of his rights. At least three of the policemen simultaneously opened fire with their service revolvers, fatally shooting the would-be assassin between the eyes. His accomplice on the street, hearing the commotion and looking up to see the flash of gunfire, managed to flee into the crowd.

In that one frozen moment, in a dusty Tehran square, all the strands of the local German covert program had come together: the fanatical desire to hit the Allies wherever they could, the use of the Luftwaffe to supply the operation, the mingling of Axis and paid paramilitary units, and the ultimate betrayal. Ettel and others listened to the breathless report of what had happened later that morning. They deemed it best to hurriedly change their accommodations, and in some cases to leave Iran altogether, but avoided arrest. Not surprisingly, there was a spirited discussion about who had sold them out to the authorities. Some said a local rug trader and Nazi sympathizer who went by the telling nickname Adolf had been captured and tortured into revealing the plot. No one ever saw him again, anyway, although Ettel wrote in the privacy of the diary, "One wonders about the wrestlers."

* * *

In June 1943, Hitler began to show a marked interest in the prospect of regime change in one or more of his enemy powers. So far as we know, there was never a written order over the führer's signature to that effect. Historians have long grappled with the question of why Hitler even tacitly endorsed a plan that might not deliver the desired strategic benefits and would likely increase the odds of a retaliatory strike. The most common answer is that consumed by homicidal rage, he and his myrmidons had developed a sort of fixation on the removal of their enemies, and then put it into practice, relentlessly and unwaveringly. There was a "straight path," in other words, from the foam-flecked rants about Churchill being a drunk and Roosevelt a Jewish puppet, and the events in Iran in the second half of 1943. The alternative explanation is that there wasn't a single path at all. There were many paths and dead-ends, detours, and reversals on the way to Tehran. Until the late summer of 1943, there was no clearly defined program of state-sponsored assassination, and, as with the larger horror of the Final Solution, measures were often improvised and muddled, driven by competing visions and political rivalries. As late as May of that year, when the tide of the war had unmistakably turned against them, the Nazi leadership was still unsure about the wisdom of targeting its human adversaries. "Are Roosevelt and Churchill to be tolerated, defeated and imprisoned, or simply put to death?" Goebbels wondered in a letter addressed to his stepson Harald Quandt.

We know that Heinrich Himmler, who by then combined the roles of chief of German police and minister of the interior, discussed the matter directly with Walter Schellenberg in a series of meetings between late May and the middle of June 1943.[13] Both men were ready to act, but less keen to have their names openly linked with the plot. Himmler was then in a particularly delicate position since he also happened to be in the early stages of furtively seeking a peace settlement with the Allies, an initiative he accelerated, prudently enough, in conditions of the utmost secrecy, at intervals over the course of the next eighteen months. Any abrupt change of government in one of his partners in negotiation (as he delusionally thought of the Allies) might compromise his efforts and thus deny him the Nobel Peace Prize he seems to have coveted while simultaneously helping direct the killing of an estimated 12–14 million European men, women, and children.

For his part, Schellenberg was enthusiastic enough about the plan but not about the prospect of collaborating with the despised Admiral Canaris, whom he continued to regard with a mixture of pity and scorn. "He was a highly intelligent man," Schellenberg later wrote of his intelligence-service rival. "But [I saw] the weakness of his organization, which was a highly over-inflated unit.... Canaris was often twisted around by his own subordinates. In many ways, he was a mystic and sensitive man. And not the most efficient one, either."[14] Into this stew of ferocious mistrust and misunderstanding came a new "spectacular" initiative which the SD chief thought would give him a jump on his Abwehr counterpart.

Schellenberg went back to Himmler on June 5, 1943, and told him he would "unilaterally take responsibility for spread[ing] agents throughout Iran," as well as for "develop[ing] those special initiatives we discussed." But he had one further proviso: he wanted to knock off Charles de Gaulle, the Free French leader, first. Schellenberg seems to have reasoned that de Gaulle would be an easier target than the Big Three and may even have had the Frenchman in mind as a sort of dummy run for the main event. Earlier that spring, de Gaulle had boarded a British Wellington bomber at an airfield outside London to fly to a briefing in Scotland. The plane had been hurtling down the runway, about to lift off, when it suddenly veered to a halt amid a cloud of smoke and the smell of burning rubber. On inspection, it was found that the Wellington's control rod had been sabotaged with acid. No one was ever charged in the affair, which de Gaulle thought equally likely to have been the work of the German intelligence services or one of his numerous enemies at the senior levels of the Allied governments. He never again flew in Britain.

Could de Gaulle's close call, or for that matter the Leslie Howard incident that followed soon afterward, have been the preliminary step to the "spectacular" later planned in Iran? Again, no written order has ever come to light for either event; they simply just happened. There is no known record of any meetings about disposing of the troublesome leader of the Free French, or of murdering a middle-aged English screen actor, whose birth name happens to have been Steiner and who was of at least partly Jewish descent. The Germans as a rule remained, and arguably still remain, commendably keen on paperwork and due process, refining it into a system that regulates every last detail of the individual citizen's life. On the other hand, it was part of the peculiar criminal genius of the Nazi regime to carry out the most barbaric aspects of state policy under conditions of tomblike stealth that would be difficult to envision today. As Himmler remarked, "When the Führer entrusts us with a job, we know how to deal with it correctly, without causing useless uproar."[15]

* * *

Walter Schellenberg's sumptuous fourth-floor office in a requisitioned Jewish old people's home on Berkaerstrasse, on the south side of central Berlin, was a study in contrasts. As we've seen, there was a pervasive air of paneled walls and framed portraits, something like that of an exclusive gentlemen's club, but, invisible to the visitor, also a steel-helmeted soldier sitting at the controls of a light machine gun, ready to deal with any trouble. The overall feel to the room, as to Schellenberg, lay somewhere between a European statesman's place of business and the lair of a particularly hardboiled 1930s Chicago gangster.

It was to this same office that Schellenberg summoned the lawyer-sleuth Winifred Oberg in June 1943. Oberg was the SD chief's eyes and ears on the ground in Tehran, not only when it came to coordinating the various sabotage efforts of Ernst Merser, Franz Mayr and company, but, he was now reminded, to reporting back to Schellenberg each week on the saboteurs themselves. These were far from the only orders then issued from the fourth floor at Berkaerstrasse. Schellenberg was also hard at work overseeing the training of 2,000–3,000 recruits, many of them captured Red Army soldiers, into a large-scale fifth column operation designed to infiltrate the Soviet Union. In the host of Mad Hatter tea party scenes that characterize much of the wartime intelligence-gathering effort by the Allies and Axis powers alike, this last initiative, codenamed Zeppelin, must have a high place. One SD officer later commented that if losses among their turncoat agents "were not over 90 percent, we were satisfied."[16]

Hard on the heels of Oberg's visit to SD headquarters came that of another of the cold-eyed, elegantly tailored Nazi functionaries who so stimulated historical curiosity in the years 1939–45. This was 26-year-old

3. "One Wonders About the Wrestlers" 75

Werner Baumbach, a mechanical engineer-turned-Luftwaffe pilot who was then mustering an elite bomber squadron, designated KG 200, to support clandestine overseas operations. "It is not to go on the record," Goring had informed him. "Just put it together quietly, in a hurry."

Schellenberg wanted Baumbach to significantly step up the pace of the Junkers airlift program in Iran, and Baumbach in turn replied by pointing out how stretched his resources already were for any operations outside of the all-important Russian front. In the subterranean jungle of Nazi politics, such a gesture was as futile as that of a mortally wounded lion flicking its tail to ward off the attention of a circling vulture in the African bush. Perhaps Schellenberg's finger even tentatively reached for the concealed button under his desk, but whatever he said or did it was enough to persuade the Luftwaffe ace to do his bidding. Yes, Baumbach agreed; perhaps he could spare more planes after all. Sending his precious bombers thousands of miles to deposit men and materiel, for unspecified ends, over mountainous, enemy-held terrain in the dead of night might, he privately conceded, run counter to the strict requirements of military logic. Nonetheless, he would deliver as many assets to the inhospitable foothills of Western Asia as Schellenberg desired, he agreed, confirming the point with a smart click of his heels. Baumbach had no idea of what such men might get up to once on the ground in Iran, nor did he particularly care, although he came to learn that each SD paratrooper was given a set of simple orders to follow once in the drop zone.

> If you are injured on landing, pretend to be dead; wait until the enemy approach; then select one of them and kill him! Kill him with gun, bayonet, or knife. Rip his throat with your teeth. Do not die without leaving behind you an enemy corpse.[17]

* * *

The third and most terrifying arrival in Walter Schellenberg's office that early summer of 1943 was the striking figure of Captain Otto Skorzeny, the decorated Russian Front veteran, and latterly head of the newly created Waffen SS Special Forces unit, who went on to physically remove the ruling Horthy family from office in Budapest. Born into a military family in 1908, the adult Skorzeny cut an imposing figure. He stood six feet four, bore deep dueling scars on his face, spoke in a booming, parade-ground voice, and was not considered a martyr to false modesty. He had been in his native Austria at the time of the Anschluss in March 1938, when, according to his account, he saved the state president Wilhelm Miklas from a marauding lynch mob. There were other stories, too, some plausible—such as his having led a covert SS unit to within sight of the Kremlin bell towers in the late summer of 1941, with the aim of opening the sluices of the Moscow-Volga canal and thus flooding the Soviet capital into surrender—and others that perhaps existed only in Skorzeny's fertile imagination, many of them involving a whole litany of romantic adventures that would have aroused the envy of Don Juan at his most libertine.

Now Schellenberg had a daring new proposal for his visitor at Berkaerstrasse. He wanted him to form a network of agents under the name Group S, to handle "unusual assignments" such as infiltrating Allied lines while wearing enemy uniforms, "with special emphasis on the Asian theater." Skorzeny listened to what Schellenberg had to say and responded with typical self-confidence. Yes, of course, he would be prepared to personally parachute into Iran and fulfill whatever duties the SS Oberführer might be pleased to give him. The final mission remained a secret, even to Skorzeny, and the forces at his disposal in Iran were little more than a patchwork of ad-hoc formations of widely varying quality. Nonetheless, if matters developed as Schellenberg believed they would, its ultimate success or failure could at a stroke determine the outcome of the war. "This may prove the hinge of fate," he added with a characteristic rhetorical flourish.

"Whenever Skorzeny heard the word 'Secret' he lit up, knowing it to be a prelude to a special mission," Schellenberg later wrote. "He left my office that June morning with a leer of excitement on his ugly face."[18]

* * *

By the midsummer of 1943, it was possible to say that any future high-level Allied conference would be in a position to contemplate victory. The tide on the Eastern front had turned decisively at Stalingrad; the Axis forces had surrendered en masse in north Africa; and there were increasing signs of discontent at all levels of Italian life that their nation's young soldiers had become cannon fodder in someone else's war. Hitler still clung to what for him had clearly become a spiritual struggle against Europe's "inferior races," but now his health was failing. Over-medicated by his physician Theo Morrell, the führer was suffering from both a heart condition and the steady onset of Parkinson's disease, sometimes displaying an uncontrollable trembling of the left arm and jerking in his left leg.[19] Following the reverses in Russia, Hitler's violent mood swings, already impressive, had become more pronounced, and Morrell, fearing a full-scale mental collapse, now prescribed his patient 28 different pills each day, most of which did nothing to head off, and may even have exacerbated, the long-term deterioration in his health.

Winston Churchill was in conversely good humor just then. Although similarly betraying some of the strains of office, particularly in the aftermath of the Casablanca conference, the 68-year-old premier quickly recovered his high spirits. Churchill's visit to Washington that summer had at least some of the properties of a modern-day rock-music tour. There were adoring crowds waiting for him wherever he went, some of the female contingent of which shouted out endearments or displayed signs indicating how positively they would react to any romantic overtures the cherubically portly PM might care to make to them. Churchill went on to make a stirring case for Anglo-American unity of purpose, the later so-called Special Relationship, in a speech at Harvard. "There is no halting-place at this point," Churchill informed his audience. "We have now reached a stage in the great journey where there can be no pause. We must go on.... Throughout all this ordeal and struggle which is characteristic of our age, you will find in the British Empire good comrades to whom you are united by other ties besides those of state policy and public need. They are the ties of blood and history. They are indissoluble."[20]

No one questioned the force of the Churchillian rhetoric. But there were those at the heart of the Atlantic alliance who still had doubts about the man's leadership style. "I'm nearly dead," Roosevelt complained to his secretary of labor Frances Perkins during that same visit.

"I have to talk to the PM all night, and he gets bright ideas in the middle of the night and comes pattering down the hall to my bedroom in his bare feet." They were generally good ideas, Roosevelt conceded, "but I have to get my rest." One afternoon, the sleep-deprived president had just retired to his room for a siesta. "And at that very moment in breezes Churchill, full of all sorts of things.... So vanishes the nap!"[21]

As usual, Churchill traveled with a single, lightly armed detective at his side. This was more often than not his friend Walter Thompson, who also combined the roles of a secretary, valet, and occasional drinking companion. While on duty, Thompson typically carried two brown leather bags slung over his shoulder. One contained a spare pair of binoculars in case Churchill forgot his, and the other held reinforcements of the old man's cigars and brandy. It was not security of the type we might associate with a modern head of government. Unless specifically required by the attentions of a press reporter or photographer, Churchill consistently refused to carry his regulation gas mask and steel helmet, was known to hail a taxi or proceed on foot rather than wait for his official car, if the mood struck him, and once, on a visit to Manchester, pressed the emergency button to summon Thompson to his hotel room in the early hours of the morning. When the bodyguard arrived a moment later, his weapon drawn, ready to handle the crisis, Churchill greeted him with the inquiry, "Ah, Walter.... Would you run my bath for me, please?"[22]

The incident illustrates a sharp contrast with President Roosevelt's security arrangements. For years, Mike Reilly and his team had been girding their loins to deal with a possible attack on their boss from the ground. In mid-1943 they also came to concern themselves with his protection while airborne. After studying and rejecting several models, the Secret Service reconfigured a Douglas C-54 Skymaster for presidential transport duty. The four-engined plane, nicknamed the Sacred Cow, included a two-bunk sleeping area, radiotelephone, and retractable ramp to load Roosevelt in his wheelchair. It may have been almost ludicrously primitive by today's Air Force One standards, but it qualified as near-divine status compared to Churchill's flying arrangements, which generally involved a noisy, unheated RAF surplus turboprop bomber where he counted himself lucky to be served "stale ham sandwiches, with soup and a swig of grog" en route. When Thompson once mentioned to him that Roosevelt now traveled by customized plane, with a squadron of U.S. Air Force Grumman "Hellcat" fighters in permanent attendance because he was considered a prime target for the Germans, Churchill replied simply, "Aren't we all?"

We needn't dwell on the Soviet ruler's security details as overseen by Nikolai Vlasik and others. They were corrosive enough. By 1943 Stalin was forbidden even to walk around his private quarters in the Kremlin unguarded. When the Vozhd ventured further afield to confer with his commanders or the Allied leaders, he was surrounded by four NKVD regiments—about 5,000 men in all—and his residence was defended by batteries of AA guns and convoys of fighter planes permanently circling overhead. There were two inner circles of guards by day, and three circles by night, as well as an impressive array of watch towers, floodlights, alarms, landmines, metal spikes, and attack dogs. Again, it was all some way from the world of Walter Thompson and his shopworn service revolver, and the traveling reinforcements of tobacco and spirits.

This disparity in style between the senior Allied leaders was mirrored by profound differences in strategy. The overall tide of the war may have turned, but there was still no consensus about the final path to victory. "We continue to fight as fiercely by telegraph as in the field," Churchill noted in June 1943. Stalin wanted the invasion of Europe to take place immediately. He didn't particularly care precisely where or how it did so, as long as it forced the Germans to take troops and artillery away from the Ukraine. On June 26, Churchill told his war cabinet in London that they should refrain from "sending any reply to the latest demands for action from Moscow." Once before, Churchill noted,

> We deliberately stalled in our response to a carping telegram from Marshal Stalin, with most satisfactory results ... [We] should do so again now. In due course, I shall remind the marshal that the delay [in the second front] is owing

to the decision to go to North Africa, the demands of the war with Japan, and other causes."[23]

When the eventual cable was handed to Stalin, Vlasik found that "a horrible feeling of anger at once descended" on Soviet headquarters. "[Stalin] can see that the British are going to be a problem who will act as a hair-shirt for us. We can get no definite decision from them or [Roosevelt]. The best they can do is to say they will ponder the options in Italy, while our troops bleed dry in the field. It is the devil."

* * *

Early in the morning of July 9, 1943, one of Werner Baumbach's specially modified Junkers 290 bombers broke out of the rose-tinged clouds over the Elburz mountains of northern Iran and began to descend. On this occasion the plane's mission was a more dynamic one than merely dropping money or munitions for collection by Erwin Ettel and his ground crew. Instead, the Junkers was to deposit a team of four men on the steep terrain at the eastern end of the range, from where they would make their way to the small coastal town of Bandar Torkaman. The place was then the center of the Iranian caviar industry, but the insertion team with blackened faces and Schmeisser submachine guns strapped to their backs was not there on a gastronomic tour. The men's brief was to destroy a vulnerable, timber-and-stone deck bridge lying along the route of the Trans-Iranian railway carrying vital oil supplies to the Soviet Union. By this stage of the war, the Western allies had invested heavily in new double-track rail stock, as well as in docks and modern port-loading equipment, to ship not only fuel but roughly six thousand vehicles and 300 planes a month to Russia. A single devastating blow, Schellenberg reasoned, could cut off this vast conveyor belt and in due course bring the Red Army's tanks then engaged with the Germans at Kursk to a grinding halt. Most importantly, he noted, if successful, the raid would deplete "the Communist will to fight a determined adversary to such an extent that it cannot be regained." He admitted, "The operation is a gamble," but he was a gambler who understood the value of preparation, bluffing, secrecy, and unconventional tactics. A surprise attack like this "will be the most effective way of choking the life from our enemy, because it is what they least expect."

The four-man team bailed out over the mountains as planned, and within three days had made their way 50 miles to the outskirts of Bandar Torkaman. It was then little more than a fishing village, but the British had built a jetty at one end of it, and the Russians their elevated railway bridge at the other. The German commandos came down the hillside from the east in the predawn hours of July 13. The ground beneath them was red-brown, lightly sprinkled with sand, and hard as rock. The morning air was still and already oppressively warm for anyone carrying a 40-pound load of high explosives and other equipment on their back. It was not an easy job in a region where the summer temperature often topped 120 degrees, and the dust on the roads was so thick that some of the Western military drivers had to be equipped with respirators.

The men turned into open country. Up ahead they could see the long, narrow ravine, with the bridge propped up on thin wooden stilts. The land just below was dotted with bushes that seemed to offer some cover. The team was exhausted after its long route march through mountainous enemy territory with little rest or food. They found a secluded spot at the foot of one of the bridge's trestles and settled down to sleep, spreading out in the nooks and corners, seemingly protected by a line of low-hanging trees thick with summer vegetation. Before turning in, two of the saboteurs climbed a few yards up a nearby bluff to survey their target as it loomed above them in the early morning light. "Their intention was to wait until the following nightfall, set their charges, and then withdraw by inflatable boat into the Caspian, where our submarine would collect them," Schellenberg later wrote.

This was not quite what happened. Instead, just an hour later the German commandos were rudely awakened by the crunch of boots on rock and opened their eyes to see a ragged collection of Iranian police, Russian soldiers, and curious native tribesmen standing above them pointing a variety of submachine guns and other weapons. They went quietly into captivity.

The Germans' subsequent fate is still unknown, but none of them was ever heard from again. Walter Schellenberg was left to reflect only that at that time Iran was "a nest of vipers" and that someone had clearly tipped off the authorities for a reward. "I had personally briefed the men," Schellenberg noted, "and each had affirmed his unquestioning and absolute loyalty to the Reich. There was a silent but clear understanding of the perils involved in their mission.... They did not necessarily expect to return alive." The supposedly temporary wartime railway bridge at Bandar Torkaman still stands. The Russian tanks prevailed at Kursk, meanwhile, and Hitler, in a marked reversal of their customary roles, overruled his field commander General von Manstein and ordered what remained of Manstein's Panzer divisions to withdraw. In the event the final Soviet losses were even greater. But the German forces had signally failed in their objective. It was another catastrophic blow for a Thousand-Year Reich that now had only 21 months to survive.

* * *

By the late summer of 1943, Germany had been forced on the defensive, experiencing only setbacks, in the conventional war. But her

3. "One Wonders About the Wrestlers"   81

clandestine operations would still "strike such a blow [as] will bestow victory on a people who have done so much to earn it," Wilhelm Canaris wrote early in August. These were fighting words, whether of commendable optimism or myopic self-deception, and characteristic of the Germans' illusory fantasy world that did not give way despite the mounting battlefield losses and calamities of the second half of 1943. Only by the following summer was it finally too late. At that stage, according to Canaris's aide Reinhard Spitzy, "The admiral knew everything of von Stauffenberg's plot to assassinate Hitler, and said 'It would be good if you succeed. I will protect you, but after all these immense crimes against the Jews it is not possible to deceive history through a small trick. There must be *expiation*.' He used the French word. Speaking to Stauffenberg direct, Canaris said, 'You will be judged only by one thing, your success.'"[24]

The Germans' failure to blow up the bridge at Bandar Torkaman was another tactical setback for Schellenberg's covert operations in the Middle East, but in no way discouraged his efforts there. More Quenzgut-trained agents continued to fall out of the dark Iranian skies at regular intervals that summer while others emerged dressed in flowing tribal robes and headdresses, disguised as nomads or pilgrims en route to their statutory hajj in Mecca. Still more debarked from ships out of neutral ports like Mersin or Izmir. The new recruits were well-versed in the art of assimilation. "They even had to learn to spit like Russians," Paul Leverkuehn, head of the Abwehr station in Istanbul, said of them.[25]

One way or another, it was a motley crew who had gathered in or around Tehran by the end of that summer of 1943. There was the gravedigging saboteur Franz Mayr and his sometime accomplice Roman Gamotha; the diplomat-turned mountaineer Erwin Ettel; the Swiss-born Ernst Merser, the Mercedes-driving businessman who proved tougher than he looked, with an appropriate talent for disguise; the lawyer-provocateur Winifred Oberg; the mustachioed World War I cavalryman Julius Schulze-Holthus; exotics like Horst Salomon and the superbly Prussian Major General Geldern-Crispendorf; and a supporting cast of sultry Polish emigres, rug traders, and all-in wrestlers, with the satanic visage of Otto Skorzeny now ready to insert itself in the fray. The whole place was swarming with restless individuals, some of them more ideologically motivated than others, all tunneling along their separate routes from several different directions to the same end of harassing the enemy and dealing a blow to the "hideous half–Jewish, half–Bolshevist centaur," as Erwin Ettel called the Soviet-Western alliance. Little did he or any of his accomplices know, but they would soon be in a position to decapitate the monster entirely.

4

Agent Cicero

Nazi black operations evolved quickly that summer in Iran. There were more hit-and-run missions by small teams dropped from the air or embedded on the ground, some of them of more practical value than others. There were the rising ambitions of men like Wilhelm Canaris and Walter Schellenberg, with the Waffen SS's Otto Skorzeny lurking menacingly in the wings like a black-coated pantomime villain. And now, too, there was a loosely defined but energetically pursued project to organize the various dissident tribes of southwestern Iran into a viable fifth-column fighting unit broadly along the lines of the mercenary forces who rallied behind T.E. Lawrence in the Arab Revolt a quarter of a century earlier. For Schellenberg, as the war outlook "broadened," this "clustering multitude" could hold out against the Allies indefinitely.

In practice, the tribesmen were to conduct a guerrilla campaign including but not limited to "destroy[ing] bridges, cutting supplies, wrecking train and truck convoys ... us[ing] their knowledge of a hostile environment against a more numerous and better equipped adversary" in Schellenberg's words. The plan went under the overall name of Operation Franz. Like Lawrence's desert campaign, it's widely remembered as a heroic and romantic enterprise in the midst of a period of savage and deeply impersonal industrial warfare. But while it ticks all the right boxes for gripping narrative drama, Franz may not have been the solid strategic success some later liked to claim. Three times camel-riding irregulars tried to storm the British garrison at Shiraz, built on the green plains at the foot of the Zagros mountains south of Tehran, for instance. And three times they failed. In the first attack, the tribesmen suffered 1,600 dead and wounded (a 40 percent casualty rate), and the other two fared little better. A subsequent attempt to mine the main road between Shiraz and the port city of Bushehr, thus cutting the Allied supply route, cost the marauding tribesmen an average 600 casualties per mile. They simply could not sustain the effort.

On August 6, the silk-robed Qashqai chieftain Nasr Khan, with some

25,000 loosely armed but fanatically loyal mounted fighters at his disposal, met with Julius Schulze-Holthus to exchange views on the former's continuing campaign to rid his ancestral land of the hated British occupiers. Khan said that another Junkers had been observed in the skies over Shiraz earlier that week and had dropped both men and boxes with "funny poles." These sounded to the former German army officer suspiciously like high-frequency radio transmitters. Schulze-Holthus knew nothing of any such mission and later wrote that the news "came like an electric shock" to him. He had heard about the Luftwaffe's parachute sorties over the Elburz mountains some 400 miles to the north. But this was the first hint there might be a more widespread campaign to destabilize the Allied military and political presence in Iran as a whole, thus paving the way for the final climactic strike in Tehran. "I stood for a moment with my mouth open, and then told Khan I would urgently seek details," Schulze-Holthus remembered.

At that, the old cavalryman promptly got on his horse and rode up into the area Nasr Khan had indicated. It was a desolate spot. The first evidence of human life Schulze-Holthus saw was a campfire about 2,000 feet up in the Zagros foothills, flickering at the mouth of a cave and brightly illuminating it. Several men in full SS field uniforms were crouching inside. Their commanding officer, a Hauptsturmführer Martin Kurmis, greeted their visitor without surprise.

"We've been expecting you," he said.

Schulze-Holthus later reported their dialogue as follows,

"Why are you here?" I asked.
"We're going to hot this place up a bit," Kurmis replied. "Commandos like us have been dropped everywhere—in Iraq, Palestine, and Syria. A brand new magnificent Eastern program."

Kurmis then introduced his guest to the other members of his team: two German radio operators named Piwonka and Harbers, an explosives man, an Iranian translator, and a pair of ragged-looking native guides. "We've had special training with Skorzeny," Kurmis announced, with unfeigned pride. "We're well schooled in blowing up oil pipes and pumping stations."[1]

At that, Kurmis produced a chart on which half a dozen gushing derricks and other local points of interest were crudely marked in red crayon. It almost looked like the map for a child's scavenger hunt. It suddenly struck Schulze-Holthus that the whole practical working of Operation Franz might be a touch on the haphazard side. The "crack southern-Iran SS insertion force," as they had introduced themselves, comprised these seven individuals, with a few more shadowy figures found squatting on their haunches among nearby scrub and boulder. "This was the reality of the Reich's great game in the region," Schulze-Holthus wrote after the war.

He later heard that Kurmis' little group had come out of Iran without firing a shot, although there had been a tense moment when they were making their way toward their final point of departure at Bushehr and an RAF fighter had roared down on them. Some of the men stood their ground and waved hastily improvised white flags; others ran. These were the wiser. "It was an inglorious exit," Kurmis later reflected, "and several men were destined not to return to their homeland again."

In fact, the main tangible result of the various factions going under the banner of Operation Franz was to circulate a large number of British banknotes around Tehran and the southern provinces, whether by way of private commerce or as inducements for dissident groups to rally to the swastika. But neither Schulze-Holthus nor anyone else among Germany's local assets seemed able or prepared to sweep through the jungle of conflicting interests and consolidate their efforts into one coherent or decisive assault. There were still some isolated successes along the way, such as the ambush that stopped an Anglo-American convoy escorting a delivery of oil to the western Soviet provinces in modern-day Turkmenistan, or the assassination of the confusingly named Major Major, second-in-command of the British 5th Infantry Division's summertime base on the banks of Lake Namak. But such efforts were either too few or too poorly coordinated to significantly affect the balance of local military or political power. There was also the fact that many or most of Franz's insurgent groups continued to be paid in crisp British £50 notes, each the size of a small flag, manufactured not in London but by the inmates of the Sachsenhausen camp. In the parallel world of wartime Iran, one set of operatives was thus bribing its subordinates to subvert the central, notionally Islamic regime, which was open to rival bidders, and doing so by foreign currency forged at gunpoint by enslaved Jewish laborers. When Schulze-Holthus tried to impose a sense of Germanic order on the workings of Operation Franz, he found that the chiefs of the dozens of component groups and tribes in the struggle had more practical authority than he did. "It struck me that our efforts would not turn the tide of the war, in Iran or anywhere else," he later wrote. "Something more brutal was needed."

* * *

On July 17, 1943, General Erwin Rommel, late of the Afrika Corps command, sent Hitler a secret report showing what the Wehrmacht thought of their ally in the Italian-German Pact of Steel. In Rome, Mussolini had written earlier that week to ask for an urgent high-level meeting. "I believe, Führer," he said, "that the time has come to examine closely together the situation, so as to reach conclusions conforming to the common interests of each country."[2] Hitler had accepted the invitation and asked his senior field commanders if there were any capable Italian officers. Rommel, in his report, replied, "There is no such person."

The Axis conference took place on July 19 at a private estate in Feltre, near the Italian border with Austria. Hitler characteristically dominated the five-hour discussion, his monologue interrupted only by the competing squawk of peacocks on the villa's grounds.[3] When an already demoralized Mussolini flew home, his camouflaged Savio-Marchetti bomber landed in a thick cloud of drifting black smoke. The Allied air forces had just hit Rome for the first time. The diminutive Italian head of state Victor Emmanuel III had watched by telescope the squadrons of B-17s bearing down over the city, and later ventured out with a phalanx of guards to inspect the damage. He distributed a few coins along his tour, but the people shouted, "We don't want your dirty money, we want peace!" On July 25, the king abruptly told Mussolini that he was dismissing him as prime minister in favor of the crassly opportunist Marshal Badoglio, the perpetrator of an array of war crimes in North Africa. As Mussolini left the royal palace he was arrested by the waiting carabinieri and eventually locked up in the Campo Imperatore ski hotel, halfway up Gran Sasso, the loftiest peak in the Apennines, some eighty miles from Rome and accessible only by cable car.[4]

In due course the new Italian regime signed an armistice with the West. Hitler's response to these developments was to demand immediate action to seize Rome, arrest the Badoglio government, and take the royal family hostage. The occupation duly followed, although the kidnap targets escaped. In time the Germans formed a defensive line along the river Volturno south of Rome, forcing the Allied armies to mount what became an arduous nine-month campaign to take the Italian capital. Hitler apparently decided this comparative strategic success was not enough to bolster Axis morale and ordered a daring raid to rescue his fellow dictator from his alpine fastness. Late that August, he summoned his local commander General Albert Kesselring and gave him a copy of the collected works of Nietzsche as a gift to be passed on to the liberated Mussolini. Apparently, Hitler presumed the Duce might yet have the time and inclination to reflect further on the "will to power."[5]

Kesselring in turn pointed out the practical challenges of mounting a conventional attack up a steep, rocky slope, which would presumably involve not only heavy German casualties but also give the guards time to kill their prisoner. A parachute drop presented similar difficulties, he added. At that point Hitler dismissed Kesselring and called in Walter Schellenberg to brief him on the problem. Schellenberg listened to an outline of the mission, snapped his heels, and in turn sent for the man officially designated, among his other titles, head of Department "S" (for Sabotage) of the Reich Security Office, Otto Skorzeny.

* * *

On Monday, July 26, the day Mussolini entered captivity at the Campo Imperatore, four senior German intelligence officers sat down for afternoon tea 900 miles away on the palm-fringed upstairs terrace of the Eden Hotel in central Berlin.[6] It seems mildly odd that the group—Walter Schellenberg, Wilhelm Canaris, the fanatical RSHA chief Ernst Kaltenbrunner, and Colonel Georg Hansen, head of the Abwehr's overseas field division—should have chosen to meet in one of the capital's most popular watering holes rather than any of the nearby secure offices at their disposal. Perhaps it appealed to the smoothly urbane Canaris, who had called the men together that warm afternoon. Ever the affable host, the admiral first inquired into his colleagues' health and that of their families, trusting that they had each enjoyed their weekend. But it was all business once the waiters had withdrawn and the security chiefs adjourned to a small anteroom, where they seated themselves at a baize-topped oval table. It was a curious sidelight on the fate of the Nazi regime that three of the attendees would be judicially executed within a few years of their tea party, only Schellenberg escaping the noose.

Canaris began the proceedings by revealing that Operation Franz had so far proved only a mixed tactical success. Regrettably, the Qashqai tribesmen of southern Iran were less amenable to proper military discipline than might be thought ideal by a German field commander. The British compound at Shiraz was still open for business. There had been a series of successful parachute drops throughout Iran, Canaris noted, although nothing definite had been learned of the fate of Hauptsturmführer Kurmis and his team of irregulars in the Zagros foothills. Nonetheless, the admiral insisted, there was every prospect that these individuals would in short order make contact with the Abwehr's men on the ground in Tehran, with all that implied for further intensified attacks on Allied positions.

At this stage, Canaris's subordinate Colonel Hansen took a decisive part in the discussion.

There was information, Hansen said, lowering his voice to a suggestive murmur, that there might yet be a target or targets of altogether greater value to the Reich than merely those of the British garrison at Shiraz or the local oil convoys. In fact, his department was in possession of intercepted cables suggesting that the three Allied heads of government would soon meet to discuss matters relating to the long-awaited invasion of Europe. There was as yet no consensus on the likely date or even the location of the conference. Alaska had reportedly been mentioned by the Americans. Stalin evidently preferred the merits of Baghdad or Basra in Iraq, possibly because he could reach these destinations by train. And Churchill had more recently proposed Tehran.

Schellenberg conceivably repressed a smile. His knowledge of this subject, never well hidden, was now an openly acknowledged secret, registered with every new report received from his sleepers in Iran. Kaltenbrunner asked about the matter of timing, and Hansen quietly, almost regretfully, replied: "It might be August. Or September. Or October. But it most assuredly will occur."

"This is a priority for Hitler," Canaris added. "He does not wish to be surprised once more." This was evidently a reference to the Anglo-American summit at Casablanca six months earlier, when Roosevelt had made his demand for unconventional surrender. "The führer has made it clear that failure in the matter is not an option he will tolerate," Canaris concluded.

Strong men had often quailed at a lesser implied threat of Hitler's wrath, but, in a remarkable show of self-control, the four state security chiefs finished their tea with only the mutual promise that they would meet again.

* * *

When we hear words like "spy" or "agent," we perhaps think of a highly trained operative with a clear, state-sponsored mission, often tinged by a more personal motivation—honor, patriotism, revenge, love—and equipped with a full array of concealed cameras, poison-tipped shoes, or watches that become miniature dart guns, and all the other accessories needed to confront an equally well-provided enemy. Our hero may actively seek opportunities to engage in these gladiatorial contests, as in some martial-arts movies, or it may be that he or she is of the more ironic, postmodern school, with a complicated inner life and only ambivalent views about the tangled governmental system issuing their orders. Taken as a whole, the operations taking place in and around Tehran in the late summer and early fall of 1943 would seem to fall into the second of these categories. The men and women involved were unconcerned with gadgetry and the other James Bond paraphernalia, but for the most part they were fiercely dedicated, often commendably moral, sometimes crassly mercenary, and, above all, fully human.

There was, for instance, the one-time popular wrestling champion Misbah Ebtehaj. By August of that year, Ebtehaj was in the happy position of supplementing his ring money with no fewer than four weekly cash-filled envelopes from distinct or competing bodies: the Americans, the British, the Germans, and a cabal of corrupt local Iranian politicians. He was separately informing the Allied powers about the activities of hostile splinter groups, such as the pro–Nazi Melliyun-I-Iran, operating in the capital, while furnishing the agents themselves with safe houses, supplies, and local gossip. For their part, the politicians used Ebtehaj and his crew as a sort of local SA Brownshirt equivalent, an auxiliary militia that intervened where even the famously uninhibited Tehran police feared to tread.

On August 17, two members of Ebtehaj's cutthroat band beat to death a visiting American Lutheran pastor, Walter Rauff, who had used the pulpit to propose some modest Iranian civil reforms. There were other such excesses, including the bombing of a British services' club on August 22. A week later, an opposition politician named Araki was beaten up by Ebtehaj's goons in the street. On September 2, a liberal newspaper columnist and poet, Bijan Razaee, was treated likewise. When his wife Farah remonstrated, she was first thrown to the ground, where she lay hysterically sobbing and raining curses on her husband's assailants, and then detained by the police for disturbing the peace in this way. Sent to Tehran's notorious Qasr prison, she was systematically beaten and placed at the mercy of the jail's psychotic "Doctor" Ahmadi, a physician who performed much the same perverted role as Josef Mengele at Auschwitz. When Razaee went on hunger strike to protest her treatment, the odious Ahmadi supervised her forcible feeding by means of a grimy rubber tube pushed up through her nostril. When this proved insufficiently painful for his tastes, he varied the practice by inserting tubes into his victim's rectum and her vagina, a deviation from the standard procedure that can only have been carried out for reasons of pure sadism.

Ahmadi was later tried for his crimes at Qasr and executed, age 58, by being slowly pulled off the ground by his neck by a crane set up in Tehran's Toopkhaneh Square. According to the horrified London *Times* correspondent, "Death took some twenty minutes, and brought visible distress to the condemned man."

Making the German covert operations around the area still stranger, there were the continuing activities—sometimes almost antics—of Operation Franz. Abwehr-supplied money and munitions still fell at regular intervals from the nighttime Iranian skies. There were occasional listless attacks on Allied assets in Tehran and more concerted ones on the various train and truck convoys taking oil to the Ukraine. There was still no coherent direction for Franz at a strategic level. The only effective liaison between Berlin and the seething mass of embedded or newly arrived Nazi agents, self-employed mavericks, and disaffected native bushmen was Julius Schulze-Holthus, whose governing credo seems to have had more than a touch of the schoolboy's "Let's make mischief!" to it. All of these assorted factions jostled together, spin-dryer fashion, in the Tehran of

4. Agent Cicero

1943. Perhaps it was no wonder that Louis Goethe Dreyfus, the U.S. minister to Iran, reported back to the State Department on August 9,

> There have been frequent incidents of drunkenness and rowdyism among [Allied] forces, and lawlessness in general. Recently a regular army garrison of more than a thousand men was all but eliminated as a military unit by tribesmen.[7]

Speaking of the stability or otherwise of Iran as a whole, Dreyfus had this to say:

> German parachutists continue to be dropped, and have not been apprehended.... The situation is extremely fluid. There is an almost total lack of security here and the whole country verges on anarchy.[8]

* * *

The gravedigging saboteur Frank Mayr lay at the heart of this turbulent world of spies, moles, spooks, and duplicitous oiled musclemen. Mayr was by then operating as a sort of matron to successive waves of German parachutists installed in safe houses in different parts of Tehran. He made sure they were generously supplied with food, drink, and women. He arranged for transport to carry them on their periodic sorties to attack a local camp or bomb a departing fuel train, and was waiting to welcome them back again like a coach proudly receiving a winning team in the locker room. When one of the commandos fell ill with typhus and died, Mayr, rather than alert the municipal Tehran authorities, rolled up his sleeves and dismembered the poor man's body with a machete. That night he took the parts out to a remote field and used his professional skills to bury them. After that, one eminent historian writes, there was a noticeable falling-off in aggressive fighting spirit among the surviving German operatives.

> It was as if part of themselves, whatever remained of their will, had also been buried in that lonely Iranian field. Two of the commandos headed off to the tribal areas; they had no plan beyond an eagerness to flee the city. The other survivors spent their time being ferried from one safe house to another, shepherded all the time by the protective attentions of Mayr's network.[9]

Others in Mayr's circle went off on assignments: Julius Schulze-Holthus managed to coordinate the efforts of yet another German drop team with those of Nasr Khan's horsemen long enough to wreck a fuel train on its way to Bushehr; the menthol-sniffing Roman Gamotha led a disparate crew of heavily armed toughs to a bank in Cukurca, just across the northern border with Turkey, to relieve it of a million lira, or some $370,000 (roughly $6 million today) in newly delivered banknotes; while Erwin Ettel continued in his role as the point man bringing new German arrivals down from the Elburz foothills into Tehran. They found a city of confusion. Many of their fellow Axis agents were enthusiastic, others perplexed, and some just indifferent. Few knew what was going on, including those involved in Operation Franz, since conflicting orders kept emanating from Berlin. It all seemed like an unlikely means to decisively alter the fortunes of a world war.

At a follow-up conference with Ernst Kaltenbrunner on August 12, when the prospect of a high-level Allied conference was again discussed, Admiral Canaris repeated his view that the führer was "decided upon some sharp strike—a *coup de main*" against the enemy since the German war effort was now increasingly "strained" (*angespannt*) on a number of fronts. The next twelve months would almost certainly prove decisive, the admiral said.

All this was accurate, though not very newsworthy. Every armchair strategist knew that the Allied assault on Europe would require a summer of campaigning, and so could come only in the spring; late April or May 1944 was widely regarded as the target date. Meanwhile, the Russians were in the throes of counterattacking around Kursk, dispelling any chance of German victory, or even stalemate, in the east; the Japanese imperial navy continued to take a relaxed view of Hitler's request that it block Western shipments heading for the USSR, and Italy teetered on the brink of collapse. The strategic picture as a whole was grave enough for the senior ranks of the Nazi hierarchy to speak in hushed tones of the prospects for the survival or otherwise of the Thousand Year Reich.

Henriette von Schirach has left an account of a meeting held in a private room of a fashionable Austrian restaurant that August between her husband Baldur, founder of the Hitler Youth and then Gauleiter of Vienna, and the man who in theory remained the second most powerful figure in Germany, Herman Goring.[10]

After a good deal to eat and drink, Schirach felt bold enough to again note the "strained" state of affairs and urged Goring to "speak to Hitler privately" about saving the Reich while he still could.

Men had been summarily removed by the Gestapo, never to be seen again, for speaking less directly than this. But it was too late for Schirach to stop now. The gauleiter raised his ante and made a prediction: if Goring did not do as he suggested, the Allies would win the war and in short order string them all up from the nearest lamppost. It was that simple.

"Goring responded without batting an eyelid," Henriette von Schirach wrote. "He seemed a little sad, as if he had heard this kind of thing before. Then he picked up one of his exquisite imported cigarettes, fingered it for a while, and lit it very slowly. He sank deep into his red chair and looked at us.

"To speak to Hitler alone, what an idea! I never see him alone these

4. Agent Cicero

days. Bormann is with him all the time. If I could, by God, I would have gone to see Churchill himself a long time ago. Do you think I am enjoying this damned business?"[11]

All the Reich could then reasonably hope for, Schirach wrote during his lengthy postwar confinement, was some form of *deus ex machina* to providentially deliver her from her enemies. "We had [agents] all over the world, going variously to Moscow, Washington, and all through the East, and report[ing] to Berlin every day. But only in one place did Germany spy as readers of spy novels would have us do. In London."

By August 1943, the Nazis' principal pipeline into their enemy belligerent's capital was a blond, blue-eyed 29-year-old former Hanover lawyer named Karl-Heinz Kramer, who had joined the Luftwaffe in 1937 and from there been recruited into the Abwehr. Posted to neutral Sweden in October 1942, Kramer was able to routinely photograph the incoming cables of the Swedish naval and air attachés to Great Britain, noting, for instance, that in July 1943, "Seven shipments from Stockholm are to be dispatched to England, [and] these include 75 packages of high-speed steel drills weighing 1,549.2 kilograms addressed to Bruce & Brown Ltd., 21 Rochester Road, Coventry."[12] His reports were always impressively detailed. But they dealt largely in the raw data of troops and materiel passing through Britain rather than in the timing or specifics of matters such as Churchill's periodic excursions to confer with his allies.

Quebec was next. Churchill and Roosevelt met there, hosted by Canadian prime minister William Mackenzie King, from August 17 to 24, 1943, largely to discuss the logistics of the cross-Channel invasion, while touching almost in passing on the matter of the development of the atomic bomb. Angry not to be consulted on some of the detail, Stalin dispatched a furious cable. His intelligence services had told him that Churchill was still in no hurry to open a second front. "He prefers to watch our armies bleed."[13] The USSR, Stalin wrote ominously, was tired of being the poor relation of the Alliance. "I have to tell you," his wire concluded, "that it is impossible to tolerate such a situation any longer."[14]

On reading this rebuke, Churchill was left to muse on the postwar world. "Stalin is an unnatural man," he reflected. "There will be grave troubles."

On September 1, Kramer reported back to Berlin of the Quebec conference,

> In principle, nothing has changed in the conception held up to now. A major action in northern France, which is supposed to bring a decision in the war, is not to be expected before the spring of next year. For now, [the Allies] will concentrate efforts in North Africa and Sicily for operations against Italy and Mediterranean islands.[15]

All this was true, but, again, not exactly a newsflash. The real significance of the Quebec summit, codenamed Quadrant, was that it helped focus Stalin's mind on the possibility that he might overcome his aerophobia and fly to meet his allies in some overseas destination after all. If you wanted to successfully negotiate with the imperialists, the Vozhd told his ghoulish court, you had to do so in person. Churchill, Stalin added for the record, was "the kind of man who will pick your pocket of every kopeck if you don't watch him." Roosevelt, whom Stalin was yet to meet, was "not like that. He dips his hand only for bigger coins. But Churchill? I dread him. He will do anything for a kopeck!"[16]

Stalin's anxiety would probably not have been greatly relieved had he known of certain events taking place that week in Tehran. An Armenian oiled muscleman named Musa, one of Misbah Ebtehaj's entourage, had recently fallen into a noisy, money-based quarrel with Franz Mayr. As a result, he decided to relieve Mayr of a briefcase he'd seen secreted behind the false wall of one of his Tehran safe houses. Musa had no idea what was in the briefcase, but he reasoned that it must be something of value to merit being stored in this way. He took it unopened to the British consul. It's not known how much, if anything, Musa was paid for his initiative. But whatever the outlay, it was worth it. The briefcase contained a list of the names of dozens of pro–German officers in the Iranian army, and, just as good, those of Soviet agents said to be actively engaged in snooping on their allies. The information came from moles and Western sympathizers in Tehran who believed that Germany and Russia were equally inimical to their country's long-term interests. "I did not like be[ing] tormented by a bunch of sweating Ivans who swaggered round the streets of Tehran and told me I was a stinking little Arab," Musa later noted. The consul passed the intel up the line for the attention of the American Army Counter-Intelligence Corps (CIC), who acted on it with alacrity. Between them, the CIC and Iranian police rounded up 173 suspects on the night of August 16, 1943, and in the carefully weighed words of the British foreign office, "a number of Soviet nationals were informed at that time that their presence in Tehran would be more sparingly required in future."

The Allied dragnet gathered even greater momentum during the late summer of 1943, which saw the Iranian capital transformed into "a huge cooler and even [on] occasion torture chamber," as Walter Schellenberg put it. On August 24, the *News Chronicle*, a London newspaper, reported the detention of "upwards of 300 individuals engaged in pro-Hitler activity."[17] Most of the arrested men and women were taken to the Qasr jail, although some were held in the nearby British military barracks. They were the lucky ones. According to an anonymous eyewitness, the Iranian interrogators at Qasr worked on their captives with "spades, clubs and whips." The cries of the victims "rang out" through the cellblock, whose other inmates, "unable to bear their screams, blocked their ears with torn shreds of paper or their own fingers." On a recent day, this "orgy" of beating had lasted over two-and-a-half hours. When it was over, "six of the 28 souls were dead, their skulls smashed. The others were all unconscious. The teeth of some had been knocked out, their eyes and noses bloody and hollow." Some of the jailers' efforts to loosen the tongues of their female prisoners were even more brutal than this and involved the nefarious Dr. Ahmadi at his most degenerate.

A local farmer named Muhsin Sadr, apparently picked up because he had sold food to some of Franz Mayr's recruits, was released from Qasr only in March 1945. His son greeted him at the prison gates. "He had lost a lot of weight, his head was shaved and he had no coat or jacket on. They had been taken from him by the guards in 1943, and he had spent two winters dressed in light clothes in a cell so small that the men slept on their sides, and were packed so tightly next to one another that in order for any of them to change position they all had to turn over in a wave. He would not speak of the experience beyond that."

There may have been at least one other extra-judicial roundup that summer of German assets in Iran. The Israeli historian and politician Michael Bar-Zohar writes in his biography of Lt. Paul Fackenheim, one of the few Jews to serve in Hitler's wartime Wehrmacht, that he, Fackenheim, was arrested as a spy by the British and eventually confined in an Allied POW camp in Latrun, outside Jerusalem. While in captivity, Fackenheim saw "six or seven SS prisoners who had parachuted into Iran, loaded with explosives and gold, who had then tried to bribe the Qashqai tribesmen into rebelling against the Allies. Once they ran out of money, the Qashqai turned them in to the British."[18]

* * *

It's difficult to say with any degree of certainty when the German plan to assassinate Roosevelt, Churchill, and Stalin took definite shape, let alone point to a particular date when such a decision was made. There were, in fact, two "decisions," if that term can be used to describe a process that, in each case, took several months to complete. The first evolved out of the late July teatime meeting at the Eden Hotel in Berlin and the subsequent directive for units of the SS 502nd Light Infantry Battalion under Otto Skorzeny's command to be trained for "special tasks," later defined by Skorzeny as "the degradation of the enemy control structure at the top level." In practice, this meant increasing the tempo of the existing plan to drop men and weapons into Iran, whether to create mischief for the country's Allied occupiers or to prepare for some altogether more "spectacular" strike.

The second, even more fateful decision came not in a sudden thunderclap of inspiration, but at intervals during the late summer and early autumn days of 1943, as further reports reached Berlin to give Schellenberg the impetus to "send reinforcements to significantly expand [and] more narrowly focus" the program already in hand in and around Tehran. Again, there is no known document bearing Hitler's signature authorizing the plan. As little as possible was committed to paper, and where that was unavoidable, it was standard procedure among the likes of Canaris and his associates to employ such veiled euphemisms as "extraction" or "relocation" for assassination, a word that derives from the ancient Persian *hashshashin*, or covert murder. As a rule, Hitler made clear what he wanted orally, leaving it to others to convey the necessary orders, using the formula "in accordance with the Führer's wishes."

There was a significant moment during this second gestation period when Canaris and Schellenberg met in the latter's Berkaerstrasse office to discuss what were minuted only as "matters of the first importance" involving Iran. According to the author Howard Blum, the heads of Germany's two principal security organs would henceforth agree to "alert their field agents and assets that information about the timing and location of the [Allied] tripartite meeting was now of the highest priority."[19] Further, "the tactical departments of both organizations would work together to provide, and if necessary create, the optimal weapons and explosive devices for the mission," and finally "selected commandos would begin training without being informed of the specific nature or aim of their mission." The men were to be told merely that they were employed on "work of the highest significance to the Reich," and given the identity of their targets only at the last moment.

One final piece of business remained. The secret mission, like all the best missions, needed a codename, and after considering various alternatives, Schellenberg finally decided that something suitably dynamic was needed to convey the sheer scope of what they had in mind by proposing to alter the whole course of the war in a single leap, and hit upon *Unternehmen Weitsprung*, or Operation Long Jump.

It had a certain ring to it, the rival spymasters agreed.

That the Allied troika might soon meet in person did not come as news to Schellenberg and his staff at Berkaerstrasse. Among other things, they had recently deciphered a message with details of a "most secret" war cabinet meeting in London.

Dated August 11, 1943, the document also hinted at the unresolved tension between the two Allied camps, East and West, which so differed in their political complexions and detailed long-term goals but were united by their desire to get rid of Hitler and then rebuild Europe in their image.

4. Agent Cicero 95

The paper's edited highlights, forwarded for Hitler's attention on August 15, may even have briefly revived his old hope, despite Germany's battlefield reverses, that the Western allies would yet realize that their true interests lay in joining Germany in her crusade against Bolshevism. Its logic was so obvious that it had to happen, Hitler informed Ribbentrop at another mad tea party that week in his Bavarian mountain retreat at Berchtesgaden.

The intercepted British cabinet paper began,

W.M. (43) Conclusions
11th AUGUST, 1943. 11.30 a.m. CONFIDENTIAL.
The War Cabinet were reminded that the attitude of the Russian Government had been difficult for some weeks past; and that no response had been received from Premier Stalin to the suggestions which had been made some time ago for a meeting between himself, the Prime Minister and President Roosevelt. Before his departure for Canada, [Churchill] had settled the terms of a message to be sent to Marshal Stalin as soon as security considerations allowed, informing him of the conference and suggesting that an early opportunity should be taken for holding a further meeting at which Stalin could be present. This message was dispatched on 7th August.[20]

Stalin's reply, which was attached, gave further proof of the Russian's undoubted gift for equivocation and of his positive genius for manipulating situations and people to his advantage.

"I have just returned from the front," he began, lest anyone think the Vozhd let the grass grow under his feet, "and have already become familiar with the message of the British government dated 7th August."

(1) I agree that a meeting of the Heads of the three Governments is absolutely desirable.
(2) At the same time I ought to say that in the existing situation on the Soviet-German front I, to my regret, have no opportunity to absent myself and leave my post even for a week. Although recently we have had several successes in the field, an extreme strain on the strength [sic] and exceptional watchfulness are required in regard to the new possible actions of the enemy.
Moreover, it would be necessary beforehand to agree on the scope of the questions to be discussed at any such meeting, and the drafts of the proposals which have to be accepted. No meeting can have any tangible result without that.[21]

Churchill's response to Stalin's message was in turn attached and is notable both for its brevity and its teasing use of his Soviet ally's nickname.

CONCRETE No. 85. 10th August, 1943. MOST SECRET.

1. This reply is better than I dared to hope for, and a great relief.
2. Should we not now at once agree to a meeting in principle, time, place, personnel and agenda to be decided later?
3. Uncle Joe is unaccountable.[22]

Even without the tapped British message at their disposal, Schellenberg's office had only to read the transcript of Churchill's public remarks at the conclusion of the Quadrant conference, which were widely circulated in the British and foreign press.

"Nothing is nearer to the wishes of President Roosevelt and myself," Churchill began, "than to have a threefold meeting with Marshal Stalin. If that has not yet taken place, it is certainly not because we have not tried our best, or have not been willing to lay aside every impediment and undertake further immense journeys for that purpose."

After some more in this same vein came Churchill's summation, which can only have further piqued the interest of the principal architects of Operation Long Jump.

> The President and I will now persevere in our efforts to meet Marshal Stalin. We shall be very glad to associate the Russian government with us in the political decisions which may arise out of the victories the Anglo-American forces have gained in the Mediterranean. It would be a very great advantage to everyone, and indeed to the whole free world, if unity of thought and decisions upon practical measures could soon be reached by the heads of the three great opponents of the Hitlerite tyranny.[23]

There were compelling grounds for Churchill's eagerness to meet Stalin and assure him that the British and Americans were serious about a cross-Channel invasion in 1944. He wished to prevent Russia from deserting the alliance. British codebreakers were regularly intercepting radio signals not only from Berlin but also Moscow. As late as September 1943, they were watching the Russians flirt with the possibility of a negotiated peace. Germany dangled tempting bait. If the USSR agreed to an armistice, Hitler would be content with the land already seized. German diplomatic records prove baseless the later canard of Soviet propaganda that their nation never had for a moment wavered in its determination to utterly crush their enemy and remove the specter of fascism from the face of the earth.

Churchill's fears on this issue were then particularly well founded, because even as their armies disengaged from the greatest and certainly bloodiest land battle mankind has ever known, the German and Soviet foreign ministers met secretly at Kirovograd, 200 miles into Nazi-held territory, to discuss a bilateral peace treaty, a development the British premier, alerted to the astonishing news (which appears nowhere in the Russian archives) by his ULTRA codebreakers at Bletchley Park, received with "some alarm."[24]

Hitler, for his part, was now fast withdrawing into the mental neverland of believing that the war could still be won by "by a nose," if not by conventional force then by "special" tactics. These ranged from the development of jet aircraft and unmanned rockets to using Quenzgut-trained commandos for the more immediate rescue of the imprisoned Mussolini. Though he didn't yet know it, Hitler also faced a burgeoning rebellion from within his intelligence services.

By September 1943, Canaris had crossed the line into an ideological no-man's-land in which he still sought to swiftly end the war, but not necessarily in the way Hitler intended. At a meeting with his Italian counterpart Cesare Amè at Venice's Hotel Danieli, the Abwehr chief publicly heaped praise on the Italo-German axis, promising that even now this would push back the enemy "gang" into the sea. His private remarks took a different tone. According to Amè's later testimony, Canaris insisted that Italy was well rid of its hated dictator, and that it would only be a matter of time before Germany was similarly "liberated" (*emanzipiert*).[25] Given the increasingly paranoid state of the senior Nazi hierarchy, this was perhaps an unwise confidence on the admiral's part. Walter Schellenberg also had a man in Venice, who in due course acquainted him with the Abwehr chief's duplicity. In the fevered climate of September 1943, the spies were themselves spied upon. Alice had now truly stepped through the looking glass.

Later that month, Schellenberg went to Hitler with a new proposal. He thought that everything possible should be done to liquidate Stalin, as "the Soviet regime would then no longer be able to withstand the burdens of war ... [My] scheme was to lure Stalin to the conference table and then to gun him down, whatever the personal consequences." The führer reflected for some time on the self-sacrificing details of Schellenberg's plan, but in the end felt that it might be asking for "trouble from Providence."[26]

* * *

Faced as they now were with almost certain defeat, many of Hitler's inner circle withdrew into a kind of mystical fairyland. It was a world of gods and heroes, of titanic struggle and redemption, and one of spurious and delusional crackpots. Nowhere did steely-eyed Nazi pragmatism comingle more closely with the occult arts of the séance room than in the reptilian form of Heinrich Himmler. In early September 1943, the SS chief issued orders to the commandants of the three main Berlin-area concentration camps to select any experts from among their intake proficient in "divination, chiromancy and radiesthesia," and present them to him for interview. Jean-Jacques Beguin, a prisoner at Sachsenhausen who had practiced as a magician and hypnotist in prewar Paris, later remembered a scene which, like so many of those involving Himmler, combined the sinister and the absurd.

> The Reichsführer was sitting behind a desk flanked by two uniformed SS guards. An attendant waved me to sit down and offered me a cigar. This man

posed several questions concerning my background and career. Himmler himself then spoke: "You are a Frenchman and a Jew, and we cannot expect you to be a champion of National Socialism. But this time you will perform not for money, not for fame, but for your life. If you cooperate with us and prove helpful we shall make life easy for you in the camp."[27]

According to Beguin, the overlord of the SS empire had just two questions for him. Where was Mussolini currently detained? And which three persons of particular interest to the Reich would soon convene, and where?

"I must consult the spirits."

"Do so," said Himmler.

He spoke eagerly, as if he expected something enjoyably dramatic.

Beguin drew a blank on the first point, but by a supreme act of will was able to hazard the names Roosevelt, Churchill and Stalin as the answer to the second, along with the tentative conclusion that they might seek an "Arab country" for their conference. This was enough of a demonstration of the psychic arts for Himmler to shake the Frenchman by the hand, and to give orders that he be transferred out of the main prison block to an outlying hut with a lone guard posted nearby. Two days later, Beguin was able to put his professional skills to good use by inducing the guard to fall asleep, then removing his uniform and, dressed in this, strolling out of the camp gate to catch a train to the last stop before the Swiss frontier, where he waited until dark before walking the last few miles to freedom.

The SS chief and sometime-mystic Heinrich Himmler on a tour of the Dachau concentration camp.

* * *

Six more German parachutists descended on the Elburz foothills north of Tehran in the early hours of September 2, 1943. They included the 23-year-old SS Untersturmführer Joseph Schnabel, the man who recalled his training at Quenzgut as largely a question of being taught to hate.[28] In due course, Schnabel found himself a house guest of the short and tubby Winifred Oberg, the former lawyer and sometime intimate of the late Ernst Rohm. The domestic arrangements were only partly to the fanatical young SS man's taste. Oberg's "unwanted and unnatural" advances were one thing, but it seemed to Schnabel that the prevailing atmosphere in his new quarters on Tehran's Molavi Street was more like that of an American college fraternity house than a dedicated Nazi sleeper cell. "The fact that the others mainly spoke English did not bother me," he recalled. "After all, we were in a distant land, and we had contacts among the Anglo-Americans as well as among every other people. What I could not understand, however, was how they could prepare for an action of such importance when they were dead drunk all the time."[29]

A day or two later, Schnabel shared his misgivings on the subject with the Swiss-born Ernst Merser, the elegantly shod businessman-spy whom he recognized as the "elite man" of the Tehran cell. Merser, whose sharp instinct for the realities of power had taught him to pick his fights carefully, advised Schnabel either to forget the matter, or if necessary to confront his host directly. Schnabel chose the latter option.

"I could mention a dozen people who would vouch for me, and not unimportant ones," Oberg replied with dignity, drawing himself up to his full height. "However, this can only be done if and when you take the opportunity to contact Berlin."

Schnabel in turn replied that he would be pleased to do so by way of wireless transmitter, and asked the lawyer to supply the name of a suitable reference.

"Walter Schellenberg or Ernst Kaltenbrunner," Oberg said. "Would that be satisfactory?"[30]

Three hours later, word came back from Berkaerstrasse that honorary SS Oberführer Oberg, "by order of the first authority in the Reich," was to be given every assistance.

As a result, Joseph Schnabel duly joined the game and became a man "put in place" for work of the highest strategic value, knowing that the führer approved.

* * *

Blind to the furious, invisible activity seething just below the surface, the Allies continued to consider what Churchill called the "stagnant pool" of Iran for their forum. Like so much of the Big Three's relationship in the war, it was a compromise choice. On September 4, Roosevelt cabled Stalin that "I personally can now arrange to come to a place as far as North Africa between Nov. 15 and Dec. 15."[31] However, the president added, neither the United States Constitution nor the poor health of his secretary of state, Cordell Hull, would allow for a more extended journey. Perhaps the three Allied foreign ministers could meet for a preparatory discussion in Washington, Roosevelt suggested, if such a thing was even necessary. "Mr. Hull is quite poorly, [and] no one can sign official papers for me when I am away," he added.

Stalin was as indifferent to the ways of democratic government as he was to Secretary Hull's illness. "There should be a preliminary meeting of senior ministers in Moscow," he replied, while for the summit itself, "it would be advisable to select a country where all the three powers are represented, such as *Iran*" (Stalin's emphasis).

The two men's next exchange established for all time the essential difference between the pragmatic, thrice-elected American head of state and the de facto latter-day czar and Communist martinet.

"I am delighted at your willingness [to meet]," Roosevelt cabled, "and the time about the end of November is all right.... Personally, my only hesitation is the place, but only because it is a bit further away from Washington than I had counted on." He added on a note of almost touching goodwill, "I hope that you may yet consider some part of Egypt, which is also a neutral state, and where every arrangement can surely be made for our convenience."

It was as though Roosevelt was talking to the Kremlin Wall.

"As regards our meeting," Stalin cabled with finality, "I have no objection to Tehran."

It was left only for Churchill, also a Tehran man, to suggest that a decoy security operation be set up in Cairo to help persuade the enemy that this was the true location of the meeting, a proposal to which Stalin agreed with a brief flick of his pen before turning to the pressing matter of composing a new Soviet national anthem, with foreign minister Molotov contributing to the lyrics, Dmitri Shostakovich and Sergei Prokofiev to the music, and Stalin serving in a sort of proto-George Martin role as the tune's supreme producer.

* * *

The Tehran of late 1943 was in many ways a curious spot for the entire Allied high command and their staffs to choose to assemble in one room. By September of that year the city had come to increasingly resemble one of those scenes of chaotic mass dislocation that characterize the post-apocalyptical diasporas of the *Mad Max* film franchise. More than any other middle eastern metropolis, Tehran epitomized tensions—social, spiritual, political—that signaled the turn of an era, the gradual death of the tribal wilderness and the birth of the modern petrostate.

On September 2, the young Mohammad Reza Pahlavi ordered the arrest of over 200 senior Iranian politicians and army officers on charges ranging from embezzlement to high treason. Many of those detained had expressed pro-German sentiments, and, like others before and after them, most quickly disappeared into the dungeons of Qasr. Rumors quickly spread through the bazaars and back alleys of Tehran that the occupying Allied forces were rounding up and summarily executing thousands of innocent civilians. On the night of September 6, a flat boat appeared in the water just off the coast at Sakht Sar, where the shah was spending the week at one of his numerous regional estates. A single, muffled rifle shot disposed of the lone sentry on duty at the water's edge. Then sinister dark figures appeared on the beach and started running silently toward the palace gates. The guards stationed there put up more of a fight than their fallen colleague. There was a sharp burst of machine gun fire, and in short order reinforcements appeared on the battlements to strafe the intruders below. Some brutal if disjointed close-order fighting ensued. One or two of the invaders threw grenades, but they seemed to have no definite plan of attack beyond that. In a few minutes the mysterious boat left again, moving smartly off up the dark Caspian coast. Daylight showed that the landing party had managed to lay an explosive charge just a few yards from the palace wall, but due to a faulty timer it had failed to go off. The drowned body of one of the raiders was later retrieved from the surf. The general feeling was that he and his colleagues had been members of the pro-Nazi Melliyun movement.

Two days later, back in Tehran, a jeep tore through the main market square in the middle of the afternoon, one of its passengers standing up in the back to spray machine gun bullets at a group of Iranian army officers sitting at an open-air café. Some British soldiers were caught drinking tea at a nearby table, one of them falling in the crossfire, while another young officer ran out of a barbershop, mouth agape in shaving foam, and could do more than shout hoarsely at the jeep as it raced down the street. When the smoke cleared it was found that a total of seven soldiers had been killed, and another one so badly wounded that doctors removed both his legs. A hastily produced communiqué from the Melliyun suggested that this, too, had been intended as an act of defiance against the country's Allied occupiers.

On September 10, a cable went out over the shah's signature to the foreign ministries in Berlin, Washington, London and Moscow:

Considering the hostile activities by German agents, aimed at creating disturbances and lawlessness and endangering the tranquility, security and independence of the country, the Imperial Iranian Government is obliged to declare the existence of a state of war between Iran and Germany.

Meanwhile, it fell to Otto Skorzeny to prove the mettle of his new "S" sabotage unit, and he rose to the occasion, pulling off the most audacious commando raid, buttressed by great discipline in guarding against leaks, of the war to date.

On the morning of September 10, an operator of the SS Communications Battalion 12 billeted in the attic of a requisitioned family hotel at Louveciennes, west of Paris, picked up a signal sent between an Italian army group and Marshal Badoglio's office in Rome.[32] Most such intercepts that poured into the Germans' radio room, where the teams of monitors sat around the clock with their headphones on, were routinely passed on to an assessment center. From there the information would be analyzed by an intelligence officer, and either sent up the line for further study or committed to the oblivion of a ministry filing cabinet. This particular signal, by contrast, bypassed all the normal channels and went to the desk of Walter Schellenberg in Berlin.

At two that afternoon, Schellenberg took off in a fast Condor 200 C-4 with the intercepted message secure in a briefcase chained to his wrist to fly the 400 miles to Hitler's military headquarters at Rastenburg. The flight took just over two hours, and it was another three hours before the SD chief was finally ushered into the same wooden barrack-hut conference room where Colonel Stauffenberg later carried his bomb. Hitler listened intently to Schellenberg's report and immediately issued the necessary order. At ten that night, Skorzeny was briefed by phone. By midnight, he had assembled a 107-strong team at Tempelhof airport in Berlin. Before dawn on the 11th they were mustered in a temporary camp attached to the Pratica di Mare air base southwest of Rome, which still lay in Axis hands, and were busy practicing takeoffs and landings with a small squadron of DFS gliders each towed by a two-seater Henschel 126 reconnaissance plane. Back at the Wolf's Lair, Hitler recorded an unusually sanguine radio broadcast to the German people that morning. "My right to believe unconditionally in success," he said, "is founded not only on my own life but also on the destiny of our great nation and that of our allies." Neither time nor force of arms would ever bring the Axis down.

At 1:00 p.m. on Sunday, September 12, Skorzeny and his team took off in ten gliders which, once airborne, began bucking violently on their tow lines. Their mission was to land on what appeared in photographs to be a flat, grassy meadow outside the Duce's alpine prison-hotel 110 miles away across the Apennines at Gran Sasso. The plan, nominally commanded by the 32-year-old SS Major Harald Mors, went by the codename *Unternehmen Eiche*, or Operation Oak.

An hour later, Mussolini, who had been threatening to commit suicide, was sitting by an open window, unshaven, dressed in ill-fitting civilian clothes, when a German glider suddenly swept out of the blue sky, a parachute billowing behind it to act as a brake, and landed in the field just below him. It was Skorzeny. The other gliders followed it in. Meanwhile, the valley station of the funicular railway leading up the mountain pass to the hotel was seized by two paratroop companies led by Major Mors, who promptly cut all communications to and from Rome. Shortly after 2:00 p.m., Skorzeny stepped out of his glider, machine gun in hand, and strode briskly toward the hotel's front door. Looking up, he saw Mussolini staring wide-eyed at him from his small room, number 220, just above. "Away from the window!" Skorzeny shouted in Italian, and without further ado charged through the main entrance of the hotel with a dozen of his colleagues close behind him.

In the event, the SS men had little trouble overcoming Mussolini's lightly armed guards, most of whom were found seated around a radio in the hotel's dining room listening to a broadcast of a local soccer match. Not a shot was fired, although Skorzeny paused to smash the radio with the butt of his gun before bounding up the richly carpeted stairs to fling open the door to Mussolini's room. "Duce," he announced dramatically, "you are free!" Mussolini seemed mildly bemused rather than positively ecstatic at these developments. "Are you Italian?" he asked. "No, eccellenza, we are Germans," Skorzeny replied. "The Führer has sent us." At that Mussolini seemed to recover himself, warmly embracing Skorzeny. "I knew my friend Adolf Hitler would not abandon me," he said, before enquiring about their onward travel plans. Would they be proceeding by tank or by truck, he wondered. "By air," Skorzeny replied, causing his new companion to flinch in alarm. The SS man later wrote of his surprise at the Axis dictator's appearance. "He looked confused, tired and unkempt," shuffling down the stairs on Skorzeny's arm, dressed in an old overcoat and nervously running his hand through the short, stubbly hair on top of his normally clean-shaven head.

Mussolini, a former pilot, was right to be apprehensive about his ongoing journey to freedom. But there was no time for any further discussion of the matter. Just five minutes later, he and Skorzeny were wedged together in the narrow cockpit of a light Fiesler Storch spotter plane that had followed the gliders to land on the hotel's sloping front lawn. Some of the German commandos had to seize the plane's wings to hold it back as Skorzeny revved up the engine for takeoff into the yawning valley below them. Mussolini was seen to cross himself in anticipation of the fate that seemed to await him. The plane duly bounced and shook as it then accelerated, lurching into the air before plunging sickeningly back down into the abyss, before pulling up and finally turning away toward Rome. Neither of the Storch's passengers spoke for several minutes. Only when the plane had leveled out into the clear-blue late-summer alpine sky, in "most unsoldierly fashion," did Skorzeny lay a reassuring hand on Mussolini's shoulder.[33]

After changing planes in Rome, the pair flew overnight to Vienna and Munich, finally arriving at Rastenburg on the morning of September 14. Hitler was waiting at the airstrip for them. He greeted both men effusively, in some accounts going so far as to favor his fellow Austrian with a kiss on the cheek. "You have performed a military feat which will become part of history," he said. "You have given me back my friend Mussolini."[34] But perhaps the real significance of Operation Oak lay in its propaganda value as an example of the long reach of the Reich's feared special forces. His subsequent private talks with his fellow dictator left Hitler "extraordinarily disappointed." Three days later, Mussolini was sent back to northern Italy to form a so-called Repubblica di Salo, reducing the once omnipotent Duce to the role of a German sock puppet, and one now living on borrowed time.

Nonetheless, the Skorzeny legend had been born. "This action has made the deepest impression throughout the world," Goebbels wrote in his diary on September 15, which for once was to do no more than to record the literal truth. "There has not been a single military action since the outbreak of the war that has shaken people to such an extent or called forth such enthusiasm. We may indeed celebrate a great moral victory."[35]

Ironically, perhaps the only person in the senior Nazi hierarchy not overjoyed by the results of Operation Oak was the SD chief Walter Schellenberg. The very success of the mission forever endeared Skorzeny to Hitler, who now came to look on him as a sort of personal guerrilla unit rather than as part of the established SS chain of command. "The activities of this man," Schellenberg was to complain at his postwar trial, "were covered in the strictest secrecy, and largely unknown even to me. Skorzeny was mainly engaged in special tasks entrusted to him by the highest authority, so circumventing official channels."[36]

Skorzeny's semi-detached status in the Reich intelligence system mirrored some of the strains within the RSHA as a whole, where the distance between the Canaris and Schellenberg factions was now not so much a gap as a yawning gulf. Considering what was at stake for Germany's survival, this breach within her main security services was a national humiliation, Schellenberg later wrote. The matter would come to a head late in 1943 with

4. Agent Cicero

Otto Skorzeny, seen shortly after his triumph in 1943's Operation Oak and two years later in his cell in Nuremberg.

the crisis involving a 24-year-old Canaris protégé named Erich Vermehren. The U.S. Justice Department noted in a classified report of the case,

> The Vermehren incident was an important step [in] the collapse of the entire Abwehr organization. It revealed the feud between Canaris and Schellenberg, and resulted in the taking over of the Abwehr by [its] rival.
>
> Dr. Erich Vermehren was born in 1919 in a family of high intellectual standing. In 1942 he married one Graefin Elisabeth von Plettenberg, six years his senior. She was a frail, sickly woman of good intellect and burning ambition. The members of her family were Catholic activists and she converted her husband to that faith.
>
> In the fall of 1942, Vermehren, a lawyer by training, was posted by the Abwehr to Turkey. His main job was to work on a case involving international law in the attempt to clear the titles to some French Danube ships which had left Rumania before the German occupation and were interned by the Turks. In addition, Vermehren worked on cases dealing with Egypt.
>
> Despite the order forbidding Abwehr personnel to have their wives with them, Vermehren submitted an application in the summer of 1943 to obtain permission for [Graefin] to join him in Turkey. This was disapproved. Nonetheless, later that year Mrs. Vermehren suddenly arrived in Istanbul by air, having shown her foreign office papers in Sofia and having thereby obtained permission to fly. Because of the incident, the situation became tense.
>
> One Friday morning, Vermehren reported to his office that he was ill and would not come in that day, also that he was moving to a new apartment in Istanbul. When he still did not appear at his office on Monday, a messenger

was sent to the new residence, but the place could not be found. A person dispatched to the Vermehrens' old apartment discovered that the couple had left with all their baggage after doing an unusual amount of typing in their rooms. The new address given by Vermehren did not exist.[37]

In fact, by then Vermehren and his wife were on a train that took them south through Syria to Beirut, before proceeding from there by sea to Alexandria, where they were smuggled on board a freighter bound for Gibraltar and then on to England. The British made a certain amount of capital out of the defection, believing that it might cause trouble in Germany's intelligence network in the buildup to the eventual invasion of Europe. They were right; it did. Hitler's fury at the news knew no bounds. His mood was not improved when two senior Abwehr officers, Hans von Dohnanyi and Hans Oster, were then arrested on corruption charges. The gestapo's tentacles soon reached Canaris, placing him under house arrest, the beginning of a protracted public disgrace that ended only on the Flossenburg gallows. The admiral had not helped his cause when Hitler summoned him for a final interview, and accused him of allowing the Abwehr to "fall to bits." Canaris had merely agreed that this was "not surprising, since Germany is losing the war."[38] From this point onward, Walter Schellenberg would effectively run the Reich's intelligence network under Himmler's nominal control.

Reviewing the RSHA's current operatives and their motley crew of assets on the ground in Iran, Schellenberg would come to question the wisdom of his entrusting the single greatest special-forces spectacular in modern history to a cell of rogue lawyers, freelance adventurers and barely literate all-in wrestlers, or whether instead to recruit a dedicated new team drawn from the inner ranks of the SS. One respected historian assumes Schellenberg's state of mind on the subject to write,

> He would ferret through the rolls hunting for battle-tested Germans who spoke either English or Russian. Outfit them in the uniforms of the Allied armies and then get them up close to their targets. They could go in heavily armed, without even concealing their weapons. What could be more natural than gun-toting soldiers? How he'd get them to the conference room, well, he'd just need to deal with that later, when—or if, he corrected himself—he discovered where the meeting would be held. So much was if, he silently groaned, and not for the first time.[39]

Leaving the imagined speech aside, this was just the sort of false-flag operation that had been a Schellenberg forte since he first helped Reinhard Heydrich stage the series of fake cross-border "attacks" that provided the justification for the full-scale German invasion of Poland in September 1939. But in the end he contented himself by sending a signal addressed

4. Agent Cicero

jointly to Winifred Oberg and Ernst Merser in Tehran. They were to effect "immediate changes in organization and personnel" on the ground, Schellenberg wrote, with the short-range goal of creating a "fully unified operation."[40] In September 1943, Oberg began implementing this program by recruiting three more local operatives. This is what the postwar U.S. Army investigators thought of them:

GRAGAZOLOU, Hussein
Subject is Iranian, about 50 years of age, five feet seven inches tall, and has thin grey hair. He came to Berlin in 1940 in order to enlist German aid in ridding Iran of Pahlavi. Was in contact with the Germans until 1943, in which year he returned at their request to Iran through Turkey.

GRAMAJE, Faroukh
Subject is Iranian, about 47 years of age, five feet two inches tall, has a bald head and is a hunchback. Served as an undercover agent of the SD. Was arrested for blackmail activity, but later freed.

SHAHROKH, Shah Bahram
Subject is Iranian, about 35 years of age, five feet two inches tall, has curly black hair and a mustache. He is a Zoroaster by religion. Came to Germany late in 1939 after he had become bankrupt as a merchant in Iran. He was engaged by the Ministry of Propaganda for Iranian broadcasts. Later returned to his native land. Subject is considered the most dangerous of all Iranians.

While none of these individuals actively dispelled the prevailing air of buccaneering nonconformity that clung to the overall German operation in Iran, they did significantly bolster the freelance resources available to the planners of Operation Long Jump. In time they were joined by 33-year-old SS Major Hans Ortel, an unquestioning and ruthless product of the Quenzgut academy with a pronounced taste for alcohol. Ortel had had some success serving behind the lines in southern Russia, where he was remembered for his personal courage and keen intelligence, as well as his fondness for the local dynamite-strength vodka. "I told him only generalities," Oberg later insisted of their introduction in Tehran. "For instance, that he was to participate in an operation of primary importance, something like Skorzeny's action. In those days Skorzeny's name was on everyone's lips, and we all dreamed of following his example."[41]

Oberg was right to be cautious when it came to briefing this new recruit to the ranks. Ortel promptly celebrated his commission by going out on an extended bender with a well-spoken young Armenian woman supposedly training to be a teacher in Tehran. Little did he know that the woman had read the collected works of Lenin and Gorky, and come to note the disparity between the city's urban poor and the wealthy bourgeoisie of which she was part. Her report of her conversation with the drunken SS major, passing himself off as a local rug merchant but revealing enough of his true calling to pique the young Marxist's interest, was soon on its way up the line to Moscow. Eventually a copy of it reached the desk of the NKVD chief Lavrentiy Beria, along with an attached note saying that "the name of the female informant [had] been added to the list of lunatics who pester our Mission in Iran daily." Beria read the document at length, and then ordered the clerk who had written the dismissive summary of it to be taken down to the basement and shot. That was how business was done at the NKVD. Beria had not become the second most feared man in the state by accident, nor was he inclined to take threats to the boss's life lightly.

The young Armenian woman, given the NKVD codename Marcelle, was not the only Soviet asset to play a part in the secret corridors of Iranian spycraft. In one of his frequent drinking bouts, Ortel befriended a fellow German who introduced himself as Paul Wilhelm Siebert, a middle-aged, wounded combat veteran who had been invalided out of the army and chosen to live out his days peacefully in the sunshine of Tehran. Since the whole country was then in a state of seething political turmoil, its capital city rocked by regular dissident attacks that left the downtown streets piled with "mountains of rubble" festering in the "pure, hot stink" of raw sewage, smoke, and putrefaction, this was not perhaps the first place on earth to suggest itself as an ideal spot to retire. But Ortel seems not to have pressed his new companion on the matter. The soft-spoken Siebert was good company. He could match even Ortel drink for drink, and spoke movingly of his former life fighting on the Russian front. In fact, he soared to almost poetic heights when it came to "the rustling woods, green fields waving in the wind, spruce white-painted churches and red-roofed, oak-beamed peasant cottages trimmed in shades of pink and ochre" he'd encountered on his advance with General Ludwig von Kleist through autumnal Ukraine. Perhaps Ortel was too moved by his friend's story, or too drunk to care, but he seems not to have questioned the oddly nostalgic tone of the narrative. In truth, this owed some of its detail less to Siebert's powers of observation as an intelligence officer with Kleist's Panzer group, as he claimed, and more to the fact that he had grown up in the Kiev area under the name Nikolai Ivanovich Kuznetsov.

Later that night, back in the small room he rented in Deylaman Street in central Tehran, Kuznetsov pried open a floorboard and carefully extracted a wooden crate, no bigger than a cigar box, with an incongruously ornate black-and-white check design on its outer sides. It contained a homemade crystal wireless set, involving some copper wire coiled around four wooden spools, two black and two red external terminals, the tubes from a household radio, and what looked like a small domestic lightbulb. Kuznetsov could use this device to transmit messages to a

Soviet listening post located on a hilltop some 500 miles away, near the oasis of Herat in western Afghanistan. From there the signal would be decoded and re-encrypted for onward transmission to the First Directorate in Moscow. All Kuznetsov's reports were preceded by six nines. This was his "control sign," the agreed code to indicate that he was operating of his own free will. If the signal did not start with 999999, the station in Herat would realize that it was a fake broadcast, and inform the NKVD accordingly.

There was no such problem with Kuznetsov's cable of September 27, 1943. It reported that the rug-dealing Herr Ortel was part of an embedded Nazi sleeper cell in Tehran and had spoken loosely of a future Axis operation of the "first magnitude" in the city. The paranoia in Soviet government circles at the time extended through the upper echelons of the Kremlin down to the bowels of the NKVD foreign bureau. In short order, Kuznetsov was ordered home to determine whether the German agent he and Agent Marcelle both claimed to be in contact with actually existed. On the morning of October 2, Kuznetsov was met at a military airfield outside Moscow by a team of unsmiling NKVD officers equipped with sodium pentothal. The "truth serum" only succeeded in making the Russian violently ill, but a subsequent interview involving some pliers and a hammer convinced his comrades that he was on the level. In due course, Kuznetsov was patched up and sent back to Iran with instructions to pump Ortel for further information. His interrogators had carefully avoided damaging their colleague's face, but it was noticed that he now walked with a slight limp—the result of a recent skiing mishap, he assured his German friend when they met again on October 15 at the bar of Tehran's Hotel Americano.

When Walter Schellenberg in turn further considered his options on the ground in this Wild West of espionage, he found that he was somewhat spoilt for choice, in quantity if not always in quality. There was the already established SS infiltration team, and the recent parachuted additions to their number. There were the local Iranian toughs, some of whom could have swapped their native garb for the black uniform and jackboots of the classic SS killer, while others merely existed in the state of seemingly permanent antagonism toward the established political order, their core agenda an unobtainable mixture of religious or tribal autonomy and Iranian national prestige that still characterizes the region today. There were the unflappable but intrepid professionals represented by the likes of Ernst Merser and Erwin Ettel. And now, too, there was the maverick figure of Otto Skorzeny, fresh from his triumph at Gran Sasso, and a court favorite of Hitler as a result, who would recall his führer having encouraged him to "subvert, sabotage and destroy our enemies" by whatever means it took, orders that gave the recent hero of Operation Oak a clear mandate for action outside the normal chain of command.

Perhaps it was no surprise that Schellenberg trod warily when finalizing the details of *Unternehmen Weitsprung*. "To decide to continue one's own line of policy in such circumstances required some nerve," he would later note, "for Hitler's sensitivity and pathological suspicion rose in direct ratio to the deterioration of the general situation."[42]

These same qualities of courage, sensitivity and above all extreme suspicion would be displayed in striking fashion during the following weeks in Tehran.

* * *

Winston Churchill was anxious. The British premier had had no direct word from Stalin on the question of the Allied conference since their exchange of cables early in August. Uncle Joe was indeed unaccountable, as Churchill had put it when describing his ally against Hitlerism. No sooner had Iran seemingly been agreed, than the sphinxlike Soviet dictator reversed himself to propose half a dozen alternative locations. Stalin's suspicion never slept; it was precisely his allies whom he distrusted most. If Churchill and Roosevelt had signed off on Tehran, his thinking went, what was wrong with it? Perhaps they could convene instead in Baghdad, Basra, or Beirut, the Vozhd suggested, which at least had an alliterative ring to it, if little else to appeal to the heads of government in far-off London and Washington. "What about Cairo?" Roosevelt again countered. "I understand it is attractive, and that there is a hotel and some villas out near the pyramids which could be completely segregated."

While the American and Soviet leaders continued to operate as a pair of unusually high-powered travel agents, the British premier grew increasingly agitated at the delay.

"We must act," Churchill cabled Roosevelt on October 14, for the first time using the agreed codename for the conference. "I have a new idea about EUREKA.... There is a place in the Sinai desert.... We could put up three encampments and live comfortably in perfect seclusion." The premier concluded with a biblical quotation: "See St. Matthew Chapter 17, Verse 4." The NKVD tappers promptly intercepted the cable and sent it upstairs to the boss. Although a former seminarian, Stalin could not immediately place the scriptural reference, which read: "It is good for us to be here: If thou wilt, let us make three tabernacles; one for thee, and one for Moses, and one for Elias." Perhaps it was a code within a code, the Vozhd thought, but whatever it meant he was determined to be on his guard about the enigmatic and, he was inclined to suspect, treacherous message between the two Western capitalists. "Tell them we will meet in Tehran,"

4. Agent Cicero

Stalin informed his foreign minister Molotov, a man obdurate enough in his dealings with foreigners to earn the half-admiring nickname "Old stone arse," but so servile toward the boss that he loyally remained in office even after his wife Polina was thrown in a Siberian prison camp for her "dealings with anti–Soviet individuals and free-thinkers."

* * *

A few days later, some of Misbah Ebtehaj's wrestling crew were lounging around their safe house on Firooz Street in the west end of Tehran. It was shortly before seven o'clock in the morning, and Ebtehaj had already left for a breakfast meeting with Ernst Merser and some of his other contacts. Without warning, dozens of heavily armed Soviet soldiers pulled up in a truck outside and began banging noisily at the front door. When no one answered, the visitors broke it down and ran up the stairs, batons and fists flying. They dragged one semi-dressed but belligerent wrestler into the kitchen, and once there began systematically pummeling him into submission. The house's other tenants were herded down to the street, where they were in turn kicked and punched into the waiting truck. None of the men's experience in the ring had prepared them to fight off soldiers brandishing submachine guns.[43]

The news that the wrestlers had been detained in this way plunged the German cell in Tehran into a ferment of speculation about who had betrayed them. The general feeling was that the Soviets must have tapped one of their recent radio signals and decided to act. As well as the house's drowsy residents, the Russians found a cache of Mann .25 caliber pistols of the type favored by members of the Wehrmacht in close combat, a crate of half a dozen rifles, and some street maps of Tehran marked in German. The arrested men were swiftly driven across town and frogmarched into the cellar of an anonymous-looking gray stone building on Zavesh Street. According to the Soviet archives grouped together under the title "Protocols, Resolutions and Stenographic Reports of the Party Congresses," the ideal military interrogator of the time needed to be a "combination of guard, psychologist, scholar, confidant, and scrupulous listener." It helped if he or she was also a confirmed sadist since the inevitable physical torture was likely to be both unpleasant and prolonged. None of the men detained that morning was ever seen again, although even if they had talked they would have had little information of practical use to their captors. Ebtehaj lived to fight another day.

* * *

Shortly before noon on October 26, 1943, a small, balding 39-year-old man with prominent eyebrows, lately employed as a valet to the British ambassador in Turkey, strolled side by side with two other men around the swan lake of Kugulu Park in central Ankara. An eavesdropper on their conversation would have detected nothing out of the ordinary. The group chatted about books, music and the weather, switching intermittently from Turkish to French and back again, as many of the country's educated classes then did. They parted with a handshake, and arranged to meet again in a few days' time.

The men's stroll in the park that warm autumn morning was not quite as innocent as it might have seemed. In fact, it concealed a complicated pas de trois. The valet's name was Elyesa Bazna, a Kosovo-born Albanian who had briefly trained as an opera singer before working successively as a locksmith, fireman, and petty thief, and his two companions were officials of the nearby German embassy. Earlier that morning, Bazna had knocked on their door and introduced himself with a simple proposal: he would hand them photographs of documents taken from his employer's safe, and in return they would give him envelopes stuffed full of British and American cash. Bazna, whom his handlers codenamed Cicero, produced 56 pictures of classified information he had brought with him to their first meeting. They revealed extraordinary details about inter-Allied relations, the latest thinking on the invasion of Europe, and the immediate prospects for a meeting of the Big Three leaders in Tehran.

Walter Schellenberg's station chief in Turkey, Ludwig Moyzisch, lost no time in flying a selection of Cicero's documents back to Berlin. As Schellenberg described it, the material was "breathtaking … highly secret correspondence between the British Embassy in Ankara and the Foreign Office in London. There were also private notes in the ambassador's own hand, dealing with developments between Britain and Turkey, and Britain and Russia…. Of special importance was a report from the Foreign Office on the results of the meeting of foreign ministers in Moscow," the prelude to the full-scale Tehran conference. Schellenberg immediately authorized a payment of £20,000—more than a million dollars at today's prices—with subsequent installments of £15,000 for each roll of film handed over to Moyzisch. Bazna had no particular fondness for the Nazi cause as such. In fact, before applying for the job with the British he'd worked as a valet to Albert Jenke, a German businessman in Ankara who happened to be the brother-in-law of Joachim von Ribbentrop, the Reich's foreign minister. Jenke had later fired him for stealing his mail.

As Schellenberg later acknowledged to Allied investigators, there was always the possibility that Bazna was too good to be true. A walk-in like him was perfectly placed to make mischief to the Reich by feeding his handlers false information while taking generous amounts of their money. Summoned to Berlin, however, Ludwig Moyzisch told his SD chiefs that he was convinced Cicero was on the level. Apparently the British ambassador was in the habit of dressing his diminutive valet in gaudily embroidered brocade, velvet slippers with upturned toes, and a plum-colored fez with a tassel to dance for him while he, the ambassador, played the piano. "The little fellow secretly burns with fury at his treatment," Moyzisch reported. More to the point, the Cicero documents "spoke for themselves," Schellenberg decided. The information taken from the ambassador's safe in Ankara "fit seamlessly into the general picture of the political situation as I saw it."

By early November, both Hitler and Himmler had full reports of the Cicero material on their desks. The führer was so pleased with the intelligence Bazna provided that he promised to reward him with a magnificent lakeside villa to live in after the war. The Germans had not lost all vestiges of their native caution, however, because Schellenberg saw to it that Cicero was paid in counterfeit "Bernhard pounds" rather than the genuine article. Later in the 1940s, the one-time opera singer duly served time in a Turkish prison as a result.

Though eloquent, Cicero's voice was far from the only one to assert itself in the tumultuous babel of raw intelligence reports in the region. The sheer profusion of agents centered on the Iranian capital reflected a mounting realization on all sides that only a truly spectacular breakthrough could now affect the momentum of the war. "The stakes were high for both us and the enemy, [as] conventional arms would no longer suffice," Schellenberg later remarked. "It was the moment to launch a mission of unique difficulty and danger."

The Russians were equally alive to the importance of Tehran as both a listening post and imminent rendezvous for the Big Three. As we've seen, Nikolai Kuznetsov, aka Siebert, had dusted himself off following his disagreeable interview in Moscow and resumed his bibulous dealings with Hans Ortel. Less cloak and dagger, but of equal value to the Kremlin spymasters, was the work of the All-Union Society for Cultural Exchange (or Voks), supposedly a goodwill body to promote Iran-Soviet relations, but in reality a front for NKVD operatives, saboteurs and a few old-school cat burglars who regularly helped themselves to the contents of Iranian officials' safes. According to the author Laslo Havas, there was also a Belgian-born health club operator named Paul Pourbaix, a Communist sympathizer in the habit of passing on gossip picked up from his customers who "shed their inhibitions along with their clothes while reclining in his aromatic steam-room." The Russians paid him well for his services, and before long Pourbaix found himself making things up in order to keep the fat, rial-stuffed envelopes coming. "It needed so much imagination to invent my tales that with the same effort I could have written novels," he told Havas. "The attention of my employers extended to the smallest detail. They never told me whether or not they believed me, but as they maintained our contact for six months and paid handsomely, I don't think they suspected me."[44]

It's hard to say whether Pourbaix passed anything of real value to Moscow, in so doing consigning further victims to Beria's torture chambers, or whether he was just another of those plausible fantasists who tend to accumulate on the fringes of a world crisis. But we know that he did Soviet intelligence at least one solid service. He told them that the Swiss businessman Ernst Merser had recently come to his club for a massage, and while there had laid down on the table next to another man who spoke with a German accent, and that both parties had been heard to agree that they were disinclined to return to their old civilian lives after the war, even if such a thing still existed. Instead, Merser had added, he meant "to depart in a blaze of glory."

It was impossible for Pourbaix to say whether or not his towel-clad patron had been entirely serious. "But he did not seem to me to be jesting," he noted in the report that duly went up the line to Beria's desk in Moscow.

* * *

Later that week, in an unmarked SD building on the banks of Berlin's Landwehr Canal, Otto Skorzeny discussed explosives with his fellow Austrian-born Colonel Erwin von Lahousen, the Canaris protégé who nonetheless survived in the upper echelons of German intelligence, as well as a posting to the Eastern front, to see out the war.

Skorzeny told Lahousen that he needed a "special bomb" sufficient to kill, and not merely maim, a group of people at close quarters. Did he require a device with a relatively muffled blast, his host inquired, to avoid unwanted attention? Not at all, Skorzeny replied. The louder, the better for his purposes; he wanted there to be utter chaos at the critical moment, in order for the perpetrators to make their escape. Something like a short-fuse percussive grenade might work, the hero of Gran Sasso continued, though all too many of the standard Wehrmacht "potato-masher" issue were unstable in combat conditions, where the heat from other nearby weapons could ignite their delicate firing mechanism. The men's technical exchange continued for some time until Lahousen mentioned a British invention of his acquaintance that went by the name of its designer, Captain Gammon of the First Parachute Regiment. Shaped something like an ordinary household lightbulb, the Gammon bomb consisted of a round, fabric-covered base that tapered off into a narrow, metal neck. The device had the triple advantage of being light, deadly, and easy to use. After filling the base with the required amount of high explosives, the bomber simply removed the screw-off cap, holding down the exposed fuse as he did so, and then launched it at the target. In the dry words of the British War Office manual: "The munition can be used for both anti-personnel and anti-tank purposes, and in most instances gives uniform satisfaction."

Skorzeny listened to the technical exposition with interest and then asked how many of the British bombs were currently available. Lahousen checked, and in a few minutes reported that the SD presently had two crates of Gammons in a storage facility at Zossen, twenty miles outside Berlin. They had been parachuted into occupied Belgium by the RAF for use by local resistance fighters, but a German patrol had found them first. There were 25 bombs in each crate, along with a few spares, meaning they had about sixty Gammons in total. Skorzeny's scarred face lit up with pleasure when he heard the news.

"That should be enough for us to put on our little show," he replied, speaking with all the enthusiasm of a child with a new toy.

* * *

Now that Stalin had finally agreed to Tehran, it was the Westerners' turn to dance the elaborate series of gavottes that characterized the advance preparations for the EUREKA conference. Roosevelt alone cabled the Kremlin 21 times in October.

"I regret to say that, as the head of the nation, it is impossible for me to go to a place where I cannot fulfill my obligations under our constitution."

"I have to tell you that I cannot go to Iran."

"I beg you not to forget my great obligation to the American government."

"Future generations would look upon it as a tragedy if a few hundred miles caused yourself, Mr. Churchill, and me to fail…. Please do not deny me in this crisis."

At this point the Germans probably had a better idea of the president's final itinerary than he did, because on November 2 Cicero passed another fat pile of photographs to his control in Ankara, who forwarded them posthaste to Walter Schellenberg. One of the documents was a British foreign office paper titled "Security Arrangements for Prime Minister's Visit to the Near East," which confirmed that Churchill would be accompanied throughout his journey by his friend and bodyguard Walter Thompson, along with "such supernumerary personnel as may be thought advisable." The note was left to admit that even this effort paled by comparison to the Soviet side, "which is now said to be deploying upwards of 3,000 troops to the streets of Tehran for Marshal Stalin's welfare."

5

Gathering Shadows

The final chapter of Operation Long Jump was about to open, and Winifred Oberg was determined to write himself into it. He would make a "bold play" that would demonstrate his prowess not just as a morally flexible lawyer, but as a "true and tested intelligence man," impress his superiors back in Berlin and pave the way for the climactic assault on the Allied conference. He proposed to lead a small group of sleeper agents and the remnants of Misbah Ebtehaj's wrestling crew to raid the Red Army barracks in Tehran.[1] His goal was to "reduce the number of able-bodied soldiers available to staff the garrison" while simultaneously collecting any data that might reveal the Soviet leader's address while in the city. The mission could yield important intelligence, Oberg believed. But it was also a stunt, a calculated bit of commando theater. The opportunity to further ingratiate himself with Walter Schellenberg and even more rarefied individuals like Himmler and possibly even Hitler was "intoxicating," he later told the writer Laslo Havas. Oberg was first and foremost a businessman, after all; who knew what lucrative new prospects might open up for him once Germany had won the war?

Before his assault on the Soviet stronghold, Oberg again went up into the Elburz foothills north of the city. This is how he recalled the experience to Havas:

> In November ... the arrival of an important delivery [was] announced for the next day. A large consignment of arms would be dropped in metal containers, but no parachutists would arrive this time. [I] was to take the cargo into Tehran and hide it in a safe place. The commandos who were to use the weapons would arrive later.[2]

When the small German reception party duly brought their prize back to Ernst Merser on Kakh Street,

> "It caused [us] some amazement," Oberg recalled. "In addition to Mann and Luger revolvers, G.41 and Siminov rifles, Sten and M.P. 43 submachine guns, the containers held more than a hundred Gammon grenades—enough of everything to arm at least a hundred men."

5. Gathering Shadows

In all the excitement, Oberg may have exaggerated the number of the carefully wrapped Gammon bombs falling from the Iranian night sky—Otto Skorzeny insisted there were no more than 60—but whatever the true figure it was more than enough to affect the "abrupt transition of personnel at the highest level of the Allied governments," as Oberg put it in somewhat lawyerly fashion.

* * *

In the end, the great nocturnal raid on the Soviet military bastion did not go quite as well as Oberg might have wished. The first saboteur in line had promptly blundered through a concealed tripwire set up around the building's perimeter. Blinding lights had immediately come on, and dogs started hysterically barking. Forced to improvise, the second man in line had stood up and begun shouting in Russian: "Don't shoot! We are your comrades!" The Soviet guards opened fire: three of Oberg's motley crew of Iranian musclemen and amateur commandos were killed; the rest took to their heels. Oberg, though sustaining a twisted ankle in the melee, escaped to the safe house where he kept a token number of the newly dropped Gammons, along with a generous supply of a grappa-like, high-octane local spirit with the evocative name of Aragh Sagi. "This was consumed in copious quantities," he admitted.

Oberg's sometime houseguest Joseph Schnabel had not been idle since his arrival in the city two months earlier. Schnabel was unwilling merely to wait for further orders from Berlin, and decided to hot things up on his own. At least one of his schemes, of which there were several, reads like the plot of a melodramatic spy thriller with John Belushi in the lead role. Codenamed BAZOOKA, it involved sending a stolen Mercedes careening off the stone Marnan bridge in Isfahan, south of Tehran, into the icy waters of the Zayandeh River twenty feet below. When the police came to investigate, Schnabel believed, they would find a locked briefcase on the vehicle's back seat. They would be convinced, he further deduced, that a German agent, presumed drowned, had had a car accident during a hurried attempt to meet a local contact, leaving behind a wealth of documents carefully forged to suggest that the SD in Berlin was anticipating an imminent Allied meeting not in Tehran but in Cairo. As he later described it, the authorities "would put two and two together, and the Allies would believe they had nothing to fear from us in Iran."[3]

In retrospect, it was a hopelessly byzantine plot. And it lost little time in going wrong. When the moment came, the car bumped down the muddy embankment of the Zayandeh without much enthusiasm, coming to rest with its front wheels barely touching the surface of the water. Iran was in a state of some disarray in 1943, and it took the authorities several days to finally interest themselves in the fate of an abandoned car found resting on a provincial riverbank. One of Schnabel's spotters eventually saw the vehicle being pulled away by a team of mules under Isfahan police supervision, and then, drawn by this same caravan, to potter down the road toward the municipal junkyard, but failed to chart its progress from there. As with many wartime deceptions, it's not known exactly what, if anything, BAZOOKA achieved. Perhaps nothing. The British kept a significant security force on hand in Cairo. But Schnabel came to believe that the local police were no more than "illiterate peasants, pressed [into] temporary wartime duty," and that in the end his elaborately forged papers had likely done no more than "serve some unspeakable sanitary purpose in the nearest *shithavus*."

Winifred Oberg's luck ran out early on the morning of November 7, when Soviet military police broke into his latest safe house on Tehran's Makhous Street and arrested everyone in sight. It was never fully established if the Russians had intercepted another indiscreet radio signal, or if this latest roundup owed something to the complicated double lives of men such as Nikolai Kuznetsov and Paul Pourbaix. Either way, Oberg was taken down to the cells, where his ordeal began even before he met his first interrogators. "I was made to sit on a cement floor covered in filth, clad in a thin robe. It was November, and bleak outside. I crouched in a ball, shivering half with cold, and half with nervous anticipation. Screams could be heard from the nearby cells." Then came the physical torture. "Blows and lashes were only the beginning—the entrance to hell. It went on day and night. Within a week I was so fogged by pain and sleeplessness I seemed to have entered a dream-state where one was more of a wild beast than a human being.... But I answered every demand with silence," Oberg insisted. "It was an act of will made possible by the one remaining shred of comfort I used to sustain myself in that place. *They will not kill me*, I thought."

Few aspects of Operation Long Jump show a more complete and dramatic reversal of fortune than the fate of Winifred Oberg in the second week of November 1943. Six days after being seized from the house on Makhous Street and thrown into the Soviet dungeons, he was free again. In the predawn hours of the 13th, two dozen members of Misbah Ebtehaj's newly replenished bandit gang launched a hit-and-run raid on a Soviet military post on Sepehr Street on the western side of Tehran. The main Red Army camp and NKVD torture cells were in the eastern sector. It took the Russians nearly an hour to send reinforcements to the scene of the surprise attack across town, although in reality they needn't have hurried. The raid on the Sepehr Street barracks was a diversionary feint, intended to draw troops away and allow a second guerrilla unit under Ernst Merser's

5. Gathering Shadows

command to free the relatively unguarded Oberg and his fellow captives. Almost incredibly, it went to plan without a single German or Iranian casualty. By eight that morning, Oberg was back in his new safe house, with only some broken teeth and a severely wrenched knee to show for his ordeal.

The more you study the state of hostilities around Tehran of the time, the more you find their distinguishing feature to have been their sheer breadth, reflecting the whole spectrum of military experience. The mounted charges of the nomadic Qashqai tribesmen differed little from those of biblical days; the thrust and parry of the occupying powers prefigured the divided Berlin of the Cold War. It's a composite picture. Conventional warfare and frontal attacks alternated with bouts of individual daring and brazen, sometimes almost comical buccaneering that evoke both the horrors of the Eastern Front and the picaresque adventures of Ali Baba and the Forty Thieves.

* * *

Throughout all this, the rogue valet Elyesa Bazna continued to help himself to the contents of his employer's safe at the British embassy in Ankara, and to pass this on to Schellenberg's man Ludwig Moyzisch. On November 11, Moyzisch was again summoned to a situation conference in Berlin, where, according to the official British foreign office historian,

> He was thoroughly grilled by Ribbentrop and told to stay in place until the end of November. But as Bazna would deal with him only, the information dried up and flowed again only when Moyzisch returned to Ankara. When details of the EUREKA conference were then provided by Cicero, Ribbentrop finally came to the conclusion that the material was not British disinformation. Instead, the foreign minister thought the documents showed fault lines in the Allied coalition, an interpretation which countered Schellenberg's rather more reasoned viewpoint, that the data pointed, however vaguely, to a massive Allied invasion of Europe and the destruction of Germany.[4]

Stalin meanwhile may have resigned himself to traveling the 1,500 miles to Tehran to meet his two partners in what had become an increasingly strained Allied marriage of convenience in their mutual struggle. But that did not mean he would do the conventional thing and simply inform his allies of his plans. A master both of dissimulation and acting a part, the Soviet dictator continued to insist that his presence was essential to direct military operations at the front, a view some of his senior Red Army commanders may or may not have endorsed. There's no doubt that Stalin had great gifts as an organizer and leader, but he also had the wayward child's taste for gratuitous deceit and subterfuge. Wherever possible, he preferred stealth and manipulation behind the scenes to open confrontation, keeping even—or especially—friends and allies off balance by a series of tactical feints which never for a moment lost sight of the ultimate objective, the consolidation of Stalin's power.

Secretary of State Hull, in Moscow, was soon obliged to cable Roosevelt with news of an alarming development. Stalin had personally summoned him, he wrote, "And said it might be preferable to postpone the Allied meeting until next spring, when military operations could be suspended...."[5]

Just as the Russians had intended, at that point Roosevelt suddenly found himself able to fall in with all of Stalin's wishes about the timing and logistics of the EUREKA conference. But in that world, it wasn't enough merely for the Vozhd to get what he wanted. A degree of torture of the submissive party was also good sport. On November 9, Molotov inquired of the U.S. ambassador Averell Harriman "whether he had noticed that Stalin had said that his colleagues were against his leaving the Soviet Union at this time?"[6]

It was like dealing with an "able but mentally disturbed youth," Churchill in turn remarked at a meeting of the British war cabinet, adding in terms that perhaps owed something to his service with the Scots Fusiliers on the Western Front that he was tired of being "arsed about" by the Russian leader. The minutes of the cabinet meeting are couched in more emollient tones.

> The Prime Minister said that as his colleagues were aware, for some time past he had been increasingly concerned at the way in which military operations in the Mediterranean were being hampered by [continuing] distractions involving the OVERLORD invasion of Europe, which would not take place for several months. The Prime Minister added that he thought that matters had now reached a point at which intervention on the part of the War Cabinet was necessary.[7]

Churchill's frustrations were not limited to military matters. He was also vocally unhappy that his "great and inseparable ally" in Washington had now resigned himself to flying to Tehran, but had somehow forgotten to mention the fact when they had spoken on the transatlantic phone just a day or two earlier. It was another early intimation that, in Churchill's words, America would come to treat Britain not as a blood brother united by ties of history and culture, but as "just another benign power, with whom the troubles of war had to be adjusted."

In the meantime, Churchill snapped off a cable to his close friend in the White House, "I am very glad to hear from your ambassador that you now contemplate going to Tehran on 26 November. I rather wish you had been able to let me know direct."[8]

Thanks to the work of Eleysa Bazna, Walter Schellenberg was able to read the gist of this message only two days after Roosevelt did. In fact, by now the German spymaster's primary challenge lay in finding the time to analyze the sheer quantity of material reaching him from Ankara. Unable to read much English, Bazna played it safe and took photos of everything he could lay his hands on, "from the embassy's Christmas card list to private correspondence with King George VI," as he, or his ghostwriter, later put it. He even copied a message to the ambassador warning him of a leak in his security. When British counterintelligence officers eventually arrived to interview the embassy staff, Bazna escaped suspicion because they thought the lowly valet was "too stupid to make an effective spy, and could barely comprehend anything but the most basic written English."

Miscalculations could hardly get any bigger than this. Bazna kept the "top secret" Allied documents coming in almost industrial quantities throughout November 1943. There was a certain amateurish directness about the way he worked. After each successive photography session, he simply rang his handler Ludwig Moyzisch, who picked him up on a convenient Ankara street corner in his car. Sometimes they agreed on a rendezvous by way of a message slipped between the pages of designated books in the central library. During these brief excursions, Bazna handed over the latest roll of film in return for more forged British banknotes. Then Moyzisch dropped him off, and both parties returned to their respective embassies. Bazna laid the bills flat under the carpet in his room, transferring a few to his pocket whenever the need arose. He spent some of the cash on a discreet suburban apartment where he and his mistress relaxed. Once a black car seemed to tail him when he was out with Moyzisch, but in the end he put the incident down to a simple case of road rage rather than anything more sinister. By the end of November the pile of money under the rug of Bazna's room, which he prudently kept locked, was several inches thick.

The Cicero material revealed three points of particular interest to Walter Schellenberg and the RSHA chief Ernst Kaltenbrunner. The first was that Turkey continued to resist British pressure to join the war against Germany, and the second was that the Allies planned to "maintain a threat to the enemy from the eastern end of the Mediterranean until OVERLORD"—Schellenberg had no doubt what this word meant—"is launched."

The third significant point in Cicero's material was the time, location, and agenda of the Allied conference in Tehran.

* * *

In Tehran, Hans Ortel continued his extended drinking sprees with the man known to him as Paul Siebert, but more familiar to his NKVD handlers as Nikolai Kuznetsov. Winifred Oberg was taking a well-earned break from his hectic round of arrests and escapes. His sometime SS houseguest Joseph Schnabel had returned from his adventure with the partly submerged car protruding out of the mud of the Zayandeh riverbank, and was at present trying to interest some local opium dealers in supplying him with poison-tipped cigarettes he believed could be insinuated into Stalin's private quarters in Tehran. It has to be said he (Schnabel, not Stalin) was singularly inept as an administrator. He could not delegate responsibility. He issued contradictory instructions to different sets of his co-conspirators. He created chaos whenever he tried to explain his technical requirements to the local tobacconists. Schnabel's primary contribution as regards Operation Long Jump lay in his unswerving loyalty to the Nazi cause, and his willingness to do whatever it took to hurt the enemy.

Ernst Merser had taken possession of the latest arsenal of weapons dropped into the north Iranian hills, and now slept with two boxes of Gammon bombs hidden under his floorboards as a result. He, too, was far from idle during the days before the Allied conference, for as he walked around Tehran he noted down possible enemy targets—British and Soviet guard posts, the huge tanks where the Americans stored oil on Behboodi Street, the airfield where Allied bombers refueled and, first among equals, the vulnerable outlying parts of the Trans-Iranian railway. He memorized the dimensions of freight trains, the number of their cars, the times of their departures and arrivals, and the names of the potential informers and collaborators who worked on the line. "It all depends on grasping the opportunities presented to you," he told Oberg.

The mountain-climbing diplomat Erwin Ettel had lately returned to a more conventional interpretation of his duties, passing intelligence reports as much as munitions to the leading players in a rapidly unfolding drama that, in his measured words, might "not be immaterial to Germany's interests." Franz Mayr, aka Max, still loosely controlled the pugilist Misbah Ebtehaj and the remnants of Ebtehaj's tag-team of local musclemen, pickpockets, street thieves, and petty hoodlums. Some of these individuals gathered one mild early November evening at an outdoor Tehran café called the Owl's Keen. Mayr appeared, and brought with him Hans Ortel, who was plainly drunk and "applied himself freely to a bottle of Aragh Sagi" throughout the meal. It seemed a curiously indiscreet way for the members of an assassination bureau to conduct their business, but perhaps they believed in the principle of hiding in plain sight. After several hours Ortel had declared himself to be in a Byronic mood, and in short order was swimming naked in the frigid waters of the duck pond at nearby Besat Park while his companions cheered him on. Fortunately, the only sirens they heard were mythical, and not those of the Tehran police. The

5. Gathering Shadows 123

tales told over a further nightcap back at Ernst Merser's house on Kakh Street were tall.

* * *

Back in the heady days of November 1941, Hitler had canceled a plan by his blue-eyed boy Reinhard Heydrich to land an SS hit team in the hills outside Moscow, from where they would make their way to Stalin's suburban dacha at Kuntsevo, and terminate the Vozhd and as many of his associates as might be on the premises. It could even have worked since the Soviet ruler was still surprisingly lightly guarded at that stage of the war. The whole compound was then under the control of Nikolai Vlasik, and a report made at the time of his inevitable later arrest complained that he had shown "criminal neglect [in] his duties, [but] instead covered himself in luxury while the Leader himself slept on a cot under an army blanket." But Hitler's managerial style was whimsical at best; he preferred to do business with one man at a time, and even that as infrequently as possible, rather than subject himself to the tedium of regular committee work and cabinet meetings. The führer's thinking in 1941 was that Stalin was a beaten man and would soon plead to be allowed to come to the negotiating table; far better to humiliate his opponent in this way, Hitler concluded, than to stir up a hornets' nest by his murder.

Now, two years later, the German dictator had no such compunction. The old, nuanced Hitler was not in evidence in his ruminations during the fall of 1943 on the New World Order as he saw it. "I have a duty to think of tomorrow, and the day after tomorrow," he told Peter Kleist, who headed the Eastern Department at Ribbentrop's foreign ministry. "For my population I need empty space. I cannot grant the Eastern hordes any sovereign right of independence and replace Soviet Russia with a new national Russia, which for that reason would be much more firmly knit together."[9] Stalin, then, had to go. Europe, in Hitler's latest scheme of things, would become a plunder economy of the Reich. Meanwhile, he added, "The most important part of final victory will be the exclusion of the United States from world politics for all time, and the destruction of their Jewish community.... For this purpose, Dr. Goebbels will have dictatorial authority as Governor to accomplish the total re-education of the racially mixed and inferior American people."[10] Taken as a whole, these were not the words of a man inclined to be generous when it came to the fate of the heads of government of his nation's sworn enemies.

Nowadays, high-level summits between friendly states usually end in agreement; momentum and mechanics alike drive them in that direction. Many months before their principals meet, scores of impeccably trained functionaries exchange agendas, talking points, and drafts of speeches.

Areas of disagreement are identified and then arbitrated or discreetly dropped from consideration. The actual encounter between the heads of government is only the public, or symbolic, enactment of extensive private rehearsals. Preparation is the rule and freewheeling spontaneity the exception on such occasions.

Matters were quite different in 1943. Only on November 8 did Roosevelt finally inform Stalin: "I have decided to go to Iran, and am glad to do so," before waiting a further three days to disingenuously cable Churchill, "I have just learned that UJ will come to Tehran … and I think that now there is no question that you and I can meet him there between the 27th and the 30th."

"Thus endeth a very difficult situation, and I think we can be very happy."

Thanks to Agent Cicero, Walter Schellenberg had a copy of this high-level exchange between the Atlantic allies only hours after Churchill did. By then the SD chief was already intimately familiar with the broad contours of the EUREKA conference and had had more time to actively prepare for it than any of the main attendees. Now, Schellenberg later reflected, he was ready to adapt his plans for the meeting "up to the very stroke of midnight."[11]

* * *

Yet another consignment of Nazi weapons dropped from the skies of northern Iran in the early hours of November 13, 1943. This time Misbah Ebtehaj and a half dozen of his crew went up into the hills to retrieve them. Fumbling their way back down again in the hazy light, they nearly bumped into a squad of Red Army engineers busy preparing an explosive charge apparently meant to blast out a road leading down the rockface into Tehran. The wrestlers hid for the next fifteen hours until dusk fell again, and then launched an ambush: the Russians were held at gunpoint while their weapons were added to the Iranians' stash. The team escaped back to the Tehran suburbs in a Soviet truck, which they abandoned on a quiet corner of Andisheh Park, close to today's Islamic Revolutionary Court, before melting away into the night, each man discreetly packing one of the liberated Goryunov submachine guns under his long winter coat. Back at Kakh Street, Ernst Merser now slept with a "veritable armory" of international military hardware under his bed, and could only hope that none of the regular Allied sweeps of the city decided to pay him a visit. Two days later, after carefully locking his door and drawing two sets of blinds, Merser neatly laid out all the ordnance on the floor so as to make an inventory of it. "I looked in amazement at the array of guns and bombs which filled the room from one end to another," he wrote.

5. Gathering Shadows

The Germans, then, already had more than enough materiel on hand to disrupt the proceedings of half a dozen Allied conferences. The challenge now was to consolidate the motley collection of hardcore SS operatives, disaffected Iranian freedom fighters, tribal warlords, freelance adventurers, and assorted deviants and misfits into a definite scenario for an assassination plot. The pragmatic Schellenberg disapproved of any plan to simultaneously wipe out the Allied military high command accompanying the politicians and felt it unrealistic to expect the surviving members of the enemy governments would promptly sue for peace. The ideal, Schellenberg later blandly noted, almost as if speaking of pruning some troublesome weeds in his garden, "was to lop off a few heads, [rather] than to threaten the wholesale destruction of nations."[12]

Once again, Agent Cicero stepped forward to serve the Nazi cause. The British were now clearly at work refurbishing their Tehran embassy inside and out, Schellenberg learned from a photographed document on November 16, very likely in preparation for the building to play some part in the conference. It stood close to the city center, adjacent to the Soviet mission, with a high, defensible wall around them. "Local construction crews [are] currently engaged in laying what appears to be a water or sewer line to the compound," Schellenberg read, another clear hint that a VIP guest or guests were expected there. "Tehran was a festering nest of espionage and counterespionage, [but] also of those who could be easily 'turned' by a cash incentive, heedless of any higher allegiance," he later said. In this febrile atmosphere, an ill-paid day laborer might well be tempted to supply technical information useful to the ultimate success of Operation Long Jump. This was intelligence of the most basic, practical kind.

On the other hand, was Cicero a legitimate German spy, or was he, as some still suspected, a plant? Might the profusion of material pouring out of the Ankara embassy be part of some elaborate Allied trap? The issue seemed to finally be resolved in Bazna's favor only by the results crossing Schellenberg's desk that month of high-altitude Luftwaffe reconnaissance flights over Tehran. A series of images taken on November 19 "embrace[d] the whole spectrum of the enemy's infrastructure, the enhanced transport and service facilities, work parties to the front and rear of British and Russian compounds, the improvement of enemy provisional and permanent fortifications."

Not long afterward, a British foreign office clerk made a typing error in a dispatch and corrected it in three of the four copies that went out to overseas embassies—but not to Ankara. Bazna duly photographed the flawed document, which as usual went posthaste back to Schellenberg's office in Berlin. But the British now suspected a leak, and in turn intercepted a radio message from Bazna's handler Ludwig Moyzisch, pinpointing Ankara's copy of the original foreign office paper as the one accessible to the spy. With the net closing in on him, Bazna gave his notice at the embassy, not haggling over severance pay, and returned to his civilian life as an itinerant conman, hustler, and sometime hotelier in the more louche parts of Ankara. But the damage to the Allied side had been done. Exulted Schellenberg, "The battle for intelligence about the Allies' plans in Iran was undoubtedly won by us."

* * *

The shah and his henchmen took every reasonable step to ensure the security of the Big Three leaders while they were in Tehran. Iran's borders were sealed, and her international telephone and postal communications, already a somewhat haphazard affair, were suspended. A flotilla of 24 British-built 102-class motor torpedo boats, each equipped with depth-charges, bow- and stern-mounted machine guns, a range of Oerlikon 20mm anti-aircraft cannons, and capable of speeds up to 48 knots, patrolled the nation's southern waterways in an arc from Bushehr, close to the Iraqi border in the west, to Bandar Abbas overlooking the Strait of Hormuz in the east. The shah's interior ministry took a number of exceptional steps to further safeguard their country's distinguished guests. On November 19, the directive went out over Lavrentiy Beria's signature in Moscow to the 3,000-strong Tehran-based Nazmiyeh "Order Agency" that they were to execute warrants for "preventative arrest and immediately ... detain those inimical citizens, agitators, radicals, subversives [and] felons ... gendarmes ... wreckers ... and enemies of the people" until further notice, thus placing a murderous weapon in the hands of the state. It undermined the rule of law in Iran and even the normal, somewhat fitful machinery of the nation's justice system was unable to prevent an estimated 8,000 men, women and even children from suddenly vanishing off the streets, never to be seen by their families again.

The impenetrable security cordon thrown over the Peacock Realm did not, however, extend to guarding the surrounds of the Elburz foothills north of Tehran. Between November 17 and 22, four more German parachute teams dropped there and proceeded to the capital. A further three landed near Qom, 70 miles to the south. Among those hurriedly making their way to the maze of backstreet safe houses was a hard-eyed 28-year-old, at once professionally ruthless and oddly puritanical where his private life was concerned, named Vladimir Shkvarzev. Shkvarzev was the nephew of the prewar Soviet ambassador to Berlin, and another notable addition to the cast of SS footsoldiers, freelance daredevils and borderline lunatics who distinguished the ranks of Operation Long Jump.

Here is how the author Laslo Havas describes him.

5. Gathering Shadows

Shkvarzev was a devout member of the Communist party, and an officer of the NKVD before the Gestapo caught him in 1942. The German secret services made him torture dozens of Russian prisoners of war, who were then released in the front lines so they could report that Shkvarzev was working for the Gestapo. This was to make it impossible for him to ever return home.

"The Russians then started operating in France, and at the Dumesnil barracks at Perigueux. This was where Shkvarzev came to do his recruiting. After twenty days, he reported that he had found 400 fully reliable men who were ready to die for Hitler and were eminently suited to perform special tasks."[13]

The vast majority of those Shkvarzev turned to the German side were fellow Russians who, like him, had come to question Stalin's direction of the war. Schellenberg's appetite for diehard special forces willing to lay down their lives for the Reich seems to have overcome any lingering doubts he may have had about incorporating such representatives of the "sub-human races" into the Nazi master plan in Iran. When raw courage and a certain innate sadism were combined with personal hatred of the Vozhd, as was the case with many of these individuals, Schellenberg was not inclined to stand on Aryan principle. The SD chief's personality was suddenly exposed: the middle-class former law student with his strict moral upbringing merged with the Nazi automaton, the fanatical agent of the führer's wishes, however drastic or flagrantly criminal. "Like many others, I succumbed to the temptation to commit atrocities unworthy of a German," Schellenberg would later admit. "But they were necessary for the annihilation of our people's blood enemy, [and] the final destruction of Bolshevism."[14]

* * *

One face was conspicuously missing from the final ranks of the massed German commando units arriving by parachute in the Tehran outskirts: that of Hitler's favorite freedom fighter Otto Skorzeny. There's no archival evidence as to why Skorzeny ultimately chose to absent himself from Operation Long Jump. It's known that he enjoyed a degree of personal latitude in the field when accepting or declining a mission denied less exalted officers, and it may be that on this occasion he was content to pull the levers behind the scenes rather than participate in a mission that made the rescue of Mussolini seem almost facile by comparison. We may never know, although the much-feted author Howard Blum imaginatively reconstructs the scene of Skorzeny already aboard a Junkers 290 transport, waiting on the runway to take him on his epochal date with destiny, when at the last moment he received a discouraging radio signal from Tehran.

"What should he do?" Blum writes. "There was, Skorzenzy firmly believed, honor in a soldier's death. But there was little honor, and certainly no fame, to be won walking stupidly into a trap. He and his men would be slaughtered. Or worse: captured and put on taunting display, fools mocked by the world for their incompetence."[15]

This may or may not be an accurate depiction of what happened. But Skorzeny's defection, whatever its cause, was by no means to jeopardize the unstoppable momentum of the plot as a whole. As Schellenberg later remarked, "Our blow was to be delivered with such force that the whole enemy war machine would be broken at its apex, and brought to its final destruction."

* * *

As so often happens in paramilitary actions, the planning of Operation Long Jump, once set in motion, evolved rapidly according to changing circumstances, while around it the events in which it originated altered in character and substance. The aftermath of the Kursk campaign might be said to have marked the moment at which Hitler irrevocably lost patience with his senior commanders on the Eastern Front, and in their conduct of the war as a whole. "No General will ever pronounce himself ready to attack; and no commander will ever fight a defensive battle without looking over his shoulder to a 'shorter' line," he complained at one of his periodic conferences in November 1943.[16] It's a notable fact, too, that while many of the most dynamic minds in the German intelligence services were now devoted to the question of liquidating the leaders of the three principal powers arrayed against them, elsewhere in the Wehrmacht the priority was to remove Hitler.

Meanwhile, Ernst Merser continued his untiring activities on the ground in Tehran. Sometimes these seemed to be harnessed to the higher cause of preparing the way for Operation Long Jump, while on others they had a more narrowly personal or improvised ring to them. Whatever his true motivation, by November 1943, Merser was running an impressive array of local agents. One of his many schemes was to use the services of young German or Austrian women working as servants in the homes of prominent Iranian public figures such as Ahmad Qavam, the country's once and future prime minister. The 70-year-old Qavam was known both for his elegant calligraphic handwriting, and for his habit of carelessly leaving state papers so inscribed lying around his bedroom. These efforts on Merser's part seem to have come to naught, although at least one of the women later complained of Qavam's personal advances ("His Excellency's hand rustling like dried leaves up her robe," in Merser's evocative report), and in the end the Swiss-born spymaster simply directed the local functionaries of his organization to bring him any data that might help pinpoint the location of the Allied conference, or the local residences of the heads of delegation in attendance.[17]

Dozens of items came in. There were descriptions of fortifications, airfields, and road obstructions; there were reports of overheard phone conversations and of troop movements. But perhaps the single most intriguing morsel of intelligence concerned the imposing, Palladian-like Soviet legation building on Nofel Loshato Street in east-central Tehran. The only access road to this was a long, pleasantly shaded driveway lined with pine, palm and cypress trees. At its far end, a screen of richly aromatic lavender bushes and banks of pink and blue hydrangeas parted to reveal a classical-style villa approached by a flight of broad, whitewashed steps and flanked by half a dozen Doric pillars. It looked like the country seat of some long-established British landed dynasty, or the sort of place one might now find a mid–European currency dealer or hedge-fund tycoon, and in either case somewhat removed from the brutal Soviet architectural ideal.[18]

On November 19, one of Merser's operatives reported that workmen were currently busy erecting a row of wooden guard boxes at 20-yard intervals along the building's approach road, which was now patrolled by scores of Russian soldiers with forbidding black uniforms and tommy guns slung across their backs, and that many of these sentinels were women—"immense, tough, and with square jaws that looked almost prehistoric in their crudeness," marveled the spotter. Merser in turn passed the news up the line for radio transmission back to Walter Schellenberg, who later boasted that there was hardly a rock or tree in central Tehran that he didn't know about. A few days later, at about eight in the morning, a flurry of excitement surged through Nofel Loshato Street. Even more soldiers with drawn weapons suddenly took up position there, and in short order a cortege of identical black Packard limousines with tinted passenger windows swept by at high speed and passed through the gates of the Soviet compound. Nobody was permitted to enter the front drive or approach the building's perimeter until further notice.

It was a dress rehearsal, Merser soon realized. "But it furnished the most trustworthy basis for judging our enemy's plans."

* * *

Franz Mayr and his bibulous friend Hans Ortel, frequently accompanied by the former Quenzgut SS instructor-turned-field operative Rudolf Holten-Pflug, continued to ply their clandestine trade around Tehran. As with Merser, it was sometimes hard to say with total conviction if this was directly in the service of the German Reich or tailored to more specialized ends. Late one night in the middle of November, Mayr, Holten-Pflug, and the wrestler Misbah Ebtehaj decided to visit one of Ebtehaj's colleagues, whom they suspected of sleeping with a Russian woman. Perhaps they believed this last individual was a spy, who could betray them to the Soviet authorities. Or perhaps their interest in the matter was more personal than that, and more in the spirit of a college prank. In either case, the three men arrived at the building on the outskirts of Tehran at five in the morning. The landlady recognized Ebtehaj and murmured something about being honored by so illustrious a visitor, but the men pushed past her and silently took up position at the upstairs bedroom door, revolvers in hand. A moment later, they burst in to find their quarry lying fast asleep in the arms of a sparsely clad woman, whom even in that pre-dawn light they noted for two physical attributes. "She had the largest breasts I had *ever* seen," Ortel reported. And perhaps of greater consequence to their mission, a Nazi *Reichsadler*, or imperial eagle, was plainly tattooed on her upper arm. The visitors left the room as swiftly as they had entered.

Elsewhere, not all was well in the ranks of Tehran's de facto Nazi spy ring. A Turko-Iranian oil wrestler named Kel Yusuf ran occasional errands for Ebtehaj, who in turn billed his services to Merser. It was one thing for the hardheaded Swiss businessman to haggle with his local agents—he was hardly unique in the field for that—but there were soon more serious issues. On November 18, Yusuf went to the city-center branch of the Bank Melli, a reassuringly solid-looking brick building with narrow, barred windows, to convert Merser's British pounds into Iranian rials. The transaction did not go quite as smoothly as intended. A suspicious teller discreetly summoned a manager, who in turn examined Yusuf's £50 note, which turned out to be one of those printed by the slave laborers at the Sachsenhausen prison camp. Merser wrote: "Questions were asked, and from then on many others of my acquaintance treated my money and myself with caution."

It might have been laughable, or at least trivial, had Yusuf not left a trail leading back to Merser and thence the architects of Operation Bernhard in Germany. An order immediately went out from Walter Schellenberg's office. From now on, everything in Tehran was to be done by "word of mouth," "strictly person to person," "no projects on paper," and any unavoidable cash disbursements made in "legitimate Iranian coin." In the efficient Reich way, this new set of directives was given its own code name—Guillotine—which, now that it served the ends of Operation Long Jump, was an entirely appropriate description of what was involved.

Julius Schulze-Holthus called on Merser at Kakh Street early in the morning of November 19. The middle-aged Great War cavalryman was disguised for the occasion in a shabby check suit and a noticeably lopsided brown wig, both intended, so he fondly thought, to make him look inconspicuous. Merser told him that "something big" was afoot, and as if to dramatize the fact led his visitor into a back room, where a false panel revealed a selection of devices that could have come from one of James Bond's toyshops. There were pistols that slid up a sleeve or were hidden in a toothpaste tube, thumb knives tipped in fast-acting poison, exploding briefcases, and pen-sized tear gas grenades. "You must keep all this to yourself," Merser informed his guest, perhaps unnecessarily. Later that night, Schulze-Holthus met Holten-Pflug at the Owl's Keen. "He was struck by what he had seen, and immediately described it in detail," Pflug remembered. "So impressed, in fact, that he encouraged me to make notes." The old Quenzgut hand wrote rapidly to keep up with the now more formally clad major's staccato cadence. "A solution to the war problem carried top priority. No time, money, blood, or manpower was to be spared. Today…. Herr Merser had indicated to him that the final chapter had still to be written…. It has got to be done, and will be done."

* * *

During this same period, the increasingly beleaguered German head of state largely restricted his contact with the outside world to three individuals: his unwavering propaganda chief Joseph Goebbels; his slavishly devoted private secretary Martin Bormann, the brutal enforcer of his master's will; and his Alsatian bitch Blondi. The last named was the only one in the inner circle whom Hitler treated with anything approaching affection. Aside from the strict requirements of his perfunctory daily military conference, the führer was otherwise ever more cut off from human contact, isolated in his realm of increasingly delusional megalomania. Goebbels did persuade his chief to again address the party's Old Guard in Munich on November 8, 1943, the twentieth anniversary of the failed beer-hall putsch that had first brought Hitler to the world's notice. His prepared remarks for the occasion were of a self-indulgent feebleness that at times seemed to prefigure the lyrics of "My Way," and more pertinently to offer the hint of imminent retaliation against the Allies for their bombing of German cities.

"I would like finally to say two things," Hitler concluded. "What grieves me most are the sacrifices of the homeland, especially those of the women and children."

> Our enemies are even now planning the reconstruction of the world. And I am even now planning the reconstruction of Germany. There will, however, be a difference: while the rebuilding of the world will not take place, the rebuilding of Germany through National Socialism will be carried out with precision, and according to plan! This is the first thing I have to say.
>
> The second thing is this: whether or not the Allied gentlemen believe it, the hour of retribution is nigh.

The greatest heroes in world history have always had to remain steadfast, even under the greatest strain.

Anybody can bear sunshine. But when the weather is bad and a storm is raging, then it will show who is a strong character and who is a weakling. When things get difficult, you can tell who is truly a man, one who does not lose his nerve in such an hour, but instead remains determined and steadfast, and never thinks of capitulation.... We need not despair. On the contrary, we may look to the future with total confidence![19]

Hitler left it at that, but in a speech later that week Goebbels elaborated on the theme of revenge. "What we have in mind has become a sort of people's secret. Each person knows no more than the next one. Nevertheless, I believe I may assert that in the not-too-distant future the enemy will receive a response that will assuredly make their people break out in a cold sweat."[20]

In the privacy of his diary that night, the propaganda minister wrote only that the war had become a "grim life-or-death confrontation." It would be tragic "not to seize the ability to strike back at this particular juncture, and to have to say, 'too little and too late,'" he concluded.[21]

* * *

New and ever more tragicomic misunderstandings bedeviled the rival groups of agents in play in Tehran. Signals went astray. Assorted bombing and kidnap attempts failed or were thwarted by the Nazmiyeh. To pass the time, the hotheaded young SS officer Joseph Schnabel decided he might like to have a go at personally removing the 24-year-old Mohammad Pahlavi from the throne of Iran. "His liquidation would raise the very real prospect of this government realigning its interests with those of the Reich," Schnabel wired Walter Schellenberg in Berlin. Seemingly as an afterthought, he showed a copy of his cable to Hans Ortel. Ortel may have enjoyed his Aragh Sagi, sometimes to excess, but any talk of "liquidating" his host state's well-guarded young ruler struck him as "almost insane in its intemperance, no more than a drunken raving." At that, he snatched up a copy of Schnabel's dispatch, scratched out the offending word, and then fired off his message to Berkaerstrasse to rage at "the inadmissibility and stupidity" of putting this type of comment in writing.

A coded signal came back to him.

"From the highest authority, no further messages to jeopardize success of events of extraordinary importance for present-day war situation."[22]

Ortel's reply was equally terse.

"The guilty party has been informed. No repetition now possible."

This was not the only exchange of traffic that week involving a belligerent power and its embedded Tehran cell. Late on the night of November

15, the alleged German retiree Paul Siebert, better known to his family as Nikolai Kuznetsov, again extracted the small, homemade crystal radio set from under the floorboards of his room on Deylaman Street, close to the sprawling campus of the University of Tehran. Siebert keyed in the identifying 999999 prefix so that the operator listening in the Paropamisus hills of western Afghanistan would know it was safe to forward on to Moscow. According to the notes on file in the Russian state archive, on reading the transmission Lavrentiy Beria "expressed the general dissatisfaction of the People's Commissar [Stalin]" with events in Iran, and "pointed out that there had been continued acts of sabotage carried out against Soviet interests in the region. These [were] now to be countered by all means necessary."²³

Joseph Goebbels, the Nazi propaganda chief who operated behind the scenes of Unternehmen Weitsprung. "It would be tragic not to seize the ability to strike at this particular juncture, and to have to say, 'too little and too late,'" he wrote.

Just ten days after Beria wrote these ominous words, he would be at the Vozhd's side on the ground in Tehran. The advance guard of the NKVD had just managed to complete preparing the Soviet embassy building in time for their arrival. At the last moment, it was found that there was no suitable round table on the premises, so an agent was hurriedly dispatched to a local woodworker to order one to be built overnight "to accommodate 25 for a wedding," with a matching number of formal chairs. With laconic understatement, Beria noted, "We will eventually need to sit down, and indeed Comrade Roosevelt can do little else."

Meanwhile, the NKVD chief had also ordered the construction of an underground bunker, protected by five feet of reinforced concrete, immediately below the embassy's reception hall. Luftwaffe bombers could still reach the area from their bases in the Crimea, Beria knew, but what concerned him more were the unseen threats and dangers of "wreckers"—as saboteurs were known—amongst them on the ground. It mattered little to him whether such individuals were actually planning to commit a crime. In Stalinist psychology, it was enough that a suspect was "objectively guilty." This was the principle on which the Great Purge had terrorized Russia in the 1930s and which now accounted for the disappearance of thousands of men, women, and children from the streets of Tehran.

Shortly after dusk fell over western England on November 12, 1943, the Royal Navy battlecruiser *Renown* left its base at Plymouth to carry Winston Churchill on the first leg of his journey to Cairo, where he would meet his friend President Roosevelt and Chiang Kai-shek, leader of the National Government in China, before continuing to Tehran. Roosevelt in turn left Washington that same evening aboard the USS *Iowa*. Two days out to sea, there was an incident that briefly but terrifyingly raised the specter of an enemy underwater attack on the president. In the dry words of the *Iowa*'s log:

> Nov 14th, 1943.
> 8:00 a.m.: Noted position and weather conditions. Air defense drill executed for FDR. Demonstrated ship's firepower. During the drill unexpected explosion occurred in vicinity of *Iowa*. Discovered to be a torpedo accidentally fired by USS *William D. Porter*, the anti-submarine screen to starboard. Probably caused by moisture from rough seas. Immediate investigation ordered.[24]

There was no such mishap when the official Soviet delegation took off the following week from Baku, on the west bank of the Caspian, to fly to Iran. Even so, their journey was not without incident. As he walked toward the specially modified Tupolev Tu-2 bomber waiting for him on the runway, Stalin glanced at Beria's identical Tu-2 standing next to it and decided to switch planes. "Comrade Beria has snake's eyes," Stalin remarked to his entourage once safely aloft. The boss's paranoia was an engine that never stopped ticking.

6

"The Greatest Surfeit and Concentration of Power Ever Seen"

Yet more German hardware fell into the moonlit Elburz foothills shortly after midnight on November 13. The latest parachute drop in the region included two more crates of recently captured Gammon bombs, several hardened recruits of the Quenzgut school, and, curiously, three prewar national middleweight boxing champions named Bohle, Kasche, and Trott. Good with their fists, this last trio was not otherwise especially well-suited to the needs of Operation Long Jump. After making their way into the Tehran suburbs, the party spent the next few nights at a safe house on Maragheh Street, just east of the city center, set up on a grassy knoll with a panoramic view of the rear of the Soviet embassy block.[1] There was nothing for the new arrivals to do during their first 48 hours in the capital. As a result some of the Nazi hitmen drank too much and then got into a fistfight, though whether this involved the professional boxers is not recorded. The looming danger of their mission seems to have stimulated pugnacity in the would-be assassins.

Three days later, another batch of Schellenberg's killers dropped onto the darkened hills around Qazvin, 90 miles northeast of Tehran. The more you learn of Operation Long Jump, the more you find its salient points (apart from the sometimes-comic cast of characters) to have been the sheer profusion of operatives raining down from the north Iranian skies. One estimate suggests that by the end of November, upward of 200 skilled or semi-skilled German agents were in place, variously engaged in the plot to radically disrupt their enemy's political leadership.

Unfortunately, the most recent addition to the conspirators' ranks would play little active part in the outcome. The man calling himself Paul Siebert soon learned of the November 13 drop and informed the Soviet authorities accordingly. Thanks to Hans Ortel, Siebert knew not only of the newcomers' temporary address in Tehran but also their plans to infiltrate the Allied conference disguised as Red Army guards. The historian Laslo Havas describes what followed.

> [Siebert] immediately advised the local Soviet army command of the task the men were to perform. After that, it was child's play for the NKVD to arrest them. The action was so successful that in addition to the parachutists almost 300 other men were captured around town. Since everyone wearing a Russian uniform was suspect, the members of the NKVD began arresting each other.[2]

In so far as there was any recognizable leadership of the remaining German assets in Tehran, it lay in the hands of Ernst Merser and Winifred Oberg. The former jealously guarded the arsenal of military hardware under the floorboards of his house on Kakh Street, while the latter slunk around town, searching for clues about any Allied VIPs arriving amongst them.

"From the beginning it was realized that the essence of the mission was human intelligence," Schellenberg noted.[3] Sooner or later, an Allied soldier or a civilian sub-contractor at one of the Big Three embassies would say or do something indiscreet, or the Germans would tap into a high-level radio signal and give the game away. On November 20, Oberg set up a forward operations post in an abandoned fishmonger's shop on Ghazali Street, directly opposite the Russian embassy block. "It [was] an ideal location but for its lingering odor," the fastidious lawyer wrote of his new base. The rusty sign over the entrance to the weather-beaten, two-story concrete and corrugated metal building displayed a burst of three native hieroglyphics, loosely translated as "The Captain's Cabin." Inside, the walls were cluttered with charts and menus, and even a crudely framed certificate from the Central District Licensed Victuallers Association commending the business on its "acceptable hygiene." The casual visitor would not have noticed the carefully painted-over door in the far corner of the shop's foyer that led to the upstairs room where Oberg or one of Merser's designated watchers sat over a mounted camera and a walkie-talkie. The hiding place would not evade an intensive search, but it would keep Oberg from the prying eyes of an innocent customer calling in for an ounce of cut-price local Ossetra caviar.

Oberg was duly at his post a few mornings later to see the dress rehearsal for Stalin's convoy sweep past through the gates of the Soviet compound. It was "both a terrifying and thrilling spectacle," he reported. Later that night, one of Merser's team taking the graveyard shift at Ghazali Street thought he could hear a series of heavy thumps coming from across the road. A freezing fog had descended over the city, and it was too dark for him to see what was causing the noise. He used the walkie-talkie to contact Oberg, who then happened to be fast asleep a few miles away in the arms of an Iranian sailor. Oberg thought it might be part of some last-minute construction work to fortify the embassy perimeter and promised to return first thing in the morning to investigate. But after the sun had burned off the fog a few hours later, the lookout in the fishmonger's shop was able to see that the Soviets had merely put a man on overnight guard duty at the embassy's front gate. The thuds he had heard in the dark had been caused by the hapless Russian sentry stamping his boots up and down to keep warm.

"Oberg proved to be a very good spy," Howard Blum reported. "He observed merchants making deliveries, the locations of the sentry posts, the number of troops deployed, as well as the timing of the changing of the guards. He scrutinized the walls surrounding the embassy, hunting for side doors or perhaps some hole in the fortification. Even now, he could not find a way in. He had every reason to believe the well-positioned and well-armed Allied guards would annihilate the commandos before they made it through the door."[4]

While Oberg and the other leading German players in Tehran continued to ponder their options for a frontal assault, a paid informant of the wrestler Misbah Ebtehaj arrived at Kakh Street one morning to suggest an alternative line of attack. This individual worked for the Tehran district water board and brought with him the blueprints of the city's sewer and irrigation system. Essentially, this consisted of a crisscrossing series of man-made subterranean channels called *qanats* (from the Arabic for "dig") to carry groundwater from an aquifer or well to the surface in one direction and to expel waste in the other. In 1943 there were at least 22,000 *qanats* in Iran, comprising some 170,000 miles of underground tunnels. Originally built 2,000 years ago, and constructed entirely by hand, much of the system remains operational today. According to German engineer Hans Wulff, who made a lifetime's study of Iran's infrastructure, "The *qanats* made a garden of what otherwise would have been an uninhabitable desert."[5]

As Oberg studied the technical drawings, he noticed that Tehran's water and sewer system resembled nothing so much as a giant pinwheel. The main pipes were laid out in two concentric loops spanning the city and its inner suburbs. At various points along the circumference of each loop, a well-like vertical duct, or *karez*, tapped into one of the conduits to pump water to the surface. These troughs were necessarily cold, dank, and uncongenial places, with malodorously sweating brick walls and barely adequate supplies of oxygen, and a native population of rats, turtles, snakes, and even an occasional stray cow or wild boar. Although not the sort of companions the squeamish Oberg would have chosen for himself, he noticed one salient point about Tehran's municipal irrigation system that trumped all other considerations.

Studying the blueprints, Oberg could see that each *karez* was wide enough to accommodate a fully-grown adult, and, perhaps more to the point, among the roughly 300 *karez* bringing water to the residents of central Tehran was one built directly below what was now the kitchen of the Soviet embassy building on Nofel Loshato Street.

* * *

Stalin was fickle in more than just his choice of airplanes. Before flying to Iran, the Vozhd's attention had seemed to swing between the great affairs of state and more narrowly personal issues. At a mid-November Kremlin reception to celebrate the debut of the new Soviet anthem, Stalin was somewhat unseasonably attired in a tropical white uniform with a red braid, while the normally austere Vyacheslav Molotov was seen sporting a "black number trimmed in gold, with a small dagger at the belt … much like Hitler's SS," wrote the U.S. diplomat Chip Bohlen.

A "jovial" Molotov then proceeded to overdo the Bacchic rites, reeling up to Averell Harriman's nubile daughter Kathleen and slurringly asking her if she liked the cut of his suit. After that, the famously reserved foreign minister slapped the Swedish ambassador on the back sufficiently hard for the latter to lose his balance and topple into a nearby potted palm, before going on to inform another Western diplomat that his wife appeared notably well-equipped for the feeding of the young. Stalin's childhood friend Sergey Kavtaradze, once condemned to death for counter-revolutionary activities, but now rehabilitated as Molotov's assistant, disappeared into a side room with the trade minister and future party chairman Anastas Mikoyan, where they were later found amidst "tables covered with bottles and wineglasses" in the company of two prostitutes.

Stalin remained aloof from the debauchery, as he generally did, preferring merely to watch his colleagues and potential rivals make fools of themselves and then use their indiscretions against them later. Nikita Khrushchev was present at the Kremlin to toast the new anthem, and remembered the boss "doing nothing, just sitting there at the party, which like all of them became disgusting, until it clouded your brain and made your head and whole body ache." As Khrushchev later wrote, "All this nonsense stemmed from Stalin's mind."[6]

The Soviet strongman had other pressing concerns, too, besides those of making his people safe from the fascist invader. Stalin's 22-year-old son Vasily, whose mother had committed suicide in 1932, was a hotheaded alcoholic who was in the habit of fishing by the unusual means of taking off in a Red Air Force training plane and dropping bombs into a pond

6. "The Greatest Surfeit and Concentration of Power..."   139

with delayed fuses. Somehow inevitably, this went wrong one day and the plane's pilot was killed in the explosion. Vasily survived but earned a public rebuke from his father. "I hereby dismiss Colonel VJ Stalin immediately from his regimental command, for hard drinking, lechery, and corrupting the men." Vasily's 17-year-old sister Svetlana had meanwhile been carrying on a torrid affair with the middle-aged and married Soviet screenwriter Aleksei Kapler. Stalin was not pleased. Kapler was arrested, and Svetlana long remembered her father's ire when she returned home from school that afternoon.[7] "I know the whole thing!" he roared, with an ominous yellow gleam in his eye. "I've got all your phone conversations right here!" He slapped his tunic pocket. "Your Kapler's a British spy. He's been removed. Who'd want you anyway, you little fool? He's got women all around him."

Svetlana tearfully replied, "But I love him."

"Love!" hissed Stalin, "with hatred of the very word," Svetlana wrote, and stepped forward to slap his daughter twice across the face. The girl's horrified nanny was watching the whole scene unfold. Stalin turned to her with a wild look. "Just think, nurse, how low she's sunk. A war going on, and she's busy fucking!"[8]

Stalin may or may not have been a "military leader of unyielding genius," as Churchill later generously described him, but to address the question of his day-to-day mental state is to enter the realm of psychodrama. The 40-year-old Kapler was duly dispatched to a camp at Vorkuta in the Arctic Circle and put on a starvation diet. Toward the end of his ten-year sentence, he weighed little more than the leg-irons he wore night and day.

Compounding the already baleful mood at Stalin's court, his eldest son Yakov perished in German captivity at Sachsenhausen, the headquarters of the Operation Bernhard currency-counterfeiting ring. The Nazis had earlier offered to swap Yakov for Field Marshal Paulus, the defeated Sixth Army commander at Stalingrad. The boss refused. An SS guard named Gustav Wegner would recall the fateful day at Sachsenhausen:

> Late in 1943 the prisoners were taking their exercise—Stalin wouldn't go with them, and asked to see the commandant of the camp. An SS man went to the phone to call the commandant. While he was telephoning the following happened: Yakov was walking around, and absentmindedly crossed the no-go area and went toward the [electrified] fence. The sentry shouted, "Halt!" Yakov kept straight on. The sentry then killed him. As the fatal shot was fired, Yakov simultaneously seized the high-tension line and collapsed onto the first two rows of barbed wire. He hung there in that position for 24 hours, after which his body was taken away to the crematorium.[9]

It was against the immediate backdrop of these events that Stalin elbowed Beria aside on the runway at Baku and took off into the night for what he called his meeting "to determine the fate of the whole world."

In Tehran, the cold-eyed Nazi convert Vladimir Shkvarzev had compelling personal grounds for willing the success of Operation Long Jump. Stalin had now been informed of Shkvarzev's defection, and his reaction to it made his treatment of Svetlana and her lover seem like that of a doting parent by comparison. "For the good of the Party, we must treat such scum as no more than wild dogs to be put down," the Vozhd declared. He would personally visit Shkvarzev once captured and confined in a Soviet jail, he added, and while the people's judicial system was of course famously merciful, there was a regrettable tendency for certain properly convicted prisoners to meet some fatal accident while in captivity, if not while being transferred to or from their place of detention. Such "car crashes," like the one that accounted for the life of Solomon Mikhoels, had become an occupational hazard for prominent guests of the Soviet state. Shkvarzev told Ernst Merser, as they waited for the Big Three to arrive in Tehran, "Others before me have wondered if the Party might not gain from some mild internal reforms. Shortly afterward, Moscow has witnessed these individuals' funerals." Bluntly put, it was a case of Stalin and as many of his murderous crew as possible losing their lives or Shkvarzev losing his own.

Devious, short, and balding, Shkvarzev was not the only member of the cutthroat band variously biding their time in Tehran to have brought off an ideological U-turn at some point in their career. There was Nikolai Kuznetsov, the Ukrainian national with youthful pro–German sympathies, whom the war had converted into the fanatical Soviet agent by the name of Siebert. A full revolution had brought him in a circle. Kuznetsov remained among the Russians' main espionage assets in Tehran, but this was undermined by one fact: neither Oberg nor Merser had ever thought to invite him to join them at the fishmonger's premises on Ghazali Street, nor to share their new-found interest in the city's municipal water system. Perhaps the two Operation Long Jump planners had become more security-conscious as the final hour of truth approached. No one could say with certainty how Misbah Ebtehaj and his entourage, for their part, might react once in the line of fire. They were regarded with a mixture of fear and hatred by the dipsomaniac Hans Ortel, impressed by grossly inflated accounts of the musclemen's prowess as street-fighters. Merser took a perhaps more dispassionate view. "Sometimes the wrestlers' antics strained their associates' indulgence," he wrote.

Despite Walter Schellenberg's edict, many of these individuals were still being paid in skillfully forged British banknotes, thus adding yet another potentially explosive element to the smooth running of Operation Long Jump. Thanks to Agent Cicero, Schellenberg and his colleagues in

6. "The Greatest Surfeit and Concentration of Power..."   141

Berlin had a good idea of what the Anglo-Americans were planning to discuss at Tehran, and what they hoped the Russians would in turn tell them. Schellenberg learned, for example, that the U.S. wanted to use Soviet airfields for their bombers, enabling them to fly from their bases in England straight to their targets in Germany, then to land and refuel in Minsk or Vilnius, and that Stalin for his part wanted the West to pressure Turkey to grant Russia free use of the warm water ports of the Dardanelles. Cicero, too, had been paid in duds. It later emerged that he had simultaneously been collecting information on Ludwig Moyzisch and his other German handlers, though without yet securing a double payday for himself by selling this back to the British.[10] Perhaps he had merely taken out an insurance policy against an uncertain future. The spy and the thief both trade in stolen goods on similar principles. One way or another, it was a singularly mixed cast of characters and a uniquely foreboding place the Allied leaders were heading to that November.

* * *

Within 48 hours of setting up watch on Ghazali Street, and before he'd verified Stalin's or anyone else's expected arrival time at the embassy across the street, Winifred Oberg sent a signal back to Schellenberg's office on Berkaerstrasse. "As a result of continuous superintendence operations," he puffed, "data has been recently developed from highly confidential sources indicating that a number of persons associated with combatants of the Reich will be accommodated here within a week of today's date."

Oberg still did not have any hard intelligence about the EUREKA conference to pass on to his masters in Berlin. The highly confidential sources of which he spoke largely consisted of a series of local Tehran storekeepers arriving at the embassy gates, bearing crates of chicken and game and cakes, as well as a large suckling pig borne in on a pallet by four dark-robed men as though carrying a human corpse, along with "copious amounts" of vodka, gin, and other spirits. Some of these same merchants were waylaid on their way out and proved agreeable to supplying particulars of their deliveries in exchange for a few reassuringly colorful British banknotes. Oberg named nine individuals who were either directly or indirectly "participants in this victualling operation," no doubt taking satisfaction in the fact that some of the tradesmen in question were also amenable to selling him surplus stock ("Two bottles extra-strength Armenian plum brandy and one of Aragh Sagi, unwanted by Soviet contingent," he fastidiously noted in his surveillance log) at a cash discount.

It was this same mixture of high political intrigue and low personal calculation that characterized Operation Long Jump. At six o'clock in the morning of November 20, Oberg watched an olive-green Soviet ZiS-5V three-ton truck pull up to the compound gate, and two soldiers emerge from the rear bearing a metal-framed cot and some neatly folded blankets. After a few minutes, they returned to the ZiS, and this time extracted a large film projector. On their third and final trip between the truck and the sweeping entrance steps to the building, the men were seen to be struggling under the weight of what appeared in the dim morning light to be several pairs of fur-lined boots, some books, and two gold-framed portraits, one of Lenin and the other of Stalin. The boss never left home without them.

In Berlin, Joseph Goebbels now diffidently suggested to Hitler that "natural fissures were widening within the Allied camp" and that under the circumstances perhaps the physical elimination of the enemy warlords might be counterproductive to the Axis cause.[11] As always, the German dictator preferred to distance himself from administration, even when it involved a decision of this magnitude. The general rule was for members of the senior Nazi hierarchy to try and be the last man to command the führer's attention on a given subject, and then hope that Hitler would say, "Agreed," leaving it to others to later fight about exactly what he had agreed to. It may seem absurd in today's political climate dominated by ministers, civil servants, and a plethora of lesser functionaries at every conceivable federal, state, and local level, but in the depths of the greatest armed conflict in recorded human history, decisions that affected the welfare of tens or hundreds of thousands of individuals around the globe were often taken on the basis of a grunt.

On November 21, Schellenberg passed the order to the SD's Section 6 Iranian desk to provide him with daily weather forecasts for the greater Tehran area. Roman Gamotha, the camphor-sniffing agent last seen directing a Turkish bank raid, had performed a wide range of duties since arriving in the area, and now found himself pressed into service as an amateur meteorologist. Strangely enough, Gamotha was one of the few German assets in the Middle East seemingly not familiar with the broad contours of Operation Long Jump. From his later testimony, he thought that Berlin's sudden interest in cloud formations some 2,000 miles away might be for the purpose of planning an airborne drop of propaganda leaflets on the streets of Tehran. He still had no idea that Schellenberg might have something altogether more dramatic in mind to curtail the Allies' influence in Iran, let alone the world. Nonetheless, he thought to mention this unusual request to his new acquaintance Paul Siebert. Siebert affected not to much care about the whims of a distant ministry, but suggested that the two join their mutual friend Hans Ortel for a few drinks at the Owl's Keen later that night. He would go home for his usual afternoon rest beforehand, he added. Gamotha affectionately watched the old SS man's limping shuffle disappear around the corner.

6. "The Greatest Surfeit and Concentration of Power..."   143

Once Siebert was safely back at his lodgings on Deylaman Street, however, he did not stretch out for a nap in the darkened bedroom, the still-warm air fragrant with the scent of orange and lemon blossom in the block's central courtyard, or drift off to the rumbling sound of passing trucks and motor-scooters, or the shouted orders and grumbles of nearby market traders, and all the other animation that marked a busy Eastern capital city currently accommodating the armed forces of three allied powers, as well as a less visible cross-section of their enemies.

Instead, Siebert, or Kuznetsov as his friends knew him, swiftly extracted the homemade crystal radio set from under his floorboards, keyed in the necessary prefix, and instructed whoever was listening at the other end on the hillsides of western Afghanistan to relay to Moscow Center this strange new interest the enemy was showing in the Iranian climate.

* * *

While the Anglo-American leaders steamed toward their rendezvous in Cairo, and Stalin prepared to take to the air for the first and only time in his life to join them in Tehran, yet another hastily ordered Junkers-290, under the command of the Luftwaffe's special operations Captain Karl-Edmund Gartenfeld, droned low over the darkened Elburz foothills. In due course, another nine parachutes billowed out over the rocky terrain, floating down toward a waiting ring of flickering lights the arriving Germans assumed to be those of their friendly reception committee. They were mistaken. As the men hit the ground, a brutal volley of machine-gun fire erupted, followed by a more measured salvo of rifles and small arms. They had dropped straight into a trap. The men waiting for them were not Nazi sleepers, or even friendly Qashqai tribesmen, but crack Soviet infantry units alerted by Moscow Center to expect them. Five paratroopers were either killed outright or captured and taken for questioning, never to be seen or heard from again. The other four were lucky enough to drift off course and thus escape the ambush. No longer an orderly SS formation but a chaotic rabble, they eventually managed to make their way down the mountain pass and through the back door of Ernst Merser's house on Kakh Street, one of them stumbling and breaking his leg in the descent. It was a somewhat inauspicious start to the plan to effectively neutralize the highest echelons of the Allied political command.

One of the three still-ambulatory German parachutists was named Lothar Schoellhorn, a 32-year-old ex-middleweight boxer, of whom there was now a surfeit in Tehran, of—as one account delicately put it—"not entirely unblemished character."[12] Schoellhorn was short, solid, rough-hewn, and utterly fearless. Leaving the aircraft without a helmet or combat boots, preferring his ensemble of cloth cap and rubber-soled shoes with a dagger concealed in the side, he'd hit the ground at roughly twice the recommended speed. The impact had knocked him about, he later admitted—in fact, thrown his spine out of alignment and temporarily left him seeing double—but this in no way lessened his appetite for the coming fight. Schoellhorn would soon recover his strength and go on to be a major player in the week's unfolding events.

* * *

The two Western leaders had barely set sail from their respective ports for Egypt when a counterintelligence maelstrom stirred by reports of their ongoing travel plans began to swirl in Berlin, Moscow, and Tehran. On November 21, Pavel Fitin, the rightly feared deputy head of the NKVD's foreign section, went to brief his boss Lavrentiy Beria. Even the criminally psychotic Beria seems to have treated Fitin as he might a pet cobra. "I had made a crass error [in 1941] in trying to draw a line between this individual's alerts of a fascist assault on the homeland and the highest authority of the Commissariat [Stalin], one neither party could ever let me forget," he later admitted. Fitin now told Beria that reports had reached him from Nikolai Kuznetsov and other sources suggesting that the Germans were preparing some form of aerial offensive on Tehran. It could not be entirely coincidental that this was the same final port of call for the Vozhd's meeting with his two allies. Other "enemies of the proletariat," such as the German parachutists captured in the Elburz foothills, or those detained in Tehran, had "to some degree or another, confirmed the fact."

Fitin's report was nevertheless perceived by his NKVD detractors, who were legion, as "a hatchet job ... reflecting his continuing ambition." It was "designed to be damaging to Beria and others who pursued their plan to put Stalin in harm's way in Iran," Nikita Khrushchev later wrote.[13] Nonetheless, Beria had not survived in the upper reaches of the Soviet governmental system, as pitiless in its way as that of the Amazon jungle, without recognizing the moment to catch the boss's ear when it presented itself. Stalin had thus read "all the security briefs before even stepping on the aircraft at Baku," Khrushchev recalled. Once on the ground, he would proceed by a heavily armored Packard limousine screened from curious eyes by brown velvet curtains and be enclosed at all other times in his hermetic bubble, with two concentric rings of NKVD troops joining his regular security detail, and six long-barreled KS-19 artillery pieces stationed around the Tehran embassy grounds ready to deal with any enemy aircraft straying overhead. Beria knew that if the boss somehow fell to enemy action while on his travels, his life would not be worth living.

Walter Schellenberg and his superiors back in Berlin now knew about the impending Allied conference; they also knew that the Allies knew that they knew. The only outstanding point of debate was when, exactly, the Big Three leaders might choose to sit down together in the compound on Nofel Loshato Street. The celebrated historian Howard Blum believes that the SD chief eventually determined the matter by consulting a calendar of dates of particular national or personal consequence to the Western trio.

"With his mind travelling down this new avenue of possibilities, Schellenberg scoured the list and saw that the American holiday of Thanksgiving fell on November 26 [actually, that year it was the 25th]. Yes, he thought, that would very likely be an occasion when Roosevelt would host a dinner.... But would Stalin have ideological concerns about attending a feast celebrated by American capitalists?"

After this, Blum has Schellenberg again running his finger down a menu of key dates.

"Then he saw it.

"It was the one event the Allies would all be certain to celebrate, when they'd all convene regardless of national politics or personal feuds. It was the one occasion when they'd have no concerns about putting aside their differences for an evening and acting like allies. He was certain he had what he needed."[14]

The momentous date was Tuesday, November 30, 1943, which happened to be Winston Churchill's birthday. And while there's of course again no reason to question Schellenberg's thought process as retailed by a modern-day author like Blum some 75 years after the fact, it's possible that the decision-makers at Berkaerstrasse were motivated equally by the various radio signals reaching them from the likes of Ernst Merser and Hans Ortel on the ground in Tehran, as well as by the reports of Elyesa Bazna and his handlers in Ankara, as by the happy coincidence of the British premier turning 69 while resident in Tehran.[15]

That Schellenberg's familiarity with the Allied leaders' plans might not exclusively be down to the diligence of his embedded agents in Iran was demonstrated by a report on America's NBC Radio that week, suggesting the "American and British leaders would soon descend from over the sawtoothed and snow-capped Persian mountains to meet the Soviet delegation, and in effect sign the death warrant of Nazi Germany." Speaking of the Allies' preliminary conference in Cairo, *Life* magazine in turn informed its 1.6 million readers, "Since the Germans still have bombers based in Crete, and since the Pyramids, within a stone's throw of the meeting-place, amount to the most efficient air landmarks in the world, there seem[s] reason to fear that the international conversations might be subject to rude interruption."[16] In short order, the Secret Service countered this last challenge by recruiting a team of 200 day-laborers to erect a row of half-sized dummy pyramids a few miles downriver from the originals.

From the air, the Americans believed, the dense assemblage would look sufficiently like the real thing to prevent the Luftwaffe from distinguishing one from the other as they droned high in the night sky. It worked.

Roosevelt's principal protection officer Mike Reilly was not entirely happy, even so, when it came time for him to fly ahead of the president to inspect the site of the Cairo conference.

"The city was filled with Axis spies and the price of life was cheap," Reilly wrote. "A 60-dollar fine was the general punishment meted out by the courts for killing a local. For ten dollars one could hire a professional agitator who would provide a thousand natives to create a frenzied demonstration for or against anything or anybody.... When I arrived in Cairo, heads were being bashed in by the hundreds in front of the British and French embassies in the riots associated with Axis-agitated uprisings."[17]

It was against this backdrop, in an Iran seething with factional unrest, that the Germans finally determined the contours of their master plan to eliminate the American, Soviet, and British warlords. There would be no omnipotent Skorzeny figure, nor Skorzeny himself, dropped in to direct the whole exercise. Instead, Schellenberg would call on the services of his already-significant resources in and around Tehran. The resulting mission, like all the best missions, was ingenious and simple. Essentially, Ernst Merser and Rudolf Holten-Pflug would lead an 18-man team consisting of thirteen Germans, the wrestler Misbah Ebtehaj, and a diversionary component of four native-born Iranians. When the moment came, they would infiltrate the Soviet stronghold by way of one unit silently breaching the compound's rear wall by the cover of dark while a second one made its entrance through the building's water tunnel. At least some of the men would be dressed in Russian uniform to further exploit the element of surprise. A combined assault deploying machine guns and Gammon bombs would finish the job off. It might all yet prove a close call for National Socialism in its existential struggle with the Allies, Schellenberg admitted, but "merely waiting on battlefield events" was no longer an option.

Studying the plan, the more cynical—or perhaps realistic—Franz Mayr told Merser that his chances of insinuating his men over and under the heavily guarded Soviet citadel were "practically non-existent," urging him to think again. Merser disputed this and on the moonless night of November 21, took Mayr out into the far western Tehran suburbs to settle the matter. A group of 14 men, each carrying a pack containing rocks equivalent to the weight of a full complement of firearms and explosives, were to silently invade a large, suitably secluded house while 20 of Merser's other men, ignorant of the time and scale of the attack, were to try and repel them.

Six of the assailants duly made it inside the building, one of them stumbling in the dark and spraining his wrist, where they swiftly cut the power supply and moved into the locked mock-conference room by the expedient of attaching two Model 39 pull-cord grenades to the door handle. In the subsequent melee, the raiders successfully shot blanks at three seated effigies representing Roosevelt, Stalin and Churchill, although there was some difficulty when it came to them withdrawing again. Even though fending off crack NKVD and Secret Service agents might prove trickier than simply pretending to do so, Merser acknowledged, he pronounced himself satisfied with the drill. "It does not matter if we ultimately fail to escape," he wrote in his diary, a remark he wisely chose not to share with his men. "We wait to prove ourselves.... If we die, we will have died gloriously. Soon enough, our names will be honored by those who value the preservation of our Reich, and that of the freedom of the whole world."

* * *

On November 22, the day on which Roosevelt and Churchill joined Chiang Kai-shek in the shadow of the pyramids at Giza, an advance party of NKVD troops was busy rounding up yet more "wreckers" in what became a week-long dragnet to descend 1,600 miles away in Tehran. After being bound and gagged, the detainees were taken to a tented camp set up in the royal hunting grounds—today's Sorkheh Hesar National Park—in the eastern suburbs of the city. In a gesture of defiance, some 300 wives and children of the interned gathered overnight in front of the estate's elaborately gilded front gates and demanded their loved ones' release. The following morning, the shah expressed his concern when, as the exodus of prisoners began to the camps in Russia, there were what he called "regrettable scenes ... when a large number of people complained, and some even attacked the Soviet troops."

"One after another, both low and high members of the local German colony disappeared without a trace," wrote Alexandr Lukin, a Russo-Iranian journalist who prudently said nothing of the roundups at the time but wrote of them in a best-selling book 22 years later. "When the valet of one such individual entered his bedroom in the morning, he found nothing but a pajama button remaining."[18]

A Tehran tailor named Jakob Kupferstein was one of those picked up by Red Army troops overnight on November 22–23. His offense was to have been born both German and Jewish, and thus doubly stigmatized by the Soviet security forces as representing the enemy within.

"I was taken away with my wife, my mother-in-law, and my two sons," Kupferstein wrote. "We were eventually put into a single-story building attached to a Russian barracks. There was room for thirty people at the most, but while I was there some 200 souls were brought in. Those for whom there was no room in the building were taken away every three or four days, I still don't know where."[19]

Kupferstein was one of the lucky ones. He and his sons survived the ordeal and were released on New Year's Eve as "privileged persons" who were to be "reincorporated in the national community." Both his wife and mother-in-law perished while in captivity.

* * *

In Cairo that week, Winston Churchill, accompanied by his uniformed daughter Sarah, drove out to look at the Sphinx and the pyramids, and returned to excitedly tell Roosevelt: "Mr. President, you simply must come and see the sights. I've arranged it all." Churchill's enthusiasm was such that, Sarah recalled, Roosevelt "leaned forward on the arms of his chair and seemed about to rise, when he remembered that he could not and sank back again. It was a painful scene."[20] After a moment, Churchill said, "We'll wait for you in the car." Sarah went outside with her father. "There in the shining sun," she remembered, "I saw that his eyes were bright with tears." For several minutes, the British premier sat, staring out the car window through the long fingers of palm leaf toward the distant hills where oil derricks rose like gallows straight out of the sand. Then Churchill's lips moved, though just barely, and he spoke in a voice so low his daughter had to strain to catch it from two feet away.

"I love that man," he said.

* * *

On November 23, there was a final parachute drop, this time of munitions alone, in the Elburz foothills. Ernst Merser and Hans Ortel went up to collect yet more MP40 submachine guns along with a cache of stick grenades and lightbulb-sized Blendkorper 2H smoke bombs of the type that could swiftly fill a room with a dense, choking gas and blind any of its occupants not equipped with a mask. The night's rain had stopped, and a cold, unhealthy mist hung over the Elburz. The two agents made a perilous descent before the winter sun came up over the snow-capped Mt. Damavand to the northeast. "During this same time, three or four patrols of our friends the Qashqai fighters were captured," Merser later noted. "The Russian forces were then everywhere in Tehran, and it was judged to be the worst of all possible fates to be taken by them. Death was truly to be envied in such circumstances. Among the tribes there was a deep-held belief that evil spirits called *shayatins* went abroad at night to steal men's souls and then torment them in unspeakable ways. Many I spoke to insisted that these same demons had now returned."

Merser and Ortel nonetheless made it safely back to Kakh Street in the early hours of the 24th to stow their equipment and assemble their men before holding another *Weitsprung* dress rehearsal later that night. They chose a gutted railway depot with windows you could see the moon through on the edge of the salt desert to serve as the Russian embassy, and, again, half the force was assigned to defend the high-walled building using blank-filled rifles, stun grenades, and other non-lethal weapons. It has to be said that the exercise was only a mixed success from the assailants' point of view. An attempt to blow the station's arched front door off its hinges using a Model 39 grenade backfired spectacularly, scorching the faces and hands of two of the attackers but leaving the door intact. A parallel operation to storm the depot by passing men through its nearest underground *qanat* sewer line also foundered when the tunnel was found to be impenetrably clogged with years of accumulated waste. Merser was as a rule not one for vulgarity, but he allowed himself one here. "I fear the whole enterprise turned to shit," he reported.

The final drill, held on the night of November 25, proved altogether more auspicious. This time Merser chose a friendly contact's remote two-story villa, complete with high surrounding walls and a bank of floodlit front steps, to simulate the target. The team again split into two groups and were told to spare no effort short of deadly fire in the ensuing melee. As an added spur, it was impressed on the invading force that they could expect to undergo "hard interrogation" if captured by the real enemy on the night, and thus that their only two viable options were to kill or be killed. "There was a certain sharpness to their actions as a result," Merser later noted. His speech to the men had more than a touch of the Churchillian, full of defiance and the exhortation to see Germany's glorious destiny fulfilled not just in the inland waterways of Europe but also over the broad seas that swirl around the world.

Merser monitored the proceedings from atop a large rock. Bursts of authentic-sounding gunfire could soon be heard from different parts of the house, followed by a series of explosions. The Model 39 grenades detonated satisfactorily. In short order, a billowing cloud of white fog drifted out into the night, accompanied by a wide variety of shouted commands and cries from within. In the confusion, "Roosevelt" and "Churchill" were both successfully dispatched, although the man portraying Stalin managed to crawl out the front door with two companions, wheezing violently in the acrid fumes. Merser then dropped down from his perch and ran to the foot of the house's entrance steps, where—in a gesture tantamount to suicide in real battle conditions—he fired a blank round directly at the fleeing target's chest. His subsequent report was terse but accurate: "Still some imperfections. Sorry but not surprised at losses on both sides. Mission successful."

*　*　*

With three of the most powerful men on earth about to arrive simultaneously, Tehran took on even more of the character of a besieged city. Merser long remembered the tense night of the 25th, when he and three of his men, having changed back into civilian clothes, drove home from their last dress rehearsal to the safe house on Kakh Street. "We proceeded in silence. Our recent mood of elation quickly vanished," he wrote. "Every few miles a lantern was waved at us, and we stopped to have our papers examined by a picket of machinegun-wielding soldiers." Once in the city center, he dropped Ortel at the Owl's Keen for a breakfast of Aragh Sagi and the two men took their leave of each other, quietly agreeing that they would meet again that evening.

Back home, at about three o'clock that afternoon, Ortel recollected, "We heard noises in the street from the buildings to either side of us. We heard the sound of splintering wood and crashes and ran downstairs, when the stout wooden door to the street just caved inwards. About seven or eight Reds armed with short-barreled guns rushed towards us, and one man fired a salvo into the ceiling while others shouted incomprehensibly in our faces."

The *shayatin* demons had come for Ortel and his crew in the form of an NKVD patrol acting on a tipoff that German-speaking individuals had been seen coming and going on the premises. Their active part in Operation Long Jump was over. In due course, Ortel was removed to a Siberian camp, where he seems to have been treated as merely one of the hundreds of thousands of perceived enemies of Soviet power rather than as a would-be assassin of the state leader. Despite regular searches by his guards, Ortel was able to keep a capsule of potassium cyanide wedged between his gums or elsewhere on his body, ready at all times to end his life if the circumstances required it. He eventually died in Soviet captivity of pneumonia.

*　*　*

Early on November 27, Ernst Merser came to a suburban Tehran *zurkhaneh*, or wrestling gym, to brief the men of Operation Long Jump on Ortel's capture.[21] He assured them that their mission would still proceed despite this setback but with one refinement. The assassins would now strike not in the Soviet but in the adjacent British embassy, where he had good grounds to believe the three enemy leaders would convene on the night of the 30th. The essential course of action remained unchanged. Merser would lead an abbreviated team of nine men, including Misbah Ebtehaj and his sub-crew, on a frontal assault, while Rudolf Holten-Pflug and Winifred Oberg took the underground route through the building's water tunnel. A third unit would launch a diversionary feint by detonating Gammon bombs 200 yards away at the northern perimeter of the Soviet block, thus drawing the enemy's attention from the main event. Once inside, a combination of grenades, Gammons and machine guns would do the job, and even the hardened NKVD guards would be rattled, Merser assumed, by the strange wilderness of smoke and rubble in which they suddenly found themselves. There was no guarantee of their welfare beyond that point, he noted, adding that any man could honorably withdraw at any time up to the moment they finally assembled to change into their battle dress and ready their weapons at six on the evening of November 30. None did.

Concluding that death was all but certain for some of them, Merser adopted a tone of extreme nonchalance. "Your names will be lauded through the ages. More immediately, the Reich will provide generously for your loved ones. Your widows will never need to pay for another meal again." A nervous ripple of laughter greeted this, and one or two of the men chinked glasses for a swift breakfast shot of Aragh Sagi. They would meet again the next morning at Kakh Street to study a scale model now being prepared for them of the British embassy. Their visit to the building would be short, fierce, and lethal, Merser assured them. The outer ring of Allied sentries guarding the complex would die "before they knew what hit them," and the momentum would be with the raiders throughout the subsequent assault. The men needed only to remember their training and to bear in mind that the future of the civilized world depended on them.

For all his combination of high principle and dry detail, Merser also knew that Hans Ortel was now in the hands of the NKVD, and if they chose to interrogate him, they would break him. And then they would come for the rest of them and kill them all.

For this and other reasons, the next 24 hours would test even Merser's prodigious reserves of self-control. Later that afternoon of the 27th, Misbah Ebtehaj confided that, while he and his men remained fully committed to the cause of ridding the world of the Jewish-Marxist conspiracy as represented by the Allied leaders in their midst, in the light of recent events they had talked the matter over between themselves and concluded that a further cash consideration of £10,000 would be in order for their services. After haggling, Merser forked over £4,000 and promised the balance on completion. Unbeknownst to Ebtehaj, the money that changed hands was once again the fruit of the slave laborers at Sachsenhausen rather than the staff at the Royal Mint. The total time devoted to *Weitsprung*'s financial arrangements on the afternoon of the 27th was about an hour, and to the actual mechanics of the plot, less than thirty seconds (the exchange about Ebtehaj's ideological piety quoted above).

Later that day, Merser heard the chilling news that Winifred Oberg and several of his circle had in turn been seized in another Soviet roundup of suspected "wreckers" in the city.[22] No one could immediately say whether the lawyer-saboteur's arrest was directly linked to his role in Operation Long Jump. Merser held another briefing of his surviving team later that night at Ebtehaj's gym, which, as he later mordantly wrote, "I was paying for, anyway." There were now just fifteen of them, an ungainly mixture of gimlet-eyed Nazi killers, Turko-Iranian oil wrestlers, and more mercenary figures like Ortel's boon companion Paul Siebert, who now joined the conspiracy, responding to his friend's arrest with a sanguine change of rationale. If the Russians were in fact combing through the streets of Tehran, was it not an admission that they were concerned a German cell or cells still lay concealed somewhere in the city, and that these could wreak havoc on their conference?

Merser in turn looked around the room at the faces staring back at him, and, with a composure that seemed scarcely human, told them that Oberg's capture qualified as a little local difficulty, certainly, but that the mission would still proceed as planned. In time, the men drifted away to study the promised plaster model of the British compound, apparently still committed to the collective cause. Merser later admitted to a greater degree of anxiety than he let on. "But my terror of being thought afraid by the men was greater than the terror itself." Besides, the Allied leaders were already among them. Stalin had landed in the morning of the 27th, and Roosevelt and Churchill each followed later in the day. It was now or never, Merser concluded, once again commending the men on their selfless devotion to duty. "History is watching us," he told them. It was a stirring performance, but even Merser's equanimity might have been shaken had he been able to spot the Soviet spy in their midst.

* * *

On that particular Saturday morning, Stalin did not look at his best. The Vozhd's luxuriant dark hair had been disarrayed by having his hand anxiously ruffle through it at regular intervals throughout the two-hour journey from Baku. The first-time flier had also suffered a severe nosebleed en route, and it was noted that he "reeled" from the plane to the black Packard waiting for him on the runway, possibly the result of a surfeit of in-flight vodka. A fourteen-car motorcade then sped him the five miles to his quarters at the embassy compound on Nofel Loshato Street. There were several small dachas on the grounds; Stalin lived in one, while Molotov and Beria took adjoining rooms in the main residence. Nikolai Vlasik was there as head of the boss's personal security detail, along with twelve handpicked Georgian bodyguards, a doctor, a strikingly well-endowed

6. "The Greatest Surfeit and Concentration of Power…"   153

nurse, and a food taster. After changing into a fresh white tunic, Stalin decided to pay an impromptu call on the 24-year-old shah at his palace. The boy king was "pleasantly surprised" by his visitor, who was "particularly polite and well-mannered, [and] seemed intent on making a good impression on me."[23]

No agenda for this meeting was ever formalized, which is hardly surprising, but it contained some lively personal interplay. Stalin offered the shah some surplus T-34 tanks and planes, but the gifts came with Soviet officers attached. Seeing an opportunity, the shah said that he personally would welcome both the arms and the men, if only the Russian government would also formally commit to Iran's national independence after the war. This was taking mutual goodwill too far for Stalin's taste, and he repeated only that he might see his way to adding a disused Soviet battleship to the package. "I declined with thanks," wrote the shah.

Meanwhile, the Russians had not only refurbished their half of the Nofel Loshato compound in advance of the conference, but had also generously helped to remodel the adjoining British premises. This included installing a dozen small, pencil-like listening devices buried in the wall behind each radiator in the embassy's formal rooms. These in turn were linked through thin wires running directly under the building's floorboards to a receiving station manned by two NKVD operators in one of the outlying dachas. Lavrentiy Beria's teenage son Sergo, a Moscow University engineering student who spoke fluent English, was personally summoned by the boss later on the afternoon of the 27th and given unusual instructions.

"I want to entrust you with a mission that is not quite proper and may even be reprehensible," Stalin began, at least proving that he wasn't too morally stunted to recognize the difference. "You are going to listen to the conversations Churchill will have with Roosevelt, and others. I must know everything in detail, be aware of all the shades of meaning. I am asking you to do this because it is now that the question of the second front will be settled. I know that Churchill is against it. It is important that the Americans support us in the matter."[24]

There was soon an unusual display of father-son bonding to be seen at Nofel Loshato Street, as the two Berias met early each morning to prepare their report for the boss. Sharp at eight o'clock they walked across the lawn to Stalin's modestly furnished dacha, where they handed him the transcripts of the previous day's private conversations. The Soviet dictator repeatedly expressed his astonishment at the Westerners' lack of discretion while speaking with one another, describing their candor as "bizarre."[25]

Roosevelt's own protracted journey to his rendezvous in Tehran was one of goodwill and commitment toward the Alliance, but also a wild gamble. After the near miss of the friendly-fire torpedo released at the USS *Iowa*, the president's ship had spent a week crossing the enemy-infested waters of the Atlantic and western Mediterranean before docking first at Casablanca and then at Oran on the Algerian coast. From there he transferred to his specially modified Skymaster, the so-called Sacred Cow, for the onward flight to Tunis and Cairo. Mike Reilly personally briefed the plane's pilot, Major Otis Bryan, shortly before takeoff. The Secret Service agent's tone was grave. "From now on this man's life is in your hands. The whole free world is counting on you." Only then did Reilly produce a large manila envelope, tied with string and further secured with a red seal, informing Major Bryan of his destination. Sometimes it's hard to understand the ways of government agencies. By that stage, Bryan may have been one of the few people not to have known the details of his journey, which had been widely aired in the press during the previous week.

Henry Stimson, the U.S. secretary of war, was one of several senior officials accompanying Roosevelt unhappy about the arrangements. "If I were a German commander with control of between 90 and 100 bombers and had received the news reports as to a specifically described target of unique importance, within easy range of my bases, I should stake every plane on the chance of winning such a prize."[26] As an added challenge, Reilly noted truthfully if also a little insensitively, "In the event of a forced landing, or worse, FDR would be hampered by a hard fact: he was a helpless cripple, incapable of walking unaided a single foot."[27] There was therefore some relief when the Sacred Cow touched down in a light fog at the Soviet-controlled Gale Morghe airfield, about five miles south of Tehran, and the president was discreetly lifted out to be placed in a waiting limousine and driven direct to the American legation building. At intervals during the ten-minute journey, Roosevelt glanced out the tinted window at the warm, dusty streets seemingly devoid of human life as he knew it back home in Washington. "Very dirty place, great poverty," he recorded of his first impressions.[28]

Roosevelt's plane touched down in Tehran just after three o'clock that Saturday afternoon. Ninety minutes later, the SD's paid informants at the airfield passed the news to Ernst Merser. Walter Schellenberg was notified shortly after 6:00 p.m. Berlin time that same evening.

The preference at the senior levels of the U.S. government for the extremes of advance preparation and protocol, and the British for almost comic amateurism and improvisation, underwent something of a role reversal around the time of the arrival of the two national leaders in Tehran. Belying its reputation for gentlemanly diffidence, the foreign office in London had noted as early as November 12 its "extreme concern ... that the Press Association had learnt of the Prime Minister's departure [for

6. "The Greatest Surfeit and Concentration of Power…"   155

Tehran], and discussed further censorship of this matter. The Minister of Information thought that there had clearly been some leakage about the Prime Minister's movements, and that an urgent enquiry should be instituted to find out how the Association acquired its facts."[29]

There was much more in this vein in the week of November 20–27, with a plethora of "Hush: Most Secret" documents concerning the "Personal safety of personnel on overseas state business…. Use of decoy assets to deter enemy…. Installation of destructor cannisters in prime minister's official aircraft," among several other such measures.[30] Churchill's plane landed in Tehran about 45 minutes after Roosevelt's, and neither the premier nor his immediate family members were happy with their onward transport arrangements. Nor was their traveling bodyguard Walter Thompson. Their drive into the city was "chaos," he wrote.[31] The military police jeep that escorted Churchill's car, "with the hood [top] up, thus preventing them seeing all around," went so fast that "they were soon far ahead." The VIP party was effectively abandoned, and "ripe for liquidation," Thompson noted.

Sarah Churchill described the 20-minute trip as "spine-chilling." As they neared their destination, the car slowed to walking pace through streets lined with a mixture of civilian police and turbaned Iranian soldiers with tommy guns, and curious onlookers pressing baskets of food and trinkets on the arriving party. "Anyone could have shot my father at point blank range, or just dropped a nice little grenade in our laps," Sarah recalled. "As the crowd surged around us I touched his knee, and as lightly he covered my hand with his."[32] Once finally inside the compound, Churchill ordered Thompson "in the plainest possible terms" to ratchet up security, and Thompson in turn summoned the resident Provost Marshal and told him equally bluntly that in the future "the military escort should keep close and the police on the roads should face the crowd, not the Prime Minister."

At that the Provost Marshal "became indignant that I should interfere with military matters," Thompson recalled, but then reappeared the next morning in a more chastened mood. The Marshal had just heard a report that heavily armed German paratroopers were loose somewhere in the area, and perhaps the conference attendees were in some degree of jeopardy as a result.

* * *

Another "Hush: Most Secret" cypher went out from Churchill to Roosevelt in his residence four miles away.

"My arrival here is bound to be known as I pass through [the city]. Moreover British Parliament meets this week and my absence must be explained…. Unless I hear from you to the contrary I shall allow it to be stated that I am in the region. This publicity will be unsupported cover for your own movement, which I think should still not be announced for a few days."

"You will be receiving a wire about military precautions in Tehran. Ends."[33]

And yet another "Most Urgent Cypher" telegram from Churchill back to the cabinet office in London:

> No hint or disclosure of immediate location of conference is to be given. [Tehran] *is not* to be mentioned in this context.
> Nothing will be allowed which suggests further post–Cairo meeting is taking place in the immediate future.
> It is desired that all messages should state that all the principles [sic] have now departed from North Africa for unannounced destinations.
> ENDS.[34]

Meanwhile, external events lent new urgency to Walter Schellenberg's supervision of Operation Long Jump from Berlin. In mid-November, the RAF began systematically bombing the city, forcing thousands of residents to hurriedly seek shelter in cellars or basements, or by running for the nearest subway tunnel. During the raids, which at first came only at night but then by day as well, Schellenberg had to conduct his business as best he could from an improvised bunker beneath the kitchens of the Kaiserhof Hotel, located next to the Reich Chancellery in central Berlin. There was a necessarily makeshift feel to the premises: two SS guards stood at the doorway at the end of a short corridor, beyond which, in a small vestibule, sat a civilian secretary at a plain wooden table furnished by a phone, a typewriter, and a framed photograph of the führer scowling back at her. Schellenberg's inner sanctum was no more luxurious. The only furnishings were a metal desk, two chairs, a row of ill-matched filing cabinets, and the ubiquitous Hitler portrait on the wall. The air was stuffy despite a portable generator whose shrill, monotonous whine penetrated both inner and outer offices. This was where the SD chief spent much of his waking hours in the critical week beginning November 22, when his operatives and their various associates and sub-agents were moving toward their endgame some 2,000 miles away in the Iranian capital.

On the night of Tuesday, November 23, the Kaiserhof took a direct hit from the British bombers. After the all-clear sounded, Schellenberg struggled out through the darkened streets—or what had once been streets—clogged by blackened bodies, broken glass, crockery, furniture and other debris, where the year's first drenching snowfall only added to the cheerless atmosphere. It was as if Berlin had gone to bed in a Vermeer painting and woken up in one by Hieronymus Bosch. Schellenberg's encrypted cable to Ernst Merser on the 26th showed a characteristic touch of bravado.

6. "The Greatest Surfeit and Concentration of Power…"   157

He wished his operative "health and a blessed hand," along with success "borne of your courage and our mutual hard work."

* * *

President Roosevelt faced two unforeseen developments shortly after his arrival at the American embassy in Tehran. The first was diplomatic. According to a cable awaiting him from the State Department, a 32-year-old Boston-born exotic named Theodore Morde, who successively fashioned himself a world explorer, globetrotting journalist, and spy, had made contact with the German ambassador to Turkey, the wily Franz von Papen, Hitler's one-time vice-chancellor but lately of more equivocal views on the Nazi elite. Papen now supposedly told Morde that "the time had come when the war must stop," before floating a proposal to overthrow Hitler and install himself at the head of a new government that would make peace with the West but maintain a presence on the Eastern Front "to guard against Bolshevism."[35]

The State Department in turn wondered if the president might wish to "carefully weigh this proposal while in conference" at Tehran. Roosevelt's first order of business on arrival in the city was to snap off a reply that made it clear he would not be party to any negotiating behind the Soviet dictator's back. Not only that: the department, he scribbled furiously, was to immediately take steps to revoke Morde's passport so he could not return to Turkey or "engage in further nonsensical diplomacy" anywhere else in the world. In later years, he (Morde, not Roosevelt) nonetheless went on to claim to have discovered the lost city of the Monkey God in the jungles of Honduras, and died under enigmatic circumstances, possibly a suicide, in 1954. Von Papen saw out the war, serving a brief prison sentence imposed by a German denazification court, and died at the age of 89, survived by his numerous children, equally profuse memoirs, and debts.

Roosevelt's second order of business on arrival in Tehran concerned his choice of accommodations in the city. Early on the evening of November 27, Molotov placed calls to the U.S. minister to the USSR and his British counterpart, both of whom were traveling with their respective masters in Tehran, and asked them to join him at the Soviet embassy at midnight. According to the State Department Historical Office, Stalin's foreign minister began the meeting by telling the two Western officials "very pointedly, on the basis of information which had reached him, that President Roosevelt's presence in Tehran was known to German agents there, that these agents were planning a 'demonstration,' that this might involve an attempt at assassination, and that Stalin therefore urged Roosevelt to move to either the British or the Soviet legation in the interests of his own welfare."[36]

It was a testament either to Roosevelt's pragmatic goodwill toward a key wartime ally, or, conversely, to an almost touching degree of credulousness about the Russian character, that he immediately chose to accept the Soviet offer of hospitality. In fact, the president's preference in the matter made little practical difference to Stalin, who had the British and Russian halves of the compound extensively wired for sound, thus covering all his bases. Mike Reilly put up no insuperable objection of a security nature, although when the moment came for the transfer, he recalled,

> We set up the standard motorcade with the gun-laden jeeps fore and aft, and it travelled slowly along the streets guarded by soldiers. As soon as the cavalcade left the American legation, we bundled the President into another car, put a jeep in front of him, and went tearing through the ancient side streets of Tehran, while the dummy convoy wound its way slowly through the main roads with Agent Bob Holmes, masquerading as FDR, accepting the cheers of the local citizens.[37]

By noon on November 28, Roosevelt was safely installed in a suite of rooms in the Soviet compound, if under circumstances that might have seemed to raise doubts about his privacy: a total of 37 directional microphones were concealed on the premises, along with a team of NKVD-trained domestic servants who wandered unmolested around the president's living quarters.[38] It was a bad place for the American delegation to come to discuss sensitive matters of state or, from a different perspective, a very good one.

Just after two on that same "beautiful Iranian Sunday afternoon, gold and blue, mild and sunny," Stalin, dressed in his white summer uniform, strode across his embassy lawn and knocked courteously on his distinguished houseguest's door. A young U.S. marine sergeant opened it, saluted, and withdrew, leaving the two statesmen alone in the room with just their interpreters.

"I am glad to see you. I have tried for a long time to bring this about," Roosevelt greeted his host. There was an unlikely but palpable rapport between the homicidal Red Czar and the refined New York Brahmin. Roosevelt soon went on to announce that he could "do business" with "the perceptive Mr. Stalin." The feeling was evidently mutual. Stalin later praised Roosevelt when speaking to the young Soviet diplomat Andrei Gromyko, musing poignantly, "Why did nature have to punish him so? Is he any worse than other people?" Gromyko wisely said nothing at the time, but years later wrote of his surprise at the boss's fondness for the wealthy American head of state because he "rarely bestowed his sympathy on anyone from another social system." Only occasionally did "Stalin give way to positive human emotions."[39]

At four that same Sunday afternoon, while Lavrentiy Beria personally

6. "The Greatest Surfeit and Concentration of Power..." 159

patrolled the compound gates, Churchill in turn padded across the lawn from his adjoining legation, and the Big Three leaders found themselves in the same room for the first time. The British premier marked the occasion with one of his trademark oratorical flourishes. "In our hands," Churchill announced, "is the possible certainty of shortening the war, the much greater certainty of victories, but the absolute certainty that we hold the happy future of all mankind.... At this table," he concluded, "is the greatest surfeit and concentration of power that the world has ever seen."[40]

It was this same surfeit of power that was now such a potent factor in the thinking of Walter Schellenberg and the men of *Unternehmen Weitsprung* still at large on the ground in Tehran. According to their timetable of events, the recently arrived Allied leaders had just two days left to live.

7

Zero Time

Even as he eavesdropped on his principal partners in the mutual struggle against fascism, Stalin was also busy spelling out their "comradely" vision of the postwar world.

At a glittering dinner held in the Soviet compound that Sunday night, the Vozhd dismissed any sentimental notions of charity toward the defeated enemy. It was not enough that the word "Nazi" be stricken from the language, as Roosevelt had tentatively suggested. Germany must be dismembered. The U.S. State Department felt it best to seal the minutes of the ensuing tripartite conversation for the next sixty years. They show that Stalin at every stage remained several moves ahead of the other players in the high-stakes geopolitical game that would within two years see the drop of a metaphorical iron curtain between East and West, constantly surprising them by the subtlety of his calculation, the depth of his duplicity, and above all by the lengths to which he was prepared to go to satisfy both his political needs and paranoiac concept of the world.

"In the detailed talks that followed between the three heads," the record reads, "Marshal Stalin took the lead, constantly emphasizing that the measures for the control of Germany and her disarmament were insufficient to prevent the rebirth of German militarism, and appearing to advocate even stronger steps. He, however, did not specify what he actually had in mind, except that he favored the partition of Germany." Stalin also remarked that the policy of unconditional surrender was a "terrible" idea, as it would only "unite the German people" against the Allies.

Shortly after that, Roosevelt retired for the night, leaving Churchill and Stalin alone with their interpreters to exchange further views on the eventual division of Europe over their cognac and cigars.

The minutes conclude:

> Mr. Churchill said that he could not look more than fifty years ahead, and that upon the three great nations represented at Tehran rested the grave responsibility of future measures of assuring in some manner or other that Germany would not again rise to plague the world during that period. He said that he

7. Zero Time 161

felt the conflict was largely the fault of the German leaders, and that while no distinction could be made in wartime, nonetheless with a generation of self-sacrificing, toil, and education, something might be done with the German people.

Marshal Stalin in turn expressed dissent with this, and did not appear satisfied as to the efficacy of any of the measures proposed by Mr. Churchill.[1]

Fortified by another round of industrial-strength Georgian brandy, Churchill then remarked that he "hoped the representatives of the three governments could work out some agreed understanding on the question of national frontiers.... He said that, as far as he was concerned, he would like to see Poland moved westward in the same manner as soldiers on parade execute the drill 'left close,' and illustrated his point with three matches representing the Soviet Union, Poland, and Germany.

"Marshal Stalin agreed that it would be a good idea to reach an understanding on this question, but said it was necessary to look into the matter further."

The dinner broke up on that note. Stalin went back to his nearby dacha to read an early transcript of his allies' private conversations during the day, and then to casually sign a few more of the death rolls awaiting his approval. By this stage of the war, the Vozhd had long since moved on from the officer class of the Red Army and Navy and was taking a keen interest in the staffing of his state's intelligence organs. By definition, spies were always suspect, even his spies. So when Beria oozed into the dacha shortly after 1:00 a.m., he and the boss quickly agreed that several of those at the highest levels of the NKVD, including Beria's executive assistant, would have to go. Then there was the matter of the Kalmyks, a semi-autonomous Buddhist community living in southern Russia near the Volga River basin. "Get rid of them," the Vozhd ordered, and 93,000 men, women and children would duly be herded up and forcibly resettled in Siberia as a result. And while they were at it, what about the troublesome documentary maker Aleksandr Dovzhenko? He was a Ukrainian, and his artistic error had been to shoot a propaganda film about that region's heroic resistance to the Nazis. Stalin didn't care for it. "To put it mildly," he told the salivating Beria, "this work revises history.... Dovzhenko's scenario contains the crudest sort of anti–Leninist mistakes."[2]

Stalin soon warmed to his theme, commenting that "there is no separate Ukraine! It does not exist! In fighting for the USSR you are fighting for the Ukraine also!" Truly those who forget history are condemned to repeat it. Dovzhenko was banished with another cursory flick of the Vozhd's pen. Only then did Stalin allow himself that brief, lupine contraction of the teeth and gums that passed with him for a smile, and, his day's work done, finally retired to the simple cot set up for him beside his desk, just as the first rays of the sun were coming up over the Elburz peaks to the east, shortly before four in the morning.

* * *

While the three Allied partners in the anti-fascist struggle had been at dinner exchanging their abstract views of the postwar world, heavily armed soldiers were preparing to shoot at each other less than a mile away in the heart of Tehran.

At about ten o'clock that Sunday night, a 19-year-old Red Army private named Gevork Vartanian was patrolling the city by bicycle when he noticed something unusual. Three olive-green Soviet "Polutorka" flatbed trucks, driven by men wearing Russian uniforms, were slowly making their way along Azarbayjan Street, the city's main east-west axis, each with several wooden crates stacked up in the rear. What made the scene unusual was the fact that the trucks were accompanied by a caravan of robed Qashqai warriors riding camels, in defiance of the shah's order banning them from the downtown streets. And on closer inspection, Vartanian saw that the trucks bore no red-star insignia or other proper military markings. The curious young private pedaled at a discreet distance behind the convoy until it reached a nondescript house in a cobbled mews just to the west of the royal palace, where both soldiers and riders dismounted and began carrying the boxes through the front door. Vartanian watched the proceedings for a further minute or two, and then turned his bike around and rode furiously back to the nearest NKVD base half a mile away on Syroos Street to report what he had just seen.

An hour later, a group of 32 Red Army soldiers, armed with a variety of submachine guns, pistols, and grenades, and a supporting unit equipped with a pair of wheeled FOG-2 flamethrowers, surrounded the small house, which was being used by some of Misbah Ebtehaj's entourage to store weapons for use in *Unternehmen Weitsprung*. The ensuing firefight was brutal, swift, and decisive: all but one of the wrestlers was killed outright, and the lone survivor succumbed to his wounds later that night before he could be tortured into a confession. As a result, the NKVD took possession of a large cache of guns and Gammon bombs, but still had no firm idea of if and when an attempt might be made on the Vozhd's or anyone else's life. Word of the raid reached the residents of Kakh Street early the next morning, and Ernst Merser immediately sent a message to Berlin reporting that "some men and supplies [had] been seized," but that even so the Allied leaders were now amongst them, protected, certainly, "but obligingly housed under what is in effect one roof" on Nofel Loshato Street. The response came back, "The director is extremely interested in the future movements of the tenants of

7. Zero Time

this place." Merser should "adapt [his] plans in any way necessary, and proceed."

* * *

In the end it came down to Ernst Merser, Rudolf Holten-Pflug, Misbah Ebtehaj and a dozen remnants of Schellenberg's paratroopers, along with the vestiges of Ebtehaj's camp followers and a small number of other freelance agents. They were hidden in groups of two or three in Kakh Street and other homes of local sympathizers. Following Winifred Oberg's arrest, it was thought best to lodge the surviving conspirators under separate roofs until the moment came to unleash the final assault, with no radio contact between them. If Merser needed to reach a colleague in one of the other residences, as happened twice on November 29, he did so by arranging to board the same city bus, where they would sit wordlessly at the back, side by side. Merser would alight first, leaving behind a package on the seat. He remembered that he also once passed on a blueprint of the British embassy to Ebtehaj through a brush contact, invisible to the casual observer. The wrestler had many valuable qualities as a participant in *Weitsprung*, not least that of sheer muscle. But he was only modestly gifted in the finer art of spycraft. In complete violation of Merser's instructions, Ebtehaj called him several times on his home phone, and continued to press the team leader for more of his apparently unlimited supply of British banknotes. A number of these had found their way into the tills of popular local watering holes like the Owl's Keen, where they were accepted as readily as the local currency, while others were invested in engaging a pair of *jendeh-an*, or prostitutes, in helping pass the strained hours between rehearsals and arrests. Ebtehaj did not indulge in this way, although seeming to take a relaxed view of the matter. But he sharply objected when he came back bearing the top-secret plans to the British embassy to share with three of his associates and found them supine with their guests "all dressed in clothes of the most indecent cut, or no clothes at all," and the house "thick with the aroma of *kif* smoke and spilled wine." At Ebtehaj's insistence, the men promptly sent the "impossible" women on their way, each rewarded by a forged £5 banknote for her trouble.

Merser's final recruit to the conspiracy was a 24-year-old Iranian émigré who called himself Qaleb Chapat, a day worker in the compound on Nofel Loshato Street, where among other duties he swept the floors, scrubbed the lavatories, and on occasion helped in some menial capacity in the kitchen. After Beria had summarily fired half a dozen of the existing waiters because of their "Asiatic" appearance, Chapat was even allowed to serve in the embassy's dining room, which he did with his normal inscrutable efficiency.

Chapat may have been the single dullest member of the legation staff, but he was also, it turned out, one of the most ambitious. Unbeknownst to his Soviet employers, he nursed a burning grievance toward the Moscow government, based on ideological and personal grounds. Chapat's widowed mother and teenage sister had been among an estimated 60,000 villagers forcibly removed from their homes when the Russians occupied Lithuania in June 1940, and had since perished in one of the genocidal bloodlettings that followed the early stages of Operation Barbarossa a year later. It was a powerful incentive for the young man to betray his new employers when the opportunity arose, and he seems to have applied at the embassy in the first place with that one end in mind. Chapat was privy to the behind-the-scenes workings of both halves of the Allied compound, and when approached by one of Ebtehaj's crew he held nothing back. Untypically, he did not ask for money in return for his services. The Lithuanian wanted only to be one of those allowed to squeeze the trigger when the moment came, and "watch Stalin die in his seat, cowering and feeble like a chained dog."

Working the other side of the Long Jump street were men like Paul Siebert, aka Kuznetsov, with his direct connection to Moscow Center, and the young British intelligence officer Percy Downward, who had periodically attached himself to Merser's circle at intervals during the late summer and early fall of 1943, but who seems to have had no access to the final mechanics of the plot. When you add in the oil wrestlers and the women and the counterfeit British banknotes, the conspiracy was all some way removed from the stereotypically efficient Nazi enterprise, and even within the hard core of the operation's inner group, the plates of loyalty frequently shifted around, usually in response to a payment or lack of payment, as much as being bound together by ties of mutual ideological commitment. Merser later wrote, "Many were motivated by personal fortune more than higher allegiance to the Reich, and even while plotting to kill the enemy were also busy spying on each other, as spies generally do."

In this last context, Rudolf Holten-Pflug, while at all times true to the cause of exterminating the Allied chiefs, kept his options open as to the specific means to do so. Holten-Pflug enjoyed the services of his own Iranian interpreter, Karimi, and this individual, to whom he confided the details of Operation Long Jump, considered the Merser plan wholly inadequate to the occasion. A dozen or so men could never hope to successfully infiltrate the Russian or British half of the compound, let alone assassinate their three targets and then make good their escape. What was needed were more fanatically single-minded freedom fighters prepared to do whatever it took to advance the world-shaping events on the night, and for only a modest consideration he, Karimi, knew just where such individuals might be found. Pflug later remarked that a "shadowy group of persons in native garb" had subsequently come and gone from the safe house on Kakh Street during the weekend of November 27–28, but without any definite brief as to their role, if any, in the execution of the plan. They were to liaise only with the interpreter, it was agreed, and thus they too duly joined the complex constellation of local partisan groups and Quenzgut-trained Nazi killers who constituted the human fabric of the mission.

The last significant member of the cabal was the square-jawed former boxer-turned-SS man Lothar Schoellhorn. Schoellhorn had had "a very mixed time in Iran," he admitted, since dropping in and temporarily maiming himself in the process two weeks earlier. Part of the trouble was boredom. With the enemy leaders only slowly making their way to Tehran, their would-be assassins had almost nothing to do, unless they were among those with a taste for the charms of the local *jendeh-an* or Aragh Sagi. As a result, many in the group found themselves effectively unemployed, at least until the time came for the rehearsals in the salt desert and elsewhere. Their other responsibilities were few, and as it was not done for a Nazi saboteur to advertise his presence in the city, Schoellhorn had found that his only real job was to study the various maps of the Nofel Loshato complex Merser brought him, while "endlessly cleaning and re-cleaning our assembled armory." Like most dramatic events in wartime, Operation Long Jump had moments when not much happened. "It sometimes seemed ridiculous to think that this motley crew of actors could do anything much to upset the Allied leadership," Schoellhorn remarked at one gloomy moment.

Ridiculous, perhaps, but not quite impossible.

Long Jump would have to adapt to changing circumstances. It had departed from Walter Schellenberg's original concept of a completely unanticipated flying attack on the Soviet citadel. Too many intending saboteurs had been picked up or lost along the way. The plan had required "complete cohesion, overwhelming numbers, and total shock," Merser had said, and he could now only hope for the last of the three, if even that.[3] He was also troubled, with some reason, both by the equivocal loyalty of Ebtehaj and his band, and the thought that one or more of the arrested men might already have been persuaded to talk. Deeming it too risky to stage another dress rehearsal of the full operation, Merser contented himself with a series of individual briefings of his men, sometimes conducted in one or other of their safe houses, at others by way of a silent brush drop. This was assassination on the hoof, improvised, unpredictable, and, Merser still firmly believed, "ultimately bound to triumph."

For their part, the Allies and more particularly the NKVD clearly knew that there were enemy agents at loose in Tehran. There had been too much human intelligence, too many intercepted signals, and above all too many seizures of the interested parties to permit any other conclusion. But even Lavrentiy Beria's long tentacles didn't quite extend to the inner workings of the plot. A relentless program of ethnic cleansing continued in several concentric circles emanating from Beria's Kremlin eyrie throughout 1943. After the Kalmyks came the Ingush and Chechens, where the NKVD copied SS tactics by forcing an officially tabulated 459,486 civilians onto cattle wagons bound for Siberia. At the village of Khaibakh, 900 miles south of Moscow, Beria's executioners locked 700 "non-transferable" citizens, from newborn babies to elderly grandmothers, in stables and set fire to them, machine-gunning those who broke out. Then it was the turn of the Bulkars, a Caucasian community largely composed of illiterate farmers and shepherds, 37,000 of whom were summarily herded onto trains and sent into permanent exile; and following that the Crimean Tatars, with 165,000 brutally deported, some to the salt mines, others to work as forced labor in munitions factories, along with 6,000 arrested as "wreckers" and 704 shot or hanged as "spies."[4]

Despite these horrors, perpetrated hundreds or thousands of miles away from the Kremlin walls in the name of state security, and notwithstanding the attentions of Nikolai Vlasik and his crew, Stalin's security arrangements could sometimes be surprisingly haphazard. When Mike Reilly of the Secret Service was finally able to inspect the primary conference room set up by the Russians in their Tehran embassy, he found civilians "wandering freely in and out" there, and a pair of unlocked French doors leading to the estate's rear garden where "several individuals stood admiring the ornamental ponds, unmolested by any security." Churchill's bodyguard Walter Thompson was similarly struck by "this strange gulf [between] our hosts' aggressive conduct at some levels, and their utter neglect at others." Curious crowds continued to mill about at the embassy gates throughout the EUREKA conference. "Most of the time," Thompson wrote, "I had my automatic in my hand inside my pocket, hoping that I should not be called upon to use it and thereby make a nice hole in my jacket."[5]

Ernst Merser would have known from his watch at the fishmonger's shop on Ghazali Street of the scene surrounding the embassy complex. The crowds jostling around the gates played to the saboteurs' hand. Merser could never hope to match Lavrentiy Beria in police-state tactics; few humans could. But Beria may have been better at the business of inflicting widespread pain and suffering than managing the details of one citizen's welfare. It was a strange thing, and one that gave Merser renewed hope. The renegade commando unit of Soviet prisoners had failed to materialize to join the ranks of Operation Long Jump as once promised, but Merser could at least call on the services of Qaleb Chapat to act as his inside man.⁶ When the moment came, then, there would be a surface and an underground component to the attack, with some killers dressed in enemy uniform, a diversionary feint at the flank, and a man already in place waiting to do whatever it took to remove Joseph Stalin from the face of the earth.

A sign of Britain's waning influence in the world, or possibly just one of American pragmatism, followed on the morning of Monday, November 29. Anxious to coordinate the "English-speaking position on certain matters" before the next plenary session of the conference, Churchill invited his friend Roosevelt to an informal lunch à deux. "The President however declined, and sent Harriman to me to explain that he did not want Stalin to know that he and I were meeting alone. I was surprised at this," Churchill added, "for I thought we all three should treat each other with equal confidence."⁷

To make matters worse, Roosevelt then met privately with Stalin in the embassy library, while Churchill brooded in his quarters at the far end of the building. The scene had all the ingredients of a classic stage farce, with the Vozhd in the happy position of not only knowing what the Allies were discussing in private, but knowing that they did not know he knew, which might almost have been funny were the future of the world not at stake. During their talk, Roosevelt, who had no written agenda for the conference he had been requesting for two years, mentioned that he was quite fond of the idea of the new international peace-keeping body that became the United Nations, and the Vozhd pretended to be caught unawares by this "bold proposal," despite having just pored through Sergo Beria's account of the American delegates discussing it among themselves the night before. Stalin then returned to his pet theme of Operation Overlord, and Roosevelt agreed that this was a priority, but shared certain of the logistical challenges involved in transporting 160,000 soldiers on 7,000 ships and landing vessels across what proved violently rough seas to storm a 50-mile stretch of heavily fortified French coastline, which both Stalin and his official deputy Marshal Kliment Voroshilov "refused to understand, thinking it was like crossing a Russian river on a raft."⁸

Stalin's essential negotiating technique was that of the coiled snake. He rarely if ever lost his temper, contenting himself with a swift, decisive objection, never raising his voice, if the need arose. He spent much of his time sitting silently, doodling a series of wolf heads in red crayon on the blotter in front of him, sometimes breaking off to gravely inform a speaker of his inconsistency with a sentence, or even a single word, he might have uttered more than an hour earlier. He had no more experience commanding troops than Roosevelt, and considerably less than Churchill, and tended to look for scapegoats when things went wrong at the front.

("I approve the sentence. No appeal. Inform the men," he remarked when ordering the arrest and immediate execution of several senior generals for failing to stem the German advance in the first days of Operation Barbarossa.)[9] Stalin also knew when to strike and when to hold back, sensing when an opponent would yield to flattery more than force. He enjoyed sparring with Churchill but was always deferential to Roosevelt. It was a game of triangles. Thanks to the efforts of the Beria family, Stalin knew that the American president had a high opinion of him, which allowed him to put pressure on the Englishman.

The Allied leaders were united by their mutual opposition to Hitler and his disastrous theory of who should and should not be permitted to inhabit Europe, though even then there was considerable individual latitude when it came to whether they were fighting for national self-interest or in the cause of a holy war. They had little else in common. Stalin was perfectly content to do business with bourgeois politicians like Roosevelt and Churchill, provided he got his way on the matters he deemed essential, such as imposing carbon copies of his regime in eastern Europe. The Vozhd did not necessarily adhere to the Wilsonian ideal that the world had once again to be made "safe for democracy," or that America was the "shining city upon a hill" whose example would inspire the rest of mankind. Churchill was perhaps quicker to the draw than his Atlantic ally to grasp that "Uncle Joe" was not a slightly exotic but fundamentally benign family member, so much as a cold-blooded realist, untouched by Western pieties, with dreams of an eighteenth-century Russian empire.

Politics aside, the Big Three leaders were united chiefly by their mutual enjoyment of tobacco and alcohol, and by the fact that each sired a ne'er-do-well son: both Vasily Stalin and Elliott Roosevelt (present in his father's entourage at Tehran) exploited the family name, enjoyed flying and drinking, often concurrently, and abandoned their long-suffering wives; while in future years Randolph Churchill tinkered with journalism, tried and failed to complete the definitive biography of his father, moved around between a series of glamorous women and foreign hotels, often leaving no forwarding address, and died in 1968 at the age of 57. As one of Stalin's biographers remarks, "Perhaps there is no sadder curse than the gift of a titanic father."[10]

After lunch on November 29, amidst a murmur of well-lubricated conversation, the three national delegations filed into the front hallway of the Soviet embassy, overlooking the bank of whitewashed steps and the crowds at the gate. A dozen NKVD personnel with blue uniforms and drawn, Chicago-style tommy guns shufflingly lined up to one side, one or two of them swaying slightly after the meal, and the dark-suited Mike Reilly and Walter Thompson to the other. A mysterious wooden carrying case sat on the polished table in the middle of the hall. There was a sudden silence, as though someone had abruptly pulled the plug on a gramophone, and the Big Three entered together, Roosevelt seated, Stalin wearing field gray with gold shoulder tabs, Churchill in a crumpled RAF uniform with a sprinkling of cigar ash. A Soviet military band struck up the three anthems. There was another abrupt silence. A British army private then marched to the box on the table, opened it, and extracted a bejeweled sword. The NKVD men resisted any temptation they may have had to intervene at this stage, and the soldier carefully handed the weapon to Churchill, who turned to Stalin.

"I have been commanded by His Majesty to present this sword of honour, whose blade bears the inscription 'To the steel-hearted citizens of Stalingrad, a gift from King George VI as a token of the homage of the British people.'" At that, he handed the weapon to Stalin, who, laying it across his hands, raised it to his lips and kissed it.[11] It was said that there were tears in the Vozhd's eyes. Stalin then extended the gift to Roosevelt, who uttered some polite words of appreciation, and turned to pass it to Marshal Voroshilov, who dropped it with a resounding clang. A moment of farce had intruded on the most solemn of the conference's proceedings. Stalin frowned with irritation, and gave "a frosty, grim, forced-looking smile" but made no further comment. The ceremony broke up after that, and the three national parties dispersed. Voroshilov survived, but later found himself posted to instill socialist fervor in postwar provincial Hungary; he died of natural causes in 1969 at the age of 88.

Following that, the Big Three went out on the steps for a group photograph, and then resumed their debate about whether Churchill's continued talk of Anglo-American mopping-up operations in the Balkans was a legitimate military tactic or, as Stalin believed, further proof of an unwillingness to confront the Germans in western Europe and thus relieve pressure on the Red Army.[12] After several minutes of Churchillian rhetoric on the subject, the Vozhd once again broke off from his wolf's heads and said he "wished to ask the prime minister an indiscreet question, namely do the British really believe in Overlord or are they only saying so to lull the Russians?"[13]

When Churchill went upstairs to his bedroom later that evening he talked about flying home that same night, leaving the Big Two to make arrangements for winning the war without him. His doctor and confidant Charles Moran found him in a fuming sulk, "pacing the floor, mumbling to himself, 'Nothing more can be done here.'" Moran took Churchill's pulse, which was racing.[14] Not for the first time, he advised his patient to drink less; Churchill glared back at him and poured himself another stiff whisky. Moran privately recorded his belief that Churchill would predecease

The Sword of Honour presented to Stalin in the entrance hall of the Soviet embassy in Tehran on November 29, 1943. After raising the sword to his lips and kissing it, Stalin handed it to his colleague Marshal Voroshilov. Voroshilov dropped it.

Stalin and that the "wonderfully genial" Roosevelt would outlast them both.

It was on that same day "that I realised for the first time what a small nation we are," Churchill later said. "There I sat with the great Russian bear on one side of me, with paws outstretched, and on the other side the great American buffalo, and between the two sat the poor little English donkey who was the only one of the three who knew the right way home."[15]

In due course, Churchill, deciding to stay in Tehran after all, changed and went downstairs for dinner, which he fell upon with his usual Rabelsian gusto, and proved the occasion of Stalin's ill-judged suggestion that 50,000 German troops should be rounded up and shot. At that, young Elliott Roosevelt leapt up from his seat to exclaim how positively the average American citizen would react to the Vozhd's initiative, and how sure he was that the United States Army would help to implement it.[16] It again took some time to restore Churchill's equilibrium. Drink flowed freely as

7. Zero Time

the leaders then toasted each other's health, and Stalin spoke of the need to carve up Germany and to treat France as a conquered Axis power rather than a liberated Allied one. At that stage Churchill enquired about what territorial ambitions the Vozhd might have in future years.

Stalin raised his glass once more to the Englishman. "There is no need to discourse on Russian desires at the present time, but when the moment comes we will speak," he replied.[17]

For all its apparent effort and expense, Stalin's personal security suffered a number of fundamental flaws. As we've seen, there was a surprisingly lax attitude toward vetting staff in potentially sensitive positions. A young Red Army cook named Nikolai Kaverin went to Tehran to help prepare the boss's meals. "I secured my job there not just due to my skills as a chef, but also to my sister's relationship with Beria's brother. No other qualification was required."[18] Once installed alongside Qaleb Chapat in the embassy kitchen, Kaverin was under the command of Major Gussef, who similarly owed his progress through the ranks of the NKVD to the patronage of the Beria family. "Each dish leaving the stove was first personally tasted by Gussef and only then carried to the dining-room, where

Stalin, Roosevelt and Churchill pose on the portico of the Soviet embassy immediately after the sword presentation on November 29.

other NKVD men were on hand disguised as waiters with mess jackets and striped pants" (and, in Chapat's case, a murderous secret agenda). Even these arrangements proved less than foolproof, however, because "many of the staff, including Gussef himself, were always leglessly drunk." There had been a "sadly uncouth" scene when the major "vomited copiously" into a large samovar, not so much the result of his selflessly intercepting poison intended for Stalin, Kaverin recalled, but of overdoing the "explosive-grade" vodka. As a rule, the inner guard became increasingly befuddled as the day went on, and by the time night fell, "the Boss was essentially unprotected."

The American and British security details seem to have avoided such excesses but were hamstrung by their national leaders. Roosevelt continually impressed on Mike Reilly that he wanted no "gangsterish, gun-toting cowboys" in his circle at Tehran, and on his side Churchill seems to have looked on the 53-year-old Walter Thompson more as a convivial traveling companion than a specialized, licensed-to-kill bodyguard in any modern sense of the role.

* * *

As Operation Long Jump raced to its world-shaking finale, Ernst Merser was swept up in an exhausting whirlwind of surveillance, planning, espionage, and human-resources duties. On any given day in the week of November 22 he might be coordinating intelligence gathered from the fishmonger's shop, running an inventory of his weapons, briefing one or more of his accomplices in their safe house or by way of a brush drop, yet again haggling with Misbah Ebtehaj and the oil wrestlers about money, while discouraging the latter's visits to the local jezebels, furtively communicating with Schellenberg in Berlin, pumping Qaleb Chapat for further details of the Big Three's schedule, and struggling to keep the whole ungainly enterprise from the eyes of the NKVD units now combing the city. Chapat produced a steady flow of intelligence from the kitchen at Nofel Loshato Street, which was preparing for a climactic banquet-birthday party starting at eight and notionally ending at midnight on the 30th, a seven-course epic progressing from a cheese soufflé through boiled trout and roast turkey dishes to a variety of cakes and ice cream, accompanied by a reported 24 bottles apiece of vodka and brandy, with ample reserves of Georgian white wine for the meal's 32 guests. Major Gussef had appointed two deputy food tasters under his overall command to help with the increased workload on the night.

Some of Merser's local spies proved more adept at their craft than others. Earlier that month, Misbah Ebtehaj had introduced a one-time ring colleague with the evocative name of Furkan Kunt. Kunt was short and stocky, with closely cropped hair and an insinuating, gold-toothed smile. He was also a walking monument to his former calling; both his earlobes had been twisted into purple-skinned lumps of gristle, and an opponent had left a deep scar on one cheek. More to the point, Kunt owned an elderly British-made Brough Superior motorbike, which he was known to drive at high speeds through the streets of Tehran, and as a result he proposed himself as the ideal candidate to tail the Allied leaders in their occasional excursions around the city. He convinced Merser to approve £200 as a fee for his services. The old bruiser duly roared around town for several days in a somewhat haphazard fashion, spent most of his windfall on local *jendeh-an*, caught a nasty skin rash, and eventually filed what amounted to a lengthy travelogue with little useful covert or operational information. He finally admitted to Ebtehaj that he was hopeless as a clandestine agent: "I was not cut out to be invisible."

Luckily, some of Merser's other sources proved more fertile, and by nightfall on the 29th he knew not only of the Allies' next day's dining arrangements but also their likely security plans for the occasion. According to Qaleb Chapat, there would be a heavy NKVD presence on the night, with uniformed men at the doors of each room, others drafted in to patrol the grounds, and guards stationed on the roof of both the British and Russian ends of the building. Impressive sounding as this was, however, no one could say with certainty how those individuals might react in emergency conditions. The secret enemy of many Soviet troops was alcohol. Nikolai Kaverin had first encountered this anomaly in the NKVD's routine while watching Major Gussef "upchuck in the nearest receptacle in the legation pantry." Most of those under Gussef's command struck Kaverin as hardened but histrionic, at once disciplined and rowdy, full of shifting alliances and short-lived feuds amongst themselves. "The man who appeared on duty in his perfectly pressed uniform at noon was often a stumbling buffoon by midnight."

There was also tension between the inner circle of Stalin's praetorian guard under Nikolai Vlasik and that of the ranks of Lavrentiy Beria's NKVD. The latter once wrote, "I shall not rest until I have cleaned out the OGPU [state security agency] pig-sty." The two factions "adopted an intolerable attitude to each other." Beria was continually trotting behind the Vozhd, pouring anti–Vlasik poison into his ear. Just as the leading players in Operation Long Jump occasionally seemed to fall short of the idealized Nazi fighting man, so their opponents at this pivotal moment in history sometimes showed a curious lack of the ruthless martial spirit we associate with Stalin's executioners.

It often seemed that no one quite knew where he stood in the acutely paranoiac court surrounding the Soviet political elite, and perhaps that was just how the Vozhd liked it. Once Stalin and Molotov had steered Churchill back to the dining room after the misunderstanding about their proposal for the 50,000 Wehrmacht executions, heartiness was restored at the table by the boss tormenting his long-serving minion.

"Come here, Molotov, and tell us about your pact with Hitler."[19]

The grisly psychodrama broke up shortly after one in the morning on November 30. Roosevelt was in bed fifteen minutes later; Churchill sat up for a further two hours, depleting his brandy supply and dictating a flurry of cables. Stalin padded back to his dacha in the grounds to read the reports of what his allies were saying about him behind his back while listlessly signing another order for a couple of thousand executions by quota, among them a senior officer who had complained about Vasily Stalin's drunkenness. Only the dauphin's father was permitted such lèse-majesté. After consigning the men to their deaths, the Vozhd stretched contentedly in his chair, patted the seat next to him, and called for Vlasik to join him for a late-night screening of the newly filmed Gary Cooper version of *For Whom the Bell Tolls*. Stalin thought the movie "bourgeois" but sat through the entire three hours. Then, as a sort of nightcap, he signed 142 more death warrants and finally curled up on the simple army cot he always insisted he preferred to a traditional bed.

While Stalin slept, just two miles away on Kakh Street, Ernst Merser finalized the plans for the *Gotterdammerung* of November 30. Merser would lead the frontal assault. Holten-Pflug and his party would make their dank trek through the *qanat* tunnel to emerge toward the rear of the building, where Qaleb Chapat would be waiting to usher them through the kitchen and help dispose of any opposition they might encounter from Major Gussef, then guide them to the adjacent British end of the complex. In the end there was no front-line role for the likes of Franz Mayr, and Vladimir Shkvarzev had mysteriously disappeared without a trace. Lothar Schoellhorn was in charge of the diversionary attack at the embassy's rear walls. He had put his men through rigorous physical training; each one knew how to kill soundlessly using a knife or his bare hands, which Schoellhorn wrote would "balance the numbers between us and our opponents [prior] to the fireworks of the gun and grenade course."

* * *

Tuesday, November 30, dawned bright and warm in Tehran. Franklin Roosevelt woke early, breakfasted heartily, and was wheeled into a downstairs reception room to meet some of his senior foreign policy staff and their Russian counterparts. Even Vyacheslav Molotov—"Old stone arse"— was melted by the president's superficial charm, assuring him that the Russian people were united in their admiration of the way in which he had "cast aside the veil of amity to Hitler [in 1941] and thrown American might into the anti-fascist struggle." At that, Roosevelt exhaled a puff of cigarette smoke and treated his audience to a sphinx-like smile. He was a past master in the art of allowing supplicants to think they had carried their point with him. "People would go away thinking, 'Ah, I've won,' but they hadn't," said Kathleen Harriman. "Roosevelt was the ultimate sophisticate at soft-soaping visitors."[20]

While Molotov went to pay court to the acceptable face of capitalism, the boss, tired after his exertions with the previous night's death rolls, slept soundly until noon. Like Stalin, Churchill was a night bird. He rarely appeared before lunch, having first read the newspapers and fired off another batch of cables that swung between the extremes of bombast and brevity. It was now his 69th birthday, an event, given the tumultuous state of affairs demanding his attention, he greeted with only muted enthusiasm. The premier had extended the amphibian theme while lying in his bath that morning by informing a young female secretary, taking dictation in the next room, that he sometimes felt "like a dead cat floating on the sea, but would be eventually washed up on the shores of victory." Churchill was meeting Stalin for a heart-starting drink at 12:30 p.m. before the Big Three again convened around the compound's newly acquired green baize-covered table and resumed their discussions on the future course of the war over a well-lubricated lunch.

Ernst Merser spent that same morning again checking the weaponry awaiting his assassins' collection at the sandstone house on Kakh Street. The clock was now ticking. The men would assemble at six, just as dusk was falling, and make their separate ways to the Allied compound. After carefully uncrating his remaining supply of Gammons and testing the firing

Vyacheslav Molotov seen in 1945; he remains one of the few men to have shaken hands with both Stalin and Hitler, yet survived to the age of 96.

pins of his guns, Merser applied himself to cleaning the house from top to bottom. In less than 24 hours, he knew, the NKVD would tear it apart, rip up the floorboards, smash down the walls with sledgehammers, and dismantle every stick of furniture, searching for clues about the conspirators and their paymasters. But some ingrained Swiss sense of pride made him determined that the place should look suitably sterile when they came to destroy it. Merser washed the dishes, swept the floors, and then carefully dismantled the radio set he used to communicate with SD headquarters in Berkaerstrasse, walking outside with the fragments in a plain gunnysack of the type commonly used for carrying potatoes, and discreetly tipped the contents down three separate storm-drains. His last message to Berlin had read, in uncoded form, "We have gone as far as we can and are ready to do everything for success. Heavy opposition surrounds us. But we absolutely can not yield in our duty."

Walter Schellenberg's reply read simply, "No alteration of zero time. Heil Hitler."

Shortly after two that afternoon, Rudolf Holten-Pflug conducted a last inspection of the trapdoor to the outlying *qanat* water tunnel where he and his team would muster in a few hours. Lothar Schoellhorn and his crew piled into a nondescript truck and headed for a secluded spot in Tehran's western Varjin hills for a last-minute rehearsal of their role in *Weitsprung*. Schoellhorn believed that there would be "sustained and intense [*heftig*]" opposition to their arrival on the enemy grounds, but the result would be an "incredible party" and "a bit of fun," terms he preferred when briefing his men to words such as violent, bloody, and potentially suicidal. On the road they passed a green-painted Soviet GAZ-MM truck with a couple of dozen Red Army soldiers sitting stony-faced in the back, heading in the direction of the embassy, possibly some of the very men they would engage in a firefight before the day was out. Winston Churchill would remember that the NKVD had insisted on "search[ing] our Legation from top to bottom, looking behind every door and under every cushion" before his birthday celebrations got underway that night.[21] "For the first time [in Tehran] I felt that conditions had been created that made the assassin's task, if not impossible, one which surely amounted to a sacrificial role on their part."

A similar conclusion was forming in the mind of a lesser public figure than Churchill but, in his way, one equally renowned as a fighter. Misbah Ebtehaj had never previously shied from a clash of wills with an opponent during his years in the ring. But now, at the twelfth hour, he admitted to doubts about the wisdom of a plan which called for him to run across the front lawn of a heavily guarded foreign embassy compound and up the building's grand entrance steps, some of his party fanning out to the dining-room patio doors and others continuing their progress through the main hallway, and then storming in with bombs and guns blazing to kill Roosevelt, Stalin, and Churchill. The assault was "not completely risk free," Ebtehaj noted with some restraint, and even then there remained the small matter of the men's escape. It was enough to make even the one-time all-in wrestling champion pause for thought, and now, with just hours remaining for him to consider the matter, Ebtehaj did so.

It wasn't that Ebtehaj lacked either moral fiber or the necessary pro–German fervor, he stressed in a four o'clock meeting with Ernst Merser, merely that he expected his widow and numerous orphans to be properly cared for. Merser replied coldly that he had already distributed more than enough of the Reich's hard-earned foreign capital for the wrestler and his associates to use as they saw fit, and that now was not the time to further negotiate the matter. Ebtehaj's Nazi zeal seems to have dimmed a little as a result of this rebuff, because less than an hour later he was in conference with his friend and fan Mervyn Wollheim, a wealthy American expatriate who dabbled in archaeology and was a fixture on the local martial-arts circuit. Wollheim listened to what his hero had to say, and then without further ado drove to the nearest U.S. Army base on Sa'adi Street, presented his passport to the guard, and was shown to the military police office on the top floor, stiff with suspicion that particular week and presided over by a young, gum-chewing major from Butte, Montana, called Forest Manure—another one of those faintly comic-opera names that punctuate the story—who listened intently to his visitor's opening remarks, posed a supplemental question or two, and then picked up the red phone on his desk and dialed the number of the U.S. embassy.

As these events unfolded at one end of Tehran, and Merser completed his housekeeping duties and readied his arsenal of weapons at the other, Churchill sat in a little-used upstairs library at Nofel Loshato Street to discuss matters of a "sensitive nature" over a pipe-opening glass of the chilled vodka his guest Stalin brought him as the first of many birthday toasts he received during the day. Little did either man know it, but they were now in greater personal jeopardy than at any time since the start of the war. It was another example of the strange extremes that run as a through-line to Operation Long Jump: the civilized, almost courtly debating of world affairs between the two heads of government, and only a mile or so away, in the houses and sewers of west Tehran, the gathering of the band of would-be assassins and freelance saboteurs set on killing them.

The exchange between the Marxist strongman and the apotheosis of capitalism was remarkably cordial.

Churchill began by remarking that he happened to be half-American and had a great affection for the American people. Nonetheless, there were certain things he wished to say without his friend Roosevelt being present. There had again been differences of emphasis, Churchill confided, between London's and Washington's preferred military strategies. The Americans wanted a concerted Allied amphibious attack in the Bay of Bengal against the Japanese, but Churchill didn't like it. Instead, the British wished to devote every possible resource to the long-awaited liberation of Europe in the spring. If anyone, it was Roosevelt who was now impeding the progress of what became the D-Day invasion, and he had the documents and cables to prove it.[22]

Churchill's play for Stalin's affections was at best only a partial account of the true state of affairs. As Roosevelt had made clear, he was committed both to the defeat of the Japanese and the impending launch of the second front. But Churchill had played his cards well. Stalin had walked into the meeting as a partner with Roosevelt against Churchill in the matter of Operation Overlord. He walked out again as part of a de facto alliance with Churchill against Roosevelt.

"The Prime Minister went on to say that 'Overlord' would certainly take place provided the enemy did not bring into France larger forces than the Americans and British could gather there," the minutes continue. "Supposing the Germans had thirty or forty divisions in place, he did not think the forces [the Allies] were going to put across the Channel could hold on. But if the Red Army engaged the enemy and held them in Italy, and perhaps the Yugoslavs and possibly the Turks came into the war, then he was hopeful we could win the day."

"Marshal Stalin said that as regards the Red Army the first steps of 'Overlord' would have a good effect, and that if he knew the operation was going to take place in May or June, he could prepare blows against Germany," a promise the Vozhd somehow later forgot.

In conclusion, Churchill noted that "he could not say when 'Overlord' would begin without the President, but that an answer would be given later that morning, and he thought that the Marshal would be satisfied."[23]

The Big Three then sat down to talk over lunch, and Stalin was indeed content with the result. He essentially got everything he desired. Toward the end of the meal, Roosevelt took the opportunity to read out a prepared statement of intent. "We will launch Overlord during May, in conjunction with a supporting operation against the South of France, on the largest scale that is permitted by the landing-craft available at that hour." Sometimes the Allied conference seemed almost like a board game, but with the fates of real people at stake rather than just plastic chips. In his diary, Roosevelt wrote, "The meetings have been going well—tho' I found I had to go along with the Russians on military plans. Today the British came along too, to my great relief."[24]

7. Zero Time

* * *

After the war, Walter Schellenberg similarly reflected on the strange tendency of history to turn on the most seemingly trivial of details. The Germans had devoted months of meticulous planning and "immeasurable resources—men and machines, local agents, recruitments, deceptions, bribes of every size, parachute drops into enemy terrain, and untold thousands of Reichsmarks and foreign treasure"—not to mention all those sometimes testy meetings back in Berlin with the likes of Kaltenbrunner and Canaris—and now the whole grand edifice of *Unternehmen Weitsprung* was about to crumble on the word of a single disaffected Turko-Iranian oil wrestler. "We had cleared every other obstacle, but we should not have relied on men of dubious allegiance to the Reich," Schellenberg was left to admit.[25]

Even so, Misbah Ebtehaj and his friend Mervyn Wollheim may not have been the only vipers in the *Weitsprung* nest. There was also the chain of events set in play on the night of November 28 by the sharp-eyed Red Army private Gevork Vartanian. His report of the suspicious trucks rumbling through the streets of nighttime Tehran with their camel escort led the NKVD to raid the house near the shah's palace where some of Ebtehaj's men were billeted. The Russians had taken a large supply of guns and bombs into their possession, although the building's occupants could not shed any light on the weapons' intended use. All of them were shot dead or at least mortally wounded in the raid. But it would not have escaped the most obtuse of minds—and Lavrentiy Beria's was far from obtuse—that their discovery of such a significant arsenal and the presence nearby of the Allied heads of government might not be entirely coincidental. "I want you to know that I will turn this town inside out, if necessary, to determine the nature of the plot," Beria wrote in a hitherto secret file to Molotov on November 29. "My personal opinion is that the wreckers are deeper entrenched here than we know, and their plans still proceed. We will redouble our efforts against them."[26]

Other members of the Allied security forces largely agreed with Beria. "Tehran was a fortress, but a besieged one," Mike Reilly later wrote of the conference. Nazi operatives sneaking into it were "a perpetual threat, despite those assets successfully infiltrated in their ranks." One of these was the man calling himself Paul Siebert, whose inside knowledge of Operation Long Jump had already been relayed back to Moscow. This identified Hans Ortel and Roman Gamotha as the chief conspirators. Siebert was ultimately unable to provide more current information than that, because on the night of November 29, his body was found in a Tehran alley. He had been shot twice through the back of the head, and his throat cut for good measure, by a party or parties unknown.

Lothar Schoellhorn showed as much determination for *Weitsprung* to succeed as Lavrentiy Beria did for it to fail. Schoellhorn's breach of the compound's rear walls would be "more than just a few colored rockets [*feuerwerkskorper*]," he wrote in a note now in the hands of the Russian state archive. He had other means of distracting the enemy guards: simulated raids led by *panzerschreck*, or bazooka, strikes on the embassy's northwest and northeast corners, and even a parachute drop that consisted of four molded plastic dummies launched by a catapult on a corner of nearby Nersi Street, each weighing about fifty pounds and strapped to an automatically opening Iranian *baldachin* sheet, much in the guise of a circus performer being shot out of a cannon. The idea was to keep the NKVD and Secret Service looking the other way; the upper, comparatively isolated part of the compound had to remain the attack site uppermost on their minds, with the light Russian guard there suddenly confronted by an apparent land-air invasion, and the troops at the front scrambling to reinforce them.

It might even have worked: a Russian *tekhnicheskiy chertezh* blueprint of the embassy at the time of the conference, also now in the state archives, with the numbers and locations of Beria's security forces, reflected their belief that any potential strike would come at the building's front gate, or be targeted at Stalin's dacha in the grounds. Five minutes of the mostly imaginary attack to the north would have left the way relatively clear for the Merser and Holten-Pflug units to strike simultaneously from above and below. The map shows just four NKVD men stationed in the dining room, one in each corner, where the Allies would celebrate Winston Churchill's birthday. Mike Reilly and his small Secret Service force were confined to two upstairs rooms for the evening, and, almost incredibly, with that touch of the haphazard never far removed from the British security arrangements, Churchill's guard-companion Walter Thompson had obtained permission to dine privately at his favorite Tehran curry restaurant, with the request only that he return to base by midnight.

At 5:15 that evening, 45 minutes before zero hour, Ernst Merser began distributing his carefully concealed weapons. The men then changed into a variety of dun-gray or brown two-piece tunics, some of them further staining these with tea from the Kakh Street kitchen, their faces darkened, and one or two of them topped off with dreadlocks of greenery, for an overall effect that made the killers look like shaggy-faced yetis or upright goats when they walked, but turned them into innocuous foliage when they crouched behind a shadowy brick wall.

By six o'clock, the Holten-Pflug party, their watches synchronized with Merser's, were already in place at the hatch of the outlying *qanat* water tunnel. When the moment came they would have a precisely measured 85 minutes to slosh their way through nearly three miles of narrow, fetid corrugated pipe to their rendezvous with Qaleb Chapat, and then pass swiftly through the embassy kitchen to attach themselves to Merser's team. Conventional wisdom said that you needed a force of men on the inside to successfully invade a guarded enemy base like that at Nofel Loshato, and in the immediate run-up to Operation Long Jump Chapat had managed to insinuate two more young Iranian kitchen porters onto the staff. It was strange how little attention was paid to the legation's hiring procedures that critical last week of November. Like Chapat, both nursed private grievances against the Allied occupiers, and both were physically fit and had been trained on every kind of close-combat weapon, including the enemy's. Along with Chapat, they were a cross between a fifth-column commando unit and a tribal fighting force, and each was fully prepared to die for his cause.

At 6:20 p.m., Merser and his men completed their preparations; this being 1943, nobody hugged or offered an inspiring high-five, although one or two muted words of prayer were heard around the room. The tommy guns had been oiled, the pistols loaded, and the remaining Gammon bombs carefully distributed according to need. Two civilian trucks stood around the corner, ready to drive the team the short distance to their target. Some of the men had a last ration of Aragh Sagi. One or two of the more devout Iranians kissed photographs of a *hilya*, or holy scroll, believing that doing so would protect them from trouble both in this world and the next. The pictures symbolized the connection between the higher need to sometimes shed blood in exchange for the promise of eternal salvation. "They fingered the images reverently, a tear sometimes rolling down a man's darkened cheek," Merser wrote.

While the ecumenical band of assassins stood in a tense locker-room assembly, ready to file out to their waiting trucks, their intended victims completed their final official round of talks at the embassy. President Roosevelt took the opportunity to repeat that Overlord would take place in May 1944, and hinted that George C. Marshall, the U.S. Army chief of staff, would command it. Churchill got a head start on the night's proceedings by toasting everyone present, and proposed they issue a communiqué to the world indicating that the Allies had reached military decisions of the highest importance. "The key note to be sounded is one of brevity, mystery, and a foretaste of impending doom for Germany," he added, and on that note the meeting adjourned until dinner.[27]

The final act of the conference was now about to begin, and Churchill was again at center stage. "The table that night was set with British elegance," U.S. diplomat Chip Bohlen wrote. "The crystal and silver sparkled in the candlelight." Roosevelt sat on Churchill's right, Stalin on his left, the Westerners in black tie, the boss in an unfrivolous high-collared military uniform. To the prime minister's daughter, Stalin was "a frightening figure with his slit, bear eyes [who] pounced on every remark with a dry and often sly humor."[28] The list of those toasted that night was long. A discordant note arose when Roosevelt raised his glass to Sir Alan Brooke, the British army chief of staff, and Stalin, briefly coming to his feet, remarked that Brooke had thus far "failed to display any real feelings of friendship towards the Red Army, and that [he] hoped in future he would be able to remedy this flaw." Brooke held his ground and replied that, just as Hitler had been misled by the appearance of dummy tanks and planes on the Eastern front, the Vozhd had failed to observe "those signs of goodwill I have consistently displayed to the Soviet troops."[29] Men had been removed to Siberia for less forthright responses. Stalin shook his head and continued sitting there, not actively smiling but not immediately calling for a new death list, either.

After that there was a lull in the proceedings, and it was left to Churchill to restore the convivial mood by reminding the room that he had "devoted his entire life to the cause of defending the weak and the helpless." His Soviet guest, Churchill continued, in something of a non-sequitur, had fully earned the title "Stalin the Great." Roosevelt then added his own effusive tribute to Churchill, and "express[ed] deep joy in the friendship that has developed between us during the war." In the midst of this wholesale outbreak of goodwill, it was left to Stalin to again lower the temperature by reminding his British hosts that the Red Army had fought heroically for two years but that the Russian people would have tolerated nothing less from their armed forces. The Vozhd added that those persons of medium courage, and even cowards, had bravely defended the mother country. Those who didn't, he added, were shot.[30]

* * *

As darkness fell over Tehran on the evening of Tuesday, November 30, Ernst Merser completed his weapons check, signaled for the two waiting trucks to move from around the corner to the front door of the house ready for departure, muttered a few final words of encouragement to his men, and silently prayed that there would be no last-second pounding on the door that heralded the arrival of the NKVD security forces.

It came at exactly 6:37 p.m., and was not distinguished by the restraint of the visitors' behavior.

According to the survivors' memory, it was unusually quiet in the house for a moment or two immediately beforehand, something like the stillness of a battlefield just ahead of a full-scale artillery barrage. Then they briefly felt the vibration of a heavy vehicle approaching rapidly up the street. Soon afterward, a draft of fresh air which made the curtains rustle at the upstairs window told them that the door had been opened, or kicked in, to be more exact, by one or more booted intruders. The first Russian word they heard was *Stoy!* A thunderous burst of machine gun fire reinforced the order. In less time than it took to register what was happening, Soviet troops with weapons drawn stormed in and pushed everyone against a wall. There was no real opposition, although one of Ebtehaj's surviving clique chose to jump through a closed window, whether as a suicide bid or merely to flee was never known, and fell twelve feet to the cobbled street, where he was summarily shot dead by more Red Army troops as he staggered to his feet to run off. The rest of the intending assassins went quietly into captivity. It later transpired they were the relatively lucky ones. The NKVD also took the opportunity to raid several other addresses around Tehran at the same time, and there their tactics were more those of the feral hand-to-hand combat lately seen at Stalingrad. The Russians simply pulled up outside each successive house and went in equipped with guns and explosives, throwing a preliminary grenade ahead of them as they entered. The ensuing blast was generally enough to stun anyone inside, if not to blow them to pieces.[31]

There was an especially grim scene at a residence on Kousha Street in north-central Tehran, where some of Winifred Oberg's old set had been prematurely toasting the deaths of the Allied leaders with the help of a bottle of Aragh Sagi. When the Reds came for them, one of the men sprawled in a chair in the upstairs room leaped to his feet and seized the first weapon that

Alan Brooke, the British chief of staff who dared to challenge Stalin in Tehran. Brooke preferred to spend much of his later life working with animals.

came to hand, a single-shot Panzerfaust high-explosive launcher. Trying to set off an anti-tank warhead in his drunken state, he burnt the skin off both his legs with the exhaust flame. The Russians then liberally sprayed the room with machine gun fire, tearing men and furniture to shreds. The only German to survive was the man who had incinerated the lower half of his body and fallen semi-conscious below the subsequent line of fire as a result. The NKVD soldiers dragged him to the street, his body still smoldering from the Panzerfaust blowback, and threatened to string him up unless he talked, but he died before he could tell them anything.

It remains unclear if the Soviet troops were finally tipped off by Paul Siebert before his demise, by Misbah Ebtehaj's discussions with Mervyn Wollheim and all that ensued, or by the chain of events that began with the young Red Army conscript Gevork Vartanian's spotting of the telltale truck-and-camel convoy rumbling through the streets of nighttime Tehran. Possibly it was a combination of all three; to this day the Russian archives are silent on the subject. But when the dust settled, the principals of Operation Long Jump found themselves in enemy hands, and the rest of their team either lay dead or had been marched away at gunpoint.

As two-thirds of the conspiracy broke down in chaos, and the Red Army trucks peeled away with their prisoners, Rudolf Holten-Pflug and his underground party waiting a few feet under the city streets received a coded walkie-talkie message from a lookout who had escaped detection at the other end of Kakh Street. "If attack has not already begun," it said, "halt and return to await further orders. If it has, do your best." Holten-Pflug rightly deduced that this meant he and his men were on their own, and that burrowing their way in unaccompanied to the heavily fortified embassy compound would be futile. This would not be the blaze of glory they had all sought. It would be a suicide mission. They crouched back down the sewer. Thirty minutes later, Pflug and his men silently reemerged at their starting point and melted away into the night.

Three miles away in the more refined surroundings of Nofel Loshato Street, the mood that night gradually progressed from one of comparative solemnity to something like that of a medieval banquet with submerged frat-house tendencies. There was nothing for Qaleb Chapat to do but grit his teeth and keep serving the guests copious amounts of food and drink. The nearest the evening came to disaster was when one of Chapat's colleagues wheeled out a dessert trolley containing two mountainous ice-cream pyramids with "a base of frosting one foot square and four inches deep," a flickering candle inside and a long, polished steel tube rising out of the middle on which rested a gold plate dripping in a lake of syrup and icing sugar. As this towering confection approached the table, Brooke noticed that the candle was rapidly melting the ice foundation and "now looked more like the Tower of Pisa." The British chief of staff had just time to shout a warning to his neighbors when "with the noise of an avalanche, the whole wonderful construction slid over our heads and exploded in a clatter of plates."[32] It's not recorded if Beria's watching agents reached for their weapons, but no one died as a result. Recovering first, Churchill suggested that as an "alternative continuation of the meal in accordance with the resources now available"—that is, without the ice cream—the guests restrict themselves merely to cheese, cake, fruit, brandy, and cigars. Roosevelt and Stalin agreed.

Many more toasts of a patriotic or personal nature followed as the night proceeded, concluding with a spirited communal rendition of "Happy Birthday to You" and the unusual spectacle of the stout British prime minister "dancing a gay and abandoned hornpipe."[33] In the early hours of December 1, Roosevelt was discreetly carried out of the room, and many lesser guests later followed in the same posture. Churchill wrote, "I went to bed tired out but content, feeling sure that nothing but good had been done. It certainly was a happy occasion for me."

The next morning, Roosevelt employed some crude but effective reverse psychology, "teas[ing] Churchill about his Englishness, about John Bull, about his cigars, about his habits" to win points with Stalin. It worked. "Winston got red and scowled, and the more he did so, the more Stalin smiled. Finally Uncle Joe broke out into a deep, hearty guffaw, and for the first time in three days I saw light."[34]

While the Vozhd chortled at the Briton's discomfort, Roosevelt seized the opportunity to glancingly mention the matter of Finland, then fighting on the German side, and how he hoped it would survive as an independent state, free of undue Soviet influence, after the war. Stalin abruptly stopped laughing. He was not prepared to "finally discuss the principle of self-determination at this time," he announced. Perhaps the Finns might be called upon to pay reparations for a few years, the Vozhd nonetheless continued, now seeming to consider the matter for the first time, before adding magnanimously that a full-scale Soviet presence in their country was "not inevitable." Roosevelt went on to reveal that he had decided to run for a fourth term in office—news even to his inner circle—and would prefer "not to visit the question of Poland at present," lest he commit to some stance unpopular "with the six or seven million American voters of Polish extraction." This, too, was broadly agreeable to the Soviet ruler.

Later, when Roosevelt retired for his afternoon nap, Stalin tore a sketch map out of one of the morning's newspapers, casually daubed half a dozen slashing lines on it in red crayon, and slid this across the table to Churchill, who amended it with a few strokes of his own pen. The future of millions of European citizens was being decided by two hungover men

FDR adviser Harry Hopkins, Stalin, and in the background Vyacheslav Molotov (known, with varying degrees of affection, as "Old Stone Arse") in the garden of the Soviet embassy in Tehran, December 1, 1943.

doodling on a flimsy scrap of newsprint in a small room in Iran. The British foreign secretary Anthony Eden later recalled that this was the moment he had realized that the war was effectively won. There was no joy on his face, or those of the other delegates in the room, at this particular insight. They were exhausted, and any relief they may have felt was tempered by their remaining doubts about what the future might hold in store.

* * *

As the Allied leaders were listlessly carving up the future map of Europe, a new plan was being hurriedly drawn up in a nearby darkened basement room to assassinate all three of them before they left Tehran.

After receiving the cryptic signal from the lookout on Kakh Street, Rudolf Holten-Pflug and the small subterranean component of *Unternehmen Weitsprung* had swiftly made their way back to a still-undiscovered cellar hideout a mile or so to the north, close to the site of the city's main children's hospital. It did not take them long to grasp that Ernst Merser and the rest of their co-conspirators were now in Russian hands, and that they, too, were in grave peril of capture as a result. Their minds raced over the grim variety of NKVD torture methods that might even now be in use to loosen their colleagues' tongues. At the very least, the situation called for a thorough reappraisal of their options. The original plan, parceled out between the three attack groups for a synchronized assault on the embassy, was no longer viable. But they had come too far to abandon *Weitsprung*'s central thrust altogether. That night, after a fortifying meal of stewed couscous and tea heated by a spirit stove, followed by a generous tot of Aragh Sagi, Pflug lay in his sleeping bag on the stone floor, peering through the room's barred window at the somehow suggestive flashes of lightning that periodically lit up the gothic turrets of the hospital next door. In the morning, while the men were quietly discussing matters between themselves and Holten-Pflug was checking their remaining weapons, a coded message came over their portable radio receiver. It read,

> He [the enemy] must be met while he may. It grows darker in December very fast.

A whispered conversation took place amongst the men in light of this second cryptic incoming message in less than twelve hours. The first part of Walter Schellenberg's signal seemed clear enough to the saboteurs as they huddled together in their underground retreat. They must still strike. But was the reference to the fast-approaching night an observation on the optimum moment to regroup for a final assault, or did it perhaps convey some broader reference to the war situation as a whole? Either way, they urgently needed more intelligence about the Allied leaders' plans. As the men debated the point further, they suddenly heard the noise of rapidly approaching steps above them on the street, followed a second later by an ear-splitting explosion. But then, instead of the sound of Russian boots at the door came a shriek of children's laughter. The noise had been nothing more than a firecracker being set off somewhere above their heads in early celebration of December's Suri festival. Fingers trembling, Holten-Pflug laid down the machine gun he had snatched up from the floor, and then watched as one of his colleagues carefully removed his grip from the pull cord of a "potato masher" grenade that would otherwise have detonated approximately four seconds later. "I have never been so scared in my life," he admitted.

The information Holten-Pflug sought was at a premium just then, because not even the Allies were entirely certain of their forward plans. Roosevelt had originally meant to leave Tehran at some stage the following Friday, December 3. But then the U.S. Army meteorologist accompanying the party had warned that a storm was brewing, and that the president's Skymaster could expect severe turbulence if it waited a further two days.

The money line of the report was that they should leave within 24 hours, or else be prepared to sit it out for another week or more. Shortly after lunch on December 1, Roosevelt ordered the plane to be ready for takeoff the following morning, and then signed a letter to the young Shah of Iran.

> I have received the magnificent carpet, the gracious gift of Your Majesty. This will serve to remind both myself and the American people of the generous hospitality of the Iranian nation.... Your Majesty's invitation to be a guest at your palace as well as to provide a guard of honor at the airport has been conveyed to me, and I am most appreciative. Much to my regret, the new circumstances of my visit make it impossible for me to avail myself of these kind offers, much as I would have liked to do so. I shall therefore leave Iran with regret at not having had an opportunity to extend my acquaintance with you and to have seen more of your country and your people.[35]

It was decided that after dinner that night Roosevelt would be driven to the U.S. Army base at Amirabad, ten miles north of the city and ironically close to the scene of many of the earlier German parachute drops in the Elburz hills. The following morning the president would be taken to the Gale Morghe airfield, where his waiting Skymaster would return him to Cairo. There Roosevelt planned to reconvene with Churchill, now joined by the president of Turkey, in a bid to have the last finally join the war on the Allied side. Stalin would meanwhile take his Tupolev back to Baku, and board his private train home to Moscow. The Big Three would thus all have safely left Iran by noon on December 2, ready, Churchill wrote, to "plunge Hitler into his last crisis."

At some stage in the afternoon of December 1, these plans became known to the various political and civilian staff on duty at Nofel Loshato Street, who could hardly have failed to notice the telltale signs of large numbers of uniformed personnel loading monogrammed dispatch boxes and other luggage into cars waiting in the embassy forecourt at intervals throughout the day. Around six that same evening, Qaleb Chapat managed to slip away on the pretense of "looking for mushrooms" for the Allied guests' last meal together to meet Rudolf Holten-Pflug in an ill-lit native sook where they pretended to be inspecting the goods at either end of a vegetable cart. Chapat told his contact what he knew about the Allies' preparations to leave the compound and about all the talk of planes flying out in the morning. A number of significant dots began to connect in Holten-Pflug's mind. The primary connection was that the last possible chance he or anyone else might have to see *Unternehmen Weitsprung* to fruition would be to strike the departing leaders at the airfield. The elaborate plans for the whole operation, which had involved months of preparation in the spy schools of Germany and on the ground in the darkened hills and chaotic streets of Tehran, with the expenditure of many thousands of

7. Zero Time   189

legitimate Reichsmarks and spurious British pounds, were now down to the improvised, last-ditch efforts of half a dozen determined men armed with MP 40 submachine guns and a crate of grenades. Many high-profile assassinations have succeeded with less.

* * *

When the final plenary session of the Allied conference convened at six that evening, Churchill and Roosevelt enquired of Stalin if he was prepared to at least "normalize" his country's relations with Poland after the war. The Vozhd replied smoothly that the Polish people would certainly have the opportunity to express their wishes "in the most democratic fashion." But perhaps his version of democracy was not quite that of the Western powers. It would be another 48 years until the next entirely free Polish parliamentary elections. Churchill reminded the room that "it would be difficult not to take cognizance of the fact that the British people had gone to war [in 1939] because of Poland," and, apparently jolted by this thought, Stalin replied that the Soviet Union would not only support Polish reconstruction but also an extension of her borders—west into Germany, naturally, not east into Russia. On that note, the trio ate their last meal together, shook hands, and went their separate ways.

At first light on December 2, Rudolf Holten-Pflug began his final briefing of his team on the day's activities. The plan was simple. The men would drive out to Gale Morghe and install themselves behind a suitable rocky knoll, just out of sight of any Allied security forces. A sympathetic Iranian accomplice would signal from a room overlooking the airport's main gate when the three motorcades swept past, or for that matter when any one or two of them did so. Even a single dead enemy chief would be a major coup for Holten-Pflug's purposes. When they got the word, the assassins would take off in two previously hijacked jeeps, three men in each, screech past their targets, firing tommy guns and pistols and hurling grenades, before veering off into the desert. There was nothing more sophisticated to it than that. It sounds suicidal, and it may well have been so. The killers were heavily outnumbered, and they would have to pass over nearly a half-mile of open taxiway from their hiding place to reach their victims. On the other hand, they would once again have the element of surprise, and, as Holten-Pflug reminded them, one truly determined man with a gun and a bomb, let alone half a dozen of them, can often prevail.

The rump of the original *Unternehmen Weitsprung* team enjoyed one other advantage when it came to their twelfth-hour attempt on the Allied warlords. One of the vanished Misbah Ebtehaj's wrestling companions, known only as Gorechi, had quietly entered a regional police station late on the night of December 1—not to sell out his sometime colleagues, but to confer with a contact there with inside knowledge of the Allies' travel plans. Gorechi returned to the basement hideout later that night, "beaming with pleasure." The three distinguished passengers, he announced, would arrive at Gale Morghe in a synchronized convoy shortly before ten the following morning, pose for a final group photograph, then make for their respective aircraft. The team's spotter in his room at the gate would signal at the precise moment the cars passed beneath him on their way to the waiting planes. Gorechi's contact also passed on details of the Tehran police detail expected to accompany the departing VIPs, which turned out to be surprisingly small. Lavrentiy Beria did not altogether trust the local law enforcement agencies, which he later wrote had been composed largely of "contract criminals, deviants, and shirkers from the army," and had rebuffed most of their offers of help. The Allied leaders would effectively be protected only by their traveling security teams of varying efficiency. Gorechi passed all this news on to Holten-Pflug late that Wednesday night. It was, the latter said with thumping understatement, a "not unhappy development."

But at the moment Holten-Pflug was making his final dispositions in the early hours of Thursday, the NKVD, too, was on the move, alerted by the same elements that had earlier led them to Ernst Merser and his group, possibly now reinforced by that cell's tortured confessions. Twenty-four of Beria's men quickly surrounded the subterranean hideout by the hospital at dawn on December 2. An NKVD officer with a loudhailer warned those inside in both Russian and German that anyone who attempted to escape would be shot, and at that same instant, soldiers went clattering down the narrow staircase to the room where the men crouched over their half-drawn weapons. The darkness was suddenly broken by the flash of an explosion. One of Holten-Pflug's assassins had deliberately pulled the pin from a grenade and blown himself up, severely injuring at least one of his companions in the process, preferring to take control of his destiny rather than surrender to the hated Ivans. When the smoke cleared, one man lay dead, another was on fire and screaming for help, and three others stood, paralyzed with varying degrees of shock, their hands up, pressed flat against the wall.

The NKVD officer with the loudhailer marched in, briskly beat the burning man until the flames on his back went out, and then summarily ordered all four survivors up into the street. The column set off toward a row of Red Army GAZ trucks parked on the corner, a Russian soldier holding a gun on each prisoner.

A few yards farther on, the men were led from the street into a narrow alley, supposedly to take a shortcut through it to their convoy. Once there, the Soviet guards abruptly grabbed the prisoners by the scruff of the collar, shoving them forward to stand with their faces against a wall, the cold barrel of a gun pressing into the back of each neck. There was a volley of shots. Four bodies fell to the ground. The NKVD killers left them lying there. Amazingly, Holten-Pflug survived to drag himself away and tell the tale. The Russian bullet had passed through his neck, enough to knock him, apparently lifeless, to the ground, but providentially missing the jugular vein or any other vital organs. Wisely, he played dead.

Later that morning, Holten-Pflug managed to stagger to the nearby home of a Nazi sympathizer who practiced as one of Tehran's only three licensed veterinarians. Pflug collapsed on a short table normally reserved for treating sick or malnourished dogs, of which there were many in the city, to receive a field dressing and a shot to prevent infection. If the bullet had been an inch lower, it would have struck his spinal cord and in all likelihood caused permanent paralysis.

The Tokarev pistol fire that cut down the final Long Jump operatives were not the only shots fired in anger that day in Tehran. Beria's thugs had directly or indirectly accounted for only five of the remaining assassins. A sixth man had left the basement only minutes before the Russian troops arrived, with orders to reconnoiter the street above them before they set off on their raid. It's said that this individual, Yousef Khatib, managed to escape the NKVD dragnet and make his way to the airfield by frantically pedaling a stolen wheeled kebab cart, although this last detail has proven difficult to corroborate, and when the time came to emerge from behind the rocky knoll and get off a burst of machine gun fire in the direction of a departing black Packard he took to be Stalin's. Or so Khatib later suggested. It has to be said that there are implausible points about the story, which neither Beria nor Stalin's private bodyguard Nikolai Vlasik mentioned in their later accounts of the Tehran conference, although set against this, the daily eight-page *Ettelaat* newspaper for December 4, 1943, speaks of "disturbances" [*faits*] at the airfield that morning, with "piles of turf and masonry hurled into the air as guns blazed at some unknown force" across the runway. This unknown force may have been a sniper, a profession at which many Iranians excelled. "One had the feeling that two armed groups were engaging each other even as the planes began to accelerate and then ascend," one report read.

Whatever the truth, all three Allied leaders were safely in the air not long after the hazy winter sun rose over the eastern Elburz mountains that warm Thursday morning. Operation Long Jump had finished without having achieved its objective. Two thousand miles away in Berlin, Adolf Hitler summoned his senior military advisers later that day to tell them that he was certain that Operation Overlord would take place in May the following year. The next months would be spent strengthening German defenses on a 1,700-mile-long front from Norway to the Franco-Spanish border to prepare for the climactic showdown. This, Hitler remarked, would "decide the war."[36]

* * *

On December 7, while on his way home from Cairo to Washington, Roosevelt told General Eisenhower that he would command Overlord; it was the second anniversary of the attack that had brought the U.S. into the war, and Eisenhower later wrote that the date "fittingly represented the beginning of the end" of the conflict. Churchill meanwhile came down with pneumonia and ended up convalescing at a villa in Tunisia, where Walter Thompson may have saved his chief's life after all by resuscitating him when his breathing stopped during the night.[37] For his part, Stalin appears to have been quietly content with the results of Tehran, and positively euphoric on safely reaching Baku after the second and final air journey of his life. In his moment of triumph, he decided to personally get behind the wheel of his bulletproof limousine for an inspection tour of the town but went too fast and collided with another car. The woman driving it "nearly expired" when she saw with whom she'd crashed. "It's not your fault," the Vozhd assured her, retaining his good humor. "Blame the war. Our car is armored and didn't suffer. You can repair yours."[38] Stalin would ensure that the next tripartite Allied conference took place on Russian soil.

After duly convening at Yalta in February 1945, the Big Three sat down again at Potsdam, outside Berlin, following their victory over Germany later that summer. Roosevelt had died, age 63, the previous April, so the U.S. delegation was led by his successor in office, Harry Truman. Truman had been sworn in as the nation's vice president just eleven weeks earlier, and privately complained that Roosevelt had failed to share any of his plans for the postwar world with him. By then the three-way coalition was already rapidly fracturing. The British circulated a paper among their delegates at Yalta, which, among other things, complained, "The behaviour of the Russians in Iran is in many ways at variance with our agreements, and is by no means unique in that regard."[39] The greatest April Fool's joke in history may have come that same spring when Stalin sent a cable to Eisenhower insisting that "Berlin has lost its former strategic importance" and disavowing any Soviet plans to occupy the Reich capital.

The Soviet dictator would retain his normal inscrutable pose when, on July 28, he looked across the Potsdam conference table to see Churchill's place there taken by the unassuming figure of 62-year-old Clement Attlee ("a bank clerk in both appearance and manner," the Vozhd privately noted), whose Labour party had just crushed the wartime leader's Conservatives in a general election. The new British premier's opening remark to his fellow heads of government was to make a rather strained analogy between choosing a cabinet and selecting a cricket team, neither one of them a task the Soviet hardman was personally familiar with. Perhaps Stalin allowed himself a brief reflection on the curious ways of democracy. His only previous comment on his new Allied negotiating partner had been to remark, "Mr. Attlee does not look to me like a man hungry for power."[40]

* * *

Some of the leading actors in Operation Long Jump went on to enjoy a sort of literary afterlife by putting their names to their generally self-serving memoirs. Others preferred to fade away, perhaps feeling that drawing undue attention to their wartime exploits might prove inimical to their future welfare. One or two of their number survived the upheavals of later years and actively prospered in civilian life.[41]

Ernst Merser endured several years of the NKVD's hospitality in Moscow, yet somehow ended his days living in a penthouse apartment on the French Riviera. When the author Laslo Havas tracked him down in the early 1960s, Merser genially invited him out on his private yacht for a Mediterranean cruise, where the old spymaster talked about everything but his role in *Unternehmen Weitsprung*. Rudolf Holten-Pflug similarly emerged unscathed from his brush with the Soviet firing squad to open a small bar in Buenos Aires said to be popular with former adherents of National Socialism. The ex-boxer Lothar Schoellhorn later resurfaced in the breakaway African republic of Katanga at the time of Moise Tshombe's secession and represented Tshombe in trade negotiations with John F. Kennedy's administration. Schoellhorn, who had stood in the military honor guard beside President Paul von Hindenburg's coffin, also attended JFK's funeral. The ambassador-turned-mountaineer Erwin Ettel became editor of the highbrow German weekly newspaper *Die Zeit*, where he wrote extensively on national security affairs. As we've seen, Winifred Oberg, the operation's advance man, also reappeared from Soviet captivity and earned a comfortable living as a legal adviser to a number of blue-chip American companies, among them General Electric and Coca-Cola. Joseph Schnabel managed a successful construction firm in postwar Hamburg and served on the city council as a Social Democrat. Qaleb Chapat emigrated to Beirut, where he, too, became a respectable businessman.[42] Hans von Ortel died in prison. Roman Gamotha was said to have committed suicide shortly after the war. Elyesa Bazna, or Cicero, eventually moved to Munich, where he unsuccessfully petitioned the West German government to be reimbursed for the counterfeit money he had received in Turkey during the war. No one seems to know what became of Misbah Ebtehaj or any of the other oil wrestlers.

In later years, Otto Skorzeny moved around between Spain, Egypt, and Argentina, sometimes acting as an adviser or bodyguard to one or other of their respective heads of state, and may have been involved as a security consultant at the time of the 1967 Arab-Israeli war, although it's by no means clear on which side.[43] This author was temporarily living in Moscow in 1970, where a rumor persisted in British embassy circles that Skorzeny had been seen entering the NKVD's (by then, KGB's) grim-looking headquarters on Lubyanka Square, a now "hugely obese" figure whose wavy gray hair, deeply scarred cheeks, and sallow complexion it was said made him a ringer for Boris Karloff. It's not known what, if anything, a former Waffen SS officer might have been doing in the Soviet spy center, but whatever it was it wasn't entirely out of keeping for a man who liked to keep his ideological options open. Skorzeny died of cancer in 1975, at the age of 67.

After the war, *Weitsprung*'s mastermind Walter Schellenberg stood trial at Nuremberg, where, to save himself a long prison sentence, he testified against his former associates; as noted, in the end he served two years but died at the age of 42, apparently of liver failure. Georg Hansen and Wilhelm Canaris, who joined Schellenberg at the July 1943 planning meeting in Berlin's Eden Hotel, were both victims of Hitler's maniacal revenge following the plot on his life twelve months later. The RSHA chief Ernst Kaltenbrunner, the fourth man present at the hotel that day, was convicted of war crimes and hanged at Nuremberg in October 1946, at age 43.

The British chief of staff Alan Brooke survived his exchange of dinner-party repartee with Stalin, later published a war diary that revealed a not wholly uncritical attitude to Winston Churchill, and perhaps understandably opted to spend the remaining years of his life working with animals as president of the London Zoological Society, dying in 1963, at age 79. The psychotic dwarf Lavrentiy Beria was arrested by Stalin's successors and unceremoniously shot in his cell. Beria's son Sergo, the man who transcribed Roosevelt's and Churchill's bugged conversations at Tehran, died only in 2001. Mike Reilly of the Secret Service died in 1973 while visiting his native Montana, at age 63. Walter Thompson became a somewhat unlikely star of U.S. television talk shows following the publication of his book *I Was Churchill's Shadow* and lived to be 87. Mohammad Reza Pahlavi, to date the last shah of Iran, was overthrown by the Islamic Revolution in early 1979; he died the following year, at the age of 60.

Only one of the Big Three leaders would remain at the helm of his nation's affairs when World War II finally came to a close 21 months after the Tehran conference. The principal targets of Operation Long Jump ultimately died in reverse order to the one predicted by Churchill's doctor Charles Moran. Roosevelt's loss in April 1945 "deeply affected" Stalin, who summoned the U.S. ambassador on hearing the news, crying and holding his visitor's hand for several minutes.[44] The Vozhd in turn collapsed with a massive stroke while at his dacha in March 1953. His guards were afraid to disturb him, and he lay unconscious on the floor for several hours before a doctor was summoned. According to his daughter Svetlana, Stalin's death agonies were terrible. "He literally choked to death as we watched," she wrote. "At what seemed like the very last moment he suddenly opened his eyes and cast a glance over everyone in the room. Then he lifted his left hand as though he were pointing to something up above and bringing a curse down on us all. The gesture was incomprehensible, and full of menace. The next moment, after a final effort, the spirit wrenched itself free of the flesh."[45] Winston Churchill died peacefully at home in London in January 1965, at age 90.

* * *

What if Operation Long Jump had succeeded? As things stood in December 1943, neither Stalin nor Churchill had a statutory successor. Based on what happened later, it's likely that in the event of their sudden deaths the former would have been replaced by a cabal of his senior colleagues until they, too, perished in the atmosphere the Vozhd had created of homicidal paranoia and rampant greed, and the latter by Clement Attlee.

The situation was more clear-cut in the United States, where Roosevelt's vice president at the time of the Tehran conference was 55-year-old Henry Wallace of Iowa, who was narrowly voted off the ticket in favor of Truman at the 1944 Democratic National Convention. We'll never know, but a President Wallace might have proved even more receptive to Soviet interests than Roosevelt. It's one of those intriguing what-ifs of history. In November 1942, Wallace informed an audience in New York that he was only partly convinced of the merits of the American model of government as opposed to the Russian. "Many of us in the United States believe that we have over-emphasized what might be called political or Bill of Rights democracy," the nation's vice president remarked. "Carried to its extreme form, it leads to rugged individualism, exploitation, impractical emphasis on states' rights, and even to anarchy. Russia, perceiving some of the abuses of excessive political democracy, has placed strong emphasis on economic democracy. This logically enough demands that all power be centered in *one man*, and his bureaucratic helpers."

Wallace was the Bernie Sanders figure of his day, and his presidency might conceivably have ushered in a period of political reorientation that would have been unthinkable under a continued Roosevelt administration. Whether the eventual shape of peace in 1945 would have been similarly transformed is another matter. Politics almost always has a personal dimension to it, and every U.S. president in history has sought to impose his particular vision of the world on his foreign allies and adversaries alike. It's not impossible to imagine that Wallace would have permitted the Soviet leadership to settle postwar affairs in eastern Europe largely on their terms, even more so than Truman. While it was the brutal Soviet vision of the world that led them to meddle directly or indirectly in the affairs of supposedly sovereign states such as Czechoslovakia, Poland, Hungary, Rumania, Bulgaria, and several others, what ultimately made the violation possible was the passive reaction of the West. There's still no evidence in the archives or elsewhere that Wallace would have seriously proposed peace to the Third Reich, even from a position of rapidly growing Allied military superiority in the winter of 1943–44.

Whether the deaths of Roosevelt, Stalin and Churchill at Tehran would have materially altered the future course of the war is impossible to say. More likely is that their successors in office would have pursued or even accelerated Operation Overlord, and that Germany's defeat would have become inevitable by the summer of 1944. The Allies might even have been bound closer together by the simultaneous murders of their three leaders. A catastrophic collective shock like that could have strengthened them in their support of the American ideal of a new postwar "United Nations," with a security

Then–US Secretary of Agriculture Henry Wallace leaves a meeting at the White House in 1939. As vice president, Wallace would have taken over if Roosevelt had died in 1943, and quite probably have given the Russians an even freer hand in Europe than his predecessor (Library of Congress).

council composed of the major powers to remedy the flaws of the toothless 1919 model. In such circumstances, it's also conceivable the Iron Curtain might have proved an altogether more flexible concept, or never have fallen in the first place. As it was, after Tehran the road from the World War to the Cold War that did occur was a short one.

Chapter Notes

Chapter 1

1. "Mr. Roosevelt, mentioning the matter...": see *New York Times*, December 18, 1943, pp. 1–2.
2. Churchill-Hopkins exchange: see David Khan, *Hitler's Spies*, as cited in the Bibliography, p. 175.
3. Admiral Canaris's final words: quoted in Richard Bassett, *Hitler's Spy Chief*, as cited in the Bibliography, p. 289.
4. Stalin, "A further delay would be a serious danger...": see *Stalin's Correspondence with Churchill, Attlee, Roosevelt and Truman, 1941–45* (Moscow, 1957), no. 129, March 15, 1943.
5. "I understand all your difficulties...": quoted in Martin Gilbert, *The Churchill War Papers, Vol. 2: Never Surrender* (New York: Norton, 1995), pp. 337–338.
6. Jock Colville on Churchill's anger at American equivocation: see John Colville, *The Fringes of Power: 10 Downing Street Diaries 1939–1955* (New York: Norton, 1985), p. 165.
7. Soviet reaction to Montgomery's achievement at El Alamein: see S.M. Shtemenko, *The Last Six Months* (New York: Zebra War, 1977), p. 36.
8. Roosevelt's comment to speechwriter Sam Rosenman: see Sam Rosenman, *Working with Roosevelt* (London: Hart-Davis Publishing, 1952), p. 527.
9. General Fromm's final words: quoted in Gene Mueller, *Generalolerst Friedrich Fromm* (Berlin: Primus Verlag Darmstadt, 1998), p. 76.
10. Hitler's reaction to the fall of Mussolini: see Walter Warlimont, *Inside Hitler's Headquarters* (Washington, D.C.: Praeger, 1964), pp. 242–247.
11. Hitler, "I'm accused of sympathizing with the orientals ...": see Christa Schroeder, *Er War mein Chef* (Munich: Langen Muller, 1985), p. 131.
12. Roosevelt-Churchill meeting of June 1942: see Winston Churchill, *The Hinge of Fate* (London: Cassell, 1951), pp. 380–381.
13. Roosevelt-Churchill memorandum on tube alloys: see Richard Rhodes, *The Making of the Atomic Bomb* (New York: Simon and Schuster, 1986), pp. 525–537.
14. Hitler's state of mind in February 1943: quoted in Nicolaus von Below, *At Hitler's Side* (London: Greenhill Books, 2004), p. 330.
15. Hitler's personal attitude to Churchill and the British people: see Ralf Georg Reuth, *Goebbels*, as cited in the Bibliography, p. 273.
16. Hitler's attitude to Roosevelt: see Ian Kershaw, *Hitler Vol. 2, Hubris* (New York: Norton, 1999), p. 446.
17. Hitler, "He wants to rule the world and rob us all...": see John Toland, *Adolf Hitler* (New York: Anchor, 1991), p. 693.
18. Churchill on Soviet threats of postwar reprisals against the German army: see Jon Meacham, *Franklin and Winston* (New York: Random House, 2004), p. 261.
19. Andrey Gromyko's recollection of the above incident: Gromyko to Rear-Admiral S.R. Sandford, RN, Moscow, April 1969.
20. Alexander Cadogan on the death of Admiral Darlan: quoted in Anthony Cave Brown, *The Secret Servant* (London: Sphere Books, 1989), p. 452.
21. Erich Kordt on Ribbentrop being "electrified" by the prospect of kidnapping the Windsors: see Erich Kordt, *Nicht*

aus den Akten (Stuttgart: Union Deutsche, 1950), p. 399.
22. Joseph Schnabel on the Abwehr training school at Quenzgut: quoted in Laslo Havas, *Hitler's Plot to Kill the Big Three*, as cited in the Bibliography, p. 105.
23. Walter Schellenberg, "Our experts produced a strange mechanism...": see Havas, p. 20.
24. Schellenberg on the merits of assassination, and Hitler's response: see Michael Bloch, *Ribbentrop*, as cited in the bibliography, p. 430.
25. Stalin's abandoned plans to assassinate the senior German hierarchy in July 1943: see the Reuters report, "Stalin blocked attempts to kill Hitler's generals," published in *World News Report*, May 25, 2010.
26. Hitler's mood immediately following the shooting down of the Lisbon-Bristol civilian airliner: see Ian Kershaw, as cited, p. 590.
27. Operation Foxley: see UK National Archives, "Operation Foxley 1944," Reference HS 6/624.
28. Office of HM King Simeon of Bulgaria to author, June 2021.
29. Otto Skorzeny activities in Budapest: see John Tolland, as cited, pp. 829–830.
30. Field Marshal B.L. Montgomery remarks at Staff College, Camberley, UK, August 1957.

Chapter 2

1. Schulze-Holthus description of Tehran: quoted in Bill Yenne, *Operation Long Jump*, as cited in the Bibliography, p. 35.
2. Modern history of Iran: see among others: Ervand Abrahamian, *A History of Modern Iran* (Cambridge: Cambridge University Press, 2008) and Elton L. Daniel, *The History of Iran* (Westport, CT: Greenwood Publishing, 2000).
3. Hitler's War Directive No. 32: see Howard Blum, *Night of the Assassins*, as cited in the Bibliography, p. 75.
4. Schellenberg comments on Roman Gamotha: quoted in Yenne, *Operation Long Jump*, p. 100.
5. Hans Frank comments at Nuremberg: see Record of International Military Tribunal, Nuremberg, Vol. XXIX (Washington, D.C.: U.S. National Archives and Records Administration, reference RG 238), p. 514.
6. Albert Florian letter to Bormann: see "Files of the Personal Staff of the Reichsfuhrer-SS and Chief of German Police," held on microfilm at U.S. National Archives, Group T-175.
7. Carl Weinrich note of January 22, 1943, for the record to Reich Chancellery: *Ibid.*, microfilm, Group 117.
8. "He left us in no doubt that Schellenberg was a person we should be wary of...": see Inge Haag interview of March 26, 2004, quoted in Bassett, *Hitler's Spy Chief*, as cited in Bibliography, p. 177.
9. Wilhelm Ohnesorge note of September 8, 1942: quoted in Havas, *Hitler's Plot to Kill the Big Three*, as cited in Bibliography, p. 111.
10. Alexander von Pfuhllsteinon wartime SS operations: see "Secret Report of 7th Army Interrogation Center, U.S. Army," U.S. National Archives, reference SAIC/2, filed April 10, 1945.
11. Canaris-Oster relationship: See David Kahn, *Hitler's Spies*, as cited in the Bibliography, p. 231.
12. Roosevelt remarks stating, "Africa is almost out of the question...": see "FDR's Last Instructions on Moscow," Diary of Joseph E. Davies, May 5, 1943, held in Joseph Davies Papers, U.S. Library of Congress, Washington, D.C.
13. Churchill remarks to U.S. Congress May 1943: see *U.S. Congressional Record*, Vol. 89, Pt. 4, p. 4621.
14. Churchill's reaction on learning of Roosevelt's plan to meet alone with Stalin: see *Churchill and Roosevelt: The Complete Correspondence, Vol. 2*, ed. Warren F. Kimball (Princeton, NJ: Princeton University Press, 1984), p. 278.
15. Churchill's car breakdown in Scotland: see Tom Hickman, *Churchill's Bodyguard*, as cited in the Bibliography, p. 32; the quote as reproduced here has been slightly adapted for sense.
16. Walter Thompson, as compared to the U.S. Secret Service: *Ibid.*, p. 135.
17. Churchill swimming incident in Palm Beach, FL: see Walter Thompson, *I Was Churchill's Shadow* (London: Christopher Johnson, 1951), p. 84.
18. Roosevelt on "Winston hours": see Wilson Brown Memoir, pp. 161–162, FDR

Presidential Library and Museum, Hyde Park, NY.

19. "Winston enjoyed himself hugely, making V-signs...": quoted in *The Diaries of Sir Alexander Cadogan*, ed. David Dilks (New York: Putnam, 1972), pp. 559–560.

20. The death of Zinoviev: quoted in Edvard Radzinsky, *Stalin* (New York: Anchor, 1997), p. 345.

21. Stalin's paranoia and obsession with personal security: see Michael Dobbs, *Six Months in 1945* (New York: Knopf, 2012), pp. 23–24.

22. Stalin, "Sadly, there are always fewer old cadres than needed...": see Josef Stalin, *Problems of Leninism* (Moscow: Foreign Languages Publishing House, 1945), p. 625.

23. Conditions in Sukhanovo Prison, south of Moscow: quoted in Stephen Kotkin, *Stalin, Waiting for Hitler: 1929–41* (New York: Penguin, 2017), pp. 618–619.

24. Stalin and the bananas: see, inter al., Simon Sebag Montefiore, *Stalin: The Court of the Red Tsar* (London: Phoenix, 2004), p. 629.

25. Vlasik on his treatment by Stalin: quoted in Radzinsky, pp. 554–555.

26. Roosevelt's aversion to flying: see Eleanor Roosevelt, *This I Remember* (New York: Harper, 1949), p. 279.

27. Comments of Margaret Suckley: see Geoffrey C. Ward, *Closest Companion* (New York: Simon and Schuster, Reprint edition, 2009).

28. Charles Bohlen comments on Churchill and "Unconditional surrender": quoted in Drew Middleton, *Retreat from Victory* (New York: Hawthorn, 1973); see section entitled "Roosevelt, Churchill Map 1943 War Strategy."

29. Churchill's comments on Morocco visit: see Churchill, *The Hinge of Fate*, as previously cited, p. 694.

30. Stalin's reservations about proposed Allied invasion of Sicily: see *Correspondence between the Chairman of the Council of Ministers of the USSR and the Presidents of the USA and the Prime Ministers of Great Britain During the Great Patriotic War of 1941–45* (Moscow: 1957), entry no. 129, March 15, 1943.

31. Mike Reilly on prospect of a German assault on the White House: quoted in Howard Blum, *Night of the Assassins*, as cited in the Bibliography, p. 37.

Chapter 3

1. Hitler's reaction to Paulus surrender at Stalingrad: see Walter Warlimont, *Inside Hitler's Headquarters*, as previously cited, pp. 300–309.

2. Background, history and topography of Iran: see, again, Abrahamian, *A History of Modern Iran*, and Daniel, *The History of Iran*, as previously cited.

3. Col. Hansen report of August 13, 1943: quoted in Laslo Havas, *Hitler's Plot to Kill the Big Three*, as cited in the Bibliography, p. 45.

4. Schulze-Holthus activities since arriving in Tehran: see "UK Defence Security Office, C.I.C.I. Persia, Counter-Intelligence Summary No. 25," UK National Archives.

5. Himmler's comment beginning "Our lines to Iran deserve..." appears in Havas, p. 96; the form given here has been slightly modified for sense.

6. The quote indicating "The soldiers were to act like missionaries..." *Ibid.*, p. 80.

7. Concealed radio transmitter and other activities in Schulze-Holthus's house: see Julius Schulze-Holthus, *Daybreak in Iran* (Glasgow: Staples Press, 1954), passim.

8. Description of Ernst Kaltenbrunner: see Havas, p. 36.

9. Heydrich-Canaris exchange: quoted in Richard Bassett, *Hitler's Spy Chief*, as cited in the Bibliography, p. 229.

10. Description of young SS recruits: quoted in Robert M.W. Kempner, *SS im Kreuzverhor* (Munich: Rutten and Loening verlag, 1964), p. 284.

11. Schulze-Holthus description of Erwin Ettel: see Bill Yenne, *Operation Long Jump*, as cited in the Bibliography, p. 20.

12. Ettel remarks on special-forces operations and other Iran activities in summer 1943: see *Dokumente der deutschen Politik, 1933–43*, 9 volumes (Berlin 1937–45), passim.

13. Further Ettel remarks on parachute drops and other activities in northern Iran: *Ibid.*

14. Himmler-Schellenberg exchanges May–June 1943: see Havas, p. 112.

15. Schellenberg remark on Canaris, beginning, "He was a highly intelligent

man...": quoted in private correspondence of Col. Burton C. Andrus, LOM, Commandant of Nuremberg Prison 1945–46; and see also Walter Schellenberg, *The Labyrinth* (New York: Da Capo Press reissue, 2000), passim. It's only fair to point out that certain historians have preferred to treat Schellenberg's autobiography with caution, seeing it as self-serving even by the standards of other Nazi memoirs.

16. Himmler, "When the Fuhrer entrusts us with a job...": quoted by Robert Jay Lifton, *The Nazi Doctors* (New York: Basic Books reissue, 2006).

17. Operation Zeppelin losses: quoted in David Kahn, *Hitler's Spies*, as cited in the Bibliography, pp. 360–361.

18. Instructions to SS paratroopers in the event of being injured on landing: see "General Principles to the Field Service Regulations of [German] Divisions and Armies" (Berlin, 1939).

19. Schellenberg on Skorzeny's "leer of excitement": *Ibid.*, Col. Burton C. Andrus and *The Labyrinth*.

20. Hitler's medical condition in 1943: see Fritz Redlich, *Hitler: Diagnosis of a Destructive Prophet* (London: Oxford University Press, 1998), pp. 224–225.

21. Churchill on Anglo-American relations in September 1943: see Churchill Speeches, included in Papers of President Franklin D. Roosevelt, U.S. National Archives and Records Administration; and Robert Rhodes James, ed., *Complete Speeches of Winston Churchill, Vol. 7* (New York: Chelsea House, 1974), pp. 6823–6824.

22. Roosevelt, "I'm nearly dead..." comment to Frances Perkins: see Frances Perkins Oral History 640, FDR Presidential Library and Museum, Hyde Park, NY.

23. Churchill's request about his bath: recounted, in very slightly different form, in Tom Hickman, *Churchill's Bodyguard*, as cited in the Bibliography, p. 125.

24. Churchill's intention to brief Stalin on the delay to D-Day: see Minutes of Meeting of UK War Cabinet of June 26, 1943, UK National Archives, ref. no. CAB-79-62-6.

25. Reinhard Spitzy comment on Canaris knowledge of Hitler assassination plot: see Richard Bassett, *Hitler's Spy Chief*, as cited in the Bibliography, p. 264.

Chapter 4

1. "They even had to learn to spit like Russians...": quoted in Havas, p. 66.

2. Introduction of the German radio operators and Iranian guide Farsad: see Bill Yenne, *Operation Long Jump*, as cited in the Bibliography, pp. 52–54.

3. Mussolini's 1943 message to Hitler: see *Corrispondenza imedita*, ed. Duilio su Smel (Milan: Edizioni del Borghese, 1972), pp. 187–189.

4. July 19, 1943, meeting at Feltre: see F.W. Deakin, *The Brutal Friendship* (London: Weidenfeld and Nicolson, 1962), pp. 381–382.

5. The arrest of Mussolini: see Nicholas Farrell, *Mussolini: A New Life* (London: Phoenix paperback edition, 2005), p. 388.

6. Hitler's gift of Nietzsche to Mussolini: quoted in Max Domarus, *Der Reichstag und die Macht* (Wurzburg, 1968), p. 2026.

7. Walter Schellenberg meeting with Canaris, Kaltenbrunner and Hansen: *Ibid.*, Col. Burton C. Andrus and *The Labyrinth*, passim.

8. "There have been frequent incidents of drunkenness and rowdyism...": see Laslo Havas, *Hitler's Plot to Kill the Big Three*, pp. 122–123.

9. "German parachutists continue to be dropped...": *Ibid.*

10. "It was as if part of themselves, whatever remained...": see Howard Blum, *Night of the Assassins*, as cited in the Bibliography, pp. 148–149.

11. Goring-Schirach discussion about ending the war: quoted in Henriette von Schirach, *The Price of Glory* (London: Muller, 1960), pp. 130–134.

12. Goring views on so persuading Hitler: private correspondence of Col. Burton C. Andrus.

13. Wartime traffic between Sweden and Great Britain: quoted in Ladislas Farago, *The Game of the Foxes: The Untold Story of German Espionage During World War 2* (New York: McKay, 1971), p. 549.

14. Stalin, "He preferred to watch the Soviet armies bleed...": see Edvard Radzinsky, *Stalin* (New York: Anchor, 1997), p. 495.

15. Stalin, "I have to tell you that it is impossible to tolerate...": quoted in W. Averell Harriman and Elie Abel, *Special*

Envoy (New York: Random House, 1975), p. 225.

16. Kramer report on the Allied conference in Quebec: see *Militararchiv 111 M 1000/49* (Berlin), pp. 132-133.

17. Stalin comparison of Roosevelt and Churchill: see Milovan Djilas, *Conversations with Stalin* (London: Penguin UK, 1969), passim.

18. The detention of 300 individuals engaged in pro-Nazi activity: see archive files of the *News Chronicle* (London), August 24, 1943.

19. Lt. Fackenheim experiences in British captivity: see Michael Bar-Zehar, *Hitler's Jewish Spy* (London: Sidgwick and Jackson, 1985), p. 148.

20. The author Howard Blum's remarks that German intelligence services would "alert their field agents and assets...": see Howard Blum, *Night of the Assassins*, as cited in the Bibliography, pp. 112-113.

21. The British War Cabinet meeting of August 11, 1943: see UK National Archives, Cabinet Papers, ref. no. CAB 65-39-10.

22. Stalin, "I have just returned from the front...": see Cypher Telegram delivered by Soviet Charge d' affaires, August 10, 1943; UK National Archives, ref. no. CAB 65-39-10.

23. Churchill's response to same: *Ibid.*

24. Churchill's remarks on conclusion of Quebec Conference: Broadcast from Quebec, August 31, 1943, transcript available from the International Churchill Society, winstonchurchill.org/speeches.

25. Prospect of a Soviet armistice with Nazi Germany: see Sir Basil Liddell Hart, *History of the Second World War* (Old Saybrook, CT: Konecky and Konecky edition, 2007), Chapter 28, passim.

26. Canaris private remarks on the German-Italian axis: quoted in Cesare Ame interview in *Corriere della Sera* (Milan), April 16, 1980.

27. Walter Schellenberg, "My plan was to lure Stalin once more to the conference table...": unpublished Schellenberg manuscript, quoted in David Irving, *Hitler's War* (London: Hodder and Stoughton, 1977), p. 610; see also Bloch, *Ribbentrop*, p. 430.

28. Himmler interrogation of Jean-Jacques Beguin: quoted in Laslo Havas, *Hitler's Plot to Kill the Big Three*, as cited in the Bibliography, p. 144, slightly amended for sense.

29. Schnabel, "We were taught to hate...": quoted in Bill Yenne, *Operation Long Jump*, as cited in the Bibliography, p. 77.

30. Schnabel on his accommodations at Molavi Street: see Havas, p. 220.

31. Oberg, "I could mention a dozen people...": *Ibid.*, p. 96.

32. Roosevelt, "I personally could arrange to come to a place as far as North Africa...": see 1943 Personal Papers, FDR Presidential Library and Museum, Hyde Park, NY.

33. Intercepted radio signal of September 10, 1943: see Charles Foley, *Teste Calde* (Milan: Longanesi, 1955), p. 88.

34. September 1943 rescue of Mussolini: see Otto Skorzeny, *Special Missions* (Mechanicsburg, PA: Stackpole Books edition, 1997), pp. 70-90.

35. Hitler, "You have performed a military feat which will become part of history...": *Ibid.*

36. Potential German propaganda value of Mussolini rescue: see *Josef Goebbels Diaries, Vol. 11/9* (Munich: K.G. Saur Verlag, 1993-98), pp. 567-568.

37. Walter Schellenberg, "The activities of this man...": quoted in Laslo Havas, *Hitler's Plot to Kill the Big Three*, as cited in the Bibliography, p. 167.

38. The Vermehren Incident: see Declassified Report, "U.S. Army, European Command, Intelligence Division, Wartime Activities of the German Diplomatic and Military Services During World War 2," Document HIC CT 1055.U51, declassified by the CIA under Nazi War Crimes Disclosure Act 2001.

39. Final Canaris-Hitler interview: quoted in Andre Brissaud, *Canaris* (New York: Grosset and Dunlap, 1974), p. 315.

40. The author Howard Blum on Walter Schellenberg's strategy for assassinating the Allied leaders: see Howard Blum, *Night of the Assassins*, as cited in the Bibliography, p. 153.

41. Schellenberg signal to Oberg to effect "Immediate changes" in organization: *Ibid.*

42. Oberg's remark that Ortel was to "Participate in an operation of primary importance...": see Laslo Havas, *Hitler's Plot to Kill the Big Three*, as cited, p. 169.

43. Schellenberg, "To decide to continue

one's own line of policy...": see Howard Blum, *Night of the Assassins*, as cited, p. 157.

44. For the exact chronology of events in Tehran in late October 1943, see, inter al., Havas, *Hitler's Plot to Kill the Big Three*, as cited, pp. 181–209.

Chapter 5

1. Paul Pourbaix, "It needed so much imagination to invent...": *Ibid.*, p. 176.
2. For Tehran history and topography, see: Ervand Abrahamian, *A History of Modern Iran* (Cambridge: Cambridge University Press, 2008), passim; Winifred Oberg himself is quoted in Laslo Havas, *Hitler's Plot to Kill the Big Three*, as cited in the Bibliography, pp. 181–208.
3. Oberg's recollection of an "important delivery" dropped by parachute: quoted in Havas, as cited, p. 209.
4. The success or otherwise of Operation Bazooka: Private correspondence of Col. Burton C. Andrus.
5. Early German reaction to Agent Cicero: see "'The Cicero Papers,' Further Releases concerning the Security Breach at HM Embassy, Ankara, in the Second World War": London: Foreign and Commonwealth Office Historians, March 2005, passim.
6. Molotov-Hull exchanges about possible location of Allied meeting: see Laslo Havas, as cited, p. 206.
7. Molotov-Harriman discussion on the same subject: *Ibid.*
8. British War Cabinet meeting of November 4, 1943: see UK War Cabinet Minutes, November 4, 1943, UK National Archives, ref. no. CAB 65-40-9.
9. Churchill, "I am very glad to hear from your Ambassador...": quoted in Laslo Havas, as cited, p. 212.
10. Hitler remarks to Peter Kleist: quoted in Peter Kleist, *Zwischen Hitler und Stalin* (Bonn: Athenaeum Verlag, 1950), pp. 126–128.
11. Hitler, "The most important part of final victory will be the exclusion of the United States...": quoted in Dr. Johannes von Mullern-Schonhausen, *Die Losung des Ratsel's Adolf Hitler* (Vienna: Verlag zur Forderung, 1950), pp. 220–224.
12. Walter Schellenberg's willingness to amend plans "up to the very brink of midnight": Private correspondence of Col. Burton C. Andrus.
13. Schellenberg's idea "was to lop off the heads...": *Ibid.*
13. Vladimir Shkvarzev activities in wartime France: see Laslo Havas, as cited, p. 161.
14. Schellenberg's "Jekyll and Hyde" personality, and willingness to do whatever necessary to annihilate the enemy: see Walter Schellenberg, *The Labyrinth*, as cited, passim.
15. "There was, Skorzeny firmly believed, honor in a soldier's death...": see Howard Blum, *Night of the Assassins*, as previously cited, p. 277.
16. Hitler, "No general will ever pronounce himself ready to attack...": quoted in Alan Clark, *Barbarossa* (New York: Morrow reissue edition, 1985), p. 374.
17. Ahmad Qavam's unwanted advances on female servants: private report of Major John Riley, MC, who investigated Qavam's household arrangements, made available to author.
18. See, inter al, Abrahamian, *A History of Modern Iran*, passim, as cited.
19. Hitler, "What grieves me most are the sacrifices...": Hitler speech in Munich Lowenbraukeller, November 8, 1943, transcript available from "der-fuehrer.org." Excerpts of the speech were published in the *New York Times*, November 9, 1943.
20. Goebbels, "What we have in mind has become a sort of people's secret...": see Helmut Heiber, trans. John K. Dickinson, *Goebbels* (New York: Hawthorn Books reissue, 1973), p. 277.
21. Goebbels's remark that the war had become a "grim life-or-death confrontation": see *Josef Goebbels Diaries* (Munich: K.G. Saur Verlag, 1993-98), entry dated November 7, 1943.
22. "From the highest authority..." signal of November 1943: see Bundesarchiv Koblenz (BAK), ref. no. NL 118/56.
23. Beria "expressed the general dissatisfaction...": see State Archives of the Russian Federation (formerly Central State Archive of the October Revolution), "Report of Intelligence and Conduct of Internal Surveillance by Agents in Tehran," Moscow: ref. no. F102.00, pp. 66–67; and personal reminiscence of Nikolai Kaverin, made available to author.

24. Roosevelt near-catastrophe at sea, November 14, 1943: see "Franklin D. Roosevelt Day by Day," Pare Lorentz Center, FDR Presidential Library and Museum, Hyde Park, NY.

Chapter 6

1. For Tehran history and topography, see Ervand Abrahamian, *A History of Modern Iran* (Cambridge: Cambridge University Press, 2008) and Elton L. Daniel, *The History of Iran* (Westport, CT: Greenwood Publishing, 2000), passim; the author did not personally visit the city.

2. "[Siebert] immediately advised the local Soviet army command...": see Laslo Havas, *Hitler's Plot to Kill the Big Three*, as cited, p. 218; the phrasing used here has been slightly modified for sense.

3. Walter Schellenberg, "From the beginning it was realized..." Private correspondence of Col. Burton C. Andrus.

4. "Oberg proved to be a very good spy...": see Howard Blum, *Night of the Assassins*, as cited in the Bibliography, p. 223.

5. The underground water channels of Tehran: see H.E. Wulff, "The Qanats of Iran," *Scientific American*, April 1968.

6. Nikita Khrushchev on Stalin revelries: see *Memuary Nikity Khruscheva*, excerpted in *Voprosy istorii*, No. 8 (Moscow, 1990), pp. 70–73.

7. Stalin-Svetlana exchange on love: see Simon Sebag Montefiore, *Stalin: The Court of the Red Tsar* (London: Phoenix, 2004), p. 459.

8. Further Stalin relations with Svetlana: see Edvard Radzinsky, *Stalin* (New York: Anchor, 1997), p. 494.

9. Gustav Wegner, "Late in 1943 the prisoners were taking their exercise...": Ibid., pp. 478–479.

10. Elyesa Bazna payment arrangements: see "The Cicero Papers," op. cit., passim.

11. Goebbels, "The natural fissures [are] now widening...": see *Josef Goebbels Diaries Vol 2* (Munich: K.G. Saur Verlag, 1993–98), and the same statement contained in the files of Bundesarchiv Koblenz (BAK), ref. no. NL 118/54.

12. Lothar Schoellhorn parachute drop into Iran: quoted in Laslo Havas, *Hitler's Plot to Kill the Big Three*, as cited, p. 158.

13. Pavel Fitin report "designed to be damaging to Beria...": Nikita Khrushchev to Rear-Admiral S.R. Sandford, RN, British Naval Attaché to Moscow, December 1968.

14. "Then he found it.... It was the one event the Allies would all be certain to celebrate...": see Howard Blum, *Night of the Assassins*, as cited, p. 246.

15. See "The Cicero Papers," op. cit., passim.

16. NBC Radio report, "Since the Germans still have bombers based in Crete...": Reported by Noel F. Busch, as quoted in *Life* magazine, August 13, 1945.

17. "The city was filled with Axis spies....": see Bill Yenne, *Operation Long Jump*, as cited, p. 107.

18. Alexandr Lukin, "One after another, the influential members of the Germany colony disappeared...": see Alexandr Lukin, *Operacia Dalyni Prizhok* (Moscow: Ogonok, 1965), pp. 115–117.

19. Jakob Kupferstein, "I was taken away with my wife...": quoted in Laslo Havas, as cited, p. 195.

20. "Roosevelt leaned forward on the arms of his chair...": quoted in Sarah Churchill, *A Thread in the Tapestry* (New York: Dodd Mead, 1966), pp. 62–64.

21. For background of Misbah Ebtehaj and his colleagues, see Eugeniy Bakhrovskiy, "History and Actual Image of Oil Wrestling," *International Journal of Ethnosport and Traditional Games No. 2* (Moscow, 2019).

22. Nikolai Kaverin unpublished manuscript, made available to author.

23. Stalin's impromptu visit to the Shah: see Simon Sebag Montefiore, *Stalin: The Court of the Red Tsar*, as cited, p. 474.

24. Stalin, "You are going to listen to the conversations Churchill will have with Roosevelt...": quoted in Sergo Beria, *Beria, My Father: Inside Stalin's Kremlin* (London: Bristol Classical Press edition, 2003), p. 93.

25. The two Berias present themselves to Stalin: see Charles River Editors, *The Tehran Conference of 1943* (Las Vegas, 2020), Chapter 3.

26. Henry Stimson, "If I were a [German] commander having control of between 90 and 100 JU 88 bombers...": quoted in Howard Blum, *Night of the Assassins*, as cited, p. 247.

27. Mike Reilly, "In the event of a landing, or worse...": *Ibid.*, p. 22.
28. Roosevelt's first impressions on landing at Tehran: see Simon Sebag Montefiore, *Stalin: The Court of the Red Tsar*, as cited, p. 472.
29. British cabinet meeting of November 12, 1943: see "W.M. (43) 153rd Conclusions, Nov 12 1943," UK National Archives, Cabinet Papers, ref. no. CAB 65-40-9.
30. Further British cabinet discussions of the week November 20-27, 1943: See UK National Archives, ref. no. FO-800-410-1; and War Cabinet minutes grouped together as "CAB 65 (1943)."
31. "Churchill's trip into Tehran was chaos...": quoted in Tom Hickman, *Churchill's Bodyguard*, cited in the Bibliography, pp. 168-169.
32. Sarah Churchill remarks on the same incident: see Jon Meacham, *Franklin and Winston* (New York: Random House paperback edition, 2004), p. 248.
33. Churchill cipher message to Roosevelt on Tehran arrangements: see "Tehran Conference," Document No. FO 800/411, UK National Archives.
34. Churchill to Cabinet Office, *Ibid*.
35. Von Papen's views on ending the war: quoted in Douglas Waller, *Wild Bill Donovan* (New York: Free Press edition, 2012), p. 192.
36. Molotov meeting with U.S. officials late on November 27, 1943: see Bill Yenne, *Operation Long Jump*, as cited, p. 133.
37. Mike Reilly, "We set up the standard cavalcade with the gun-laden jeeps...": *Ibid.*, p. 137.
38. Nikolai Kaverin, op. cit.
39. Stalin's apparent sympathy for Roosevelt, "Why did nature have to punish him so?": quoted in Simon Sebag Montefiore, *Stalin: The Court of the Red Tsar*, as cited, p. 492.
40. Churchill's opening remarks in Tehran: See International Churchill Society, winstonchurchill.org/speeches, among numerous published sources.

Chapter 7

1. "In the detailed discussion between the three heads...": see U.S. State Dept., Office of the Historians, "Foreign Relations of the U.S.: Diplomatic Papers, The Conferences at Cairo and Tehran, 1943."
2. Stalin, "To put it mildly, this work revises Leninism...": quoted in Edvard Radzinsky, *Stalin* (New York: Anchor, 1997), p. 501.
3. "The plan had required 'complete cohesion'...": Private Correspondence of Col. Burton C. Andrus.
4. Soviet atrocities at Khaibakh and elsewhere: see Donald Rayfield, *Stalin and His Hangmen* (New York: Random House paperback edition, 2005), p. 405.
5. Walter Thompson, "Most of the time, I had my automatic in my hand...": quoted in Tom Hickman, *Churchill's Bodyguard*, as cited in the Bibliography, p. 170.
6. Ernst Merser-Qaleb Chapat role at Soviet embassy: Private Correspondence of Col. Burton C. Andrus.
7. Churchill, "The President however declined, and sent Harriman to me...": see Winston Churchill, *Closing the Ring*, as previously cited, p. 363.
8. Stalin-Roosevelt exchange at Tehran on the logistics of D-Day landings: see Simon Sebag Montefiore, *Stalin: The Court of the Red Tsar*, as cited, p. 477.
9. Stalin, "I approve the sentence. No appeal": quoted in D.A. Volkogonov, *Stalin: Triumph and Tragedy* (New York: Grove, 1991), p. 422.
10. "Perhaps there is no sadder curse than the gift of a titanic father": quoted in Simon Sebag Montefiore, *Stalin: Court of the Red Tsar*, as cited, p. 479.
11. Presentation of the Sword of Honour to Stalin at Tehran: *Ibid.*, p. 477.
12. Stalin skepticism about British commitment to Overlord, and lack of supreme commander of same: U.S. State Dept., Office of the Historians, "The Conferences at Cairo and Tehran: Bohlen Minutes, November 29, 1943."
13. Stalin "wished to ask Mr. Churchill an indiscreet question...": *Ibid*.
14. Churchill's medical condition that same night: Charles Moran, *Churchill: Taken from the Diaries of Lord Moran: The Struggle for Survival 1940-1965* (New York: Basic Books edition, 2006), p. 148.
15. Churchill, "There I sat with the great Russian bear on one side...": see Sir John Wheeler-Bennett, et al., *Action this Day: Working with Churchill* (New York: Macmillan, 1968), p. 96.

16. Elliott Roosevelt outburst at Tehran dinner: see Elliott Roosevelt, *As He Saw It* (New York: Duell, Sloan and Pearce, 1946), p. 186.

17. Stalin: "There is no need to discourse..." see Havas, *Hitler's Plot to Kill the Big Three*, lightly amended for sense, p. 232.

18. Nikolai Kaverin, "I secured my job not just due to my skills...": Kaverin to the author, Moscow, August 1969.

19. Stalin and Molotov offend Churchill at Tehran dinner: see Simon Sebag Montefiore, *Stalin: Court of the Red Tsar*, as cited, p. 479.

20. Kathleen Harriman on Roosevelt's ability to charm: see Jon Meacham, *Franklin and Winston* (New York: Random House paperback edition, 2004), p. 16.

21. Churchill, "Searching our Legation from top to bottom": quoted in Bill Yenne, *Operation Long Jump*, as cited, p. 164.

22. Churchill-Stalin bilateral meeting at Tehran: see report included in minutes of UK War Cabinet meeting of January 7, 1944, "Record of a Conversation Between the Prime Minister and Marshal Stalin, 30 November 1943," Cabinet Papers, UK National Archives.

23. Churchill summation of Anglo-American plans for Overlord: *Ibid.*

24. The Big Three lunch at Tehran of November 30, 1943: See "Diary of Franklin D. Roosevelt, Handwritten Notes of Cairo and Tehran," FDR Presidential Library and Museum, Hyde Park, NY.

25. Walter Schellenberg on devoting "immeasurable resources": Private correspondence of Col. Burton C. Andrus.

26. Beria's comments to Molotov on unearthing the possible Tehran conspiracy were reported in *Izvestia* on January 7, 2002.

27. Discussions about the leadership of Operation Overlord: see Winston Churchill, *Closing the Ring*, as previously cited, p. 466.

28. Sarah Churchill, Stalin was "a frightening figure with his slit, bear eyes...": see Sarah Churchill, *A Thread in the Tapestry*, as previously cited, p. 65.

29. Stalin-Brooke exchange: see, inter al., Yenne, *Operation Long Jump*, p. 166.

30. Stalin on the heroic two-year fighting performance of the Red Army: see U.S. State Dept, Office of the Historians: "Boettiger Minutes of November 30, 1943."

31. The NKVD raid of November 30, 1943: Oral history of Nikolai Kaverin.

32. The cascading ice-cream cake at Churchill birthday dinner: quoted in Simon Sebag Montefiore, *Stalin: The Court of the Red Tsar*, as previously cited, p. 480.

33. Subsequent scenes of revelry at Churchill dinner: see Howard Blum, *Night of the Assassins*, as previously cited, p. 315; and Kaverin oral history.

34. "Winston got red and scowled, and the more he did so...": quoted in Frances Perkins, *The Roosevelt I Knew* (New York: Viking, 1946), p. 84.

35. Roosevelt, "I have received the magnificent carpet...": see U.S. State Dept, Office of the Historians, "Diplomatic Papers, The Conferences at Cairo and Tehran: Roosevelt letter of December 1, 1943."

36. Hitler's remarks of December 1943 regarding future Allied invasion of Europe: see *Lagebesprechungen im Fuhrerhauptquartier 1942-45*, ed. Helmut Heiber (Berlin: Damstadt, 1962), pp. 218-219.

37. Churchill's illness in January 1944, and later recovery: see Jon Meacham, *Franklin and Winston*, as previously cited, p. 271.

38. Stalin's car accident at Baku: quoted in Simon Sebag Montefiore, *Stalin: The Court of the Red Tsar*, as previously cited, p. 481.

39. British paper tabled at Yalta regarding "behaviour of the Russians in Persia": see "Cypher Message from Sir R. Bullard to Foreign Office of January 16, 1945," UK National Archives, ref. no. PER-45-6.

40. Allied conference at Potsdam, and Stalin's views on Attlee: see, inter al., Michael Dobbs, *Six Months in 1945*, as cited, p. 334.

41. Subsequent fates of principal actors at Tehran conference: see Laslo Havas, *Hitler's Plot to Kill the Big Three*, as cited in the Bibliography, pp. 257-263.

42. Later fortunes of Qaleb Chapat: Nikola Kaverin oral history.

43. Skorzeny postwar activities: see Martin Lee, *The Beast Reawakens: Fascism's Resurgence from Hitler's Spymasters to Today's Neo-Nazi Groups and Right-Wing Extremists* (New York: Little Brown, 1997), p. 185.

44. Stalin reaction on the death of Roosevelt: see Simon Sebag Montefiore, *Stalin: The Court of the Red Tsar*, as previously cited, p. 496.

45. The death of Stalin: see Svetlana Alliluyeva, *Twenty Letters to a Friend* (New York: Harper and Row, 1967), p. 18.

Bibliography

Andrus, Burton C. *I Was the Nuremberg Jailer*. New York: Coward McCann, 1969.
Bassett, Richard. *Hitler's Spy Chief: The Wilhelm Canaris Betrayal*. New York: Pegasus, 2011.
Birse, Arthur Herbert. *Memoirs of an Interpreter*. New York: Coward McCann, 1967.
Bloch, Michael. *Ribbentrop*. London: Little Brown, 2003.
Blum, Howard. *Night of the Assassins: The Untold Story of Hitler's Plot to Kill FDR, Churchill, and Stalin*. New York: HarperCollins, 2020.
Bohlen, Charles E. *Witness to History 1929-1969*. New York: Norton, 1973.
Charles River, Eds. *The Tehran Conference of 1943*. Las Vegas: Charles River, 2020.
Churchill, Winston S. *Closing the Ring*. Boston: Houghton Mifflin, 1951.
Colvin, Ian. *Admiral Canaris, Chief of Intelligence*. London: Colvin Press, 2007.
Deane, John R. *The Strange Alliance*. Bloomington: Indiana University Press, 1973.
Dulles, Allen W. *Germany's Underground*. New York: Macmillan, 1978.
Eubank, Keith. *Summit at Tehran*. New York: William Morrow, 1985.
Gilbert, G.M. *Nuremberg Diary*. New York: Da Capo Press, 1995.
Haas, William S. *Iran*. New York: Columbia University Press, 1946.
Harris, Whitney R. *Tyranny on Trial*. New York: Barnes & Noble, 1995.
Havas, Laslo. *Hitler's Plot to Kill the Big Three*. New York: Cowles, 1967.
Hickman, Tom. *Churchill's Bodyguard: The Authorised Biography of Walter H. Thompson*. London: Headline, 2005.
Kahn, David. *Hitler's Spies: German Military Intelligence in World War 2*. New York: Macmillan, 1978.
Kapuscinski, Ryszard. *Shah of Shahs*. London: Penguin, 2006.
Leahy, William D. *I Was There*. New York: McGraw-Hill, 1950.
Rayfield, Donald. *Stalin and His Hangmen*. London: Viking, 2004.
Reilly, Michael. *I Was Roosevelt's Shadow*. London: Foulsham, 1947.
Reuth, Ralf Georg. *Goebbels*. New York: Harcourt, 1993.
Skorzeny, Otto. *My Commando Operations: Memoirs of Hitler's Most Daring Commando*. Atglen, PA: Schiffer, 1998.
Wallace, Henry. *The Price of Vision: The Diary of Henry A. Wallace 1942-1946*. Boston: Houghton Mifflin, 1973.
West, Nigel. *Historical Dictionary of World War 2 Intelligence*. Lanham, MD: Scarecrow Press, 2008.
Yenne, Bill. *Operation Long Jump*. Washington, D.C.: Regnery, 2015.

Index

Amè, Cesare 97
Anglo-Persian Oil Company 34
Ankara, Turkey 113, 119, 121
Antonescu, Ion 9
Asadi, Ahmad 37
Attlee, Clement 192–193, 195
Axis conference 85

Badoglio, Pietro 8, 85, 102
Badoglio government 85
Baghdad (Iraq) 110
Bandar Torkaman (Iran) 79–81
Bar-Zohar, Michael 93
Basra (Iraq) 86, 110
Battle of the Bulge 30
Baumbach, Werner 75, 79
Bazna, Elyesa (Cicero) 112, 119–121, 126, 145, 193
BAZOOKA (code word) 118–117
Beguin, Jean-Jacques 97–98
Beirut (Lebanon) 106, 110, 193
Beria, Marshal of the USSR and NKVD chief Lavrentiy 25, 49–50, 108, 126, 133–134, 139, 144, 161, 163, 168, 173, 179–180, 190, 194
Beria, Sergo 167, 153, 194
Best, Sigismund 40
Bletchley Park (UK) 96
Blokhin, Vasily 6
Blum, Howard 94, 127, 137, 145
Bohlen, Charles "Chip" 135, 138, 181
Bonhoeffer, Dietrich 43
Bormann, Martin 39, 91, 131
Brooke, General (later Field Marshal) Sir Alan 182–183, 194
Brown, Wilson 47
Bryan, Otis 154
Burger, Ernst 22
Burkner, Leopold 42

Cadogan, Alexander 16–48
Canaris, Admiral, Chief of the Abwehr Wilhelm 4–5, 15–17, 38–43, 59, 68, 73, 81–82, 86, 90, 94, 97, 105–106, 179, 194
Chanel, Coco 68
Chapat, Qaleb 163, 164, 167, 171–174, 181, 184, 188, 193
Chemical Warfare Service 55
Chenhalis, Alfred 26
Chiang Kai-shek 134, 147
Churchill, Randolph 168
Churchill, Sarah 155
Churchill, Winston S. 2–6, 9–11, 14, 34, 44–48, 54, 77–78, 87, 91–92, 95–96, 99–100, 110, 120, 124, 134, 139, 145, 147–148, 155–156, 159–161, 167–172, 174–178, 180–182, 185, 188–189, 191, 194–195
Cicero (Elyesa Bazna) 113, 119, 124–125, 140–141, 193
Cold War 197
Colville, Jock 6
Conquest, Robert 50
Counter-Intelligence Corps (CIC) 92
Couture, Emile 48
Crimea region 64, 134, 166
Crimean Tatars 166

D'Arcy, William Knox 34
Darlan, Admiral François 16
Dasch, George 22
De Gaulle, Brigadier-General Charles 73
De Portes, Hélène 46
Dobbs, Michael 49
Dohnanyi, Hans von 106
Donovan, William "Wild Bill" 35
Dovzhenko, Aleksandr 161
Downward, Percy 61–62, 164
Dreyfus, Goethe 89
Dutch national air carrier KLM 42

Index

Early, Stephen 2
Ebtehaj, Misbah 60–61, 70–71, 87–88, 92, 111, 116, 118, 122, 124, 130, 137, 146, 150–151, 162–163, 172, 176–177, 179, 183–184, 194
Eden, Anthony 186
Edward, Duke of Windsor 17
Eisenhower, General Dwight D. 16, 30, 192
Emmanuel III, Victor 8, 85
Eran (or land of the Aryans) 34
Ettel, Erwin 37–39, 60, 65–66, 69–72, 81, 89, 109, 122, 193
EUREKA Conference 119, 124, 141, 166

Fackenheim, Paul 93
Ferguson, Peter 61–62
"Final Solution" 72
Fitin, Pavel 144
Florian, Albert 39
Foxley (code name) 27
Frank, Hans 39
Fromm, General, Friedrich 8, 29

Gabcik, Josef 22
Gamotha, Roman 36–37, 57, 81, 89, 142, 179, 193
Gartenfeld, Karl-Edmund 143
Gerstdorff, Rudolf von 29
Giraud, Henri 15
Goebbels, Joseph 11–12, 14, 16, 24, 68, 72, 104, 123, 131, 133, 142
Gorechi 189–190
Goring, Reichsmarschall, Hermann 64–65, 75, 90
Gragazolou, Hussein 107
Gramaje, Faroukh 107
Gromyko, Andrei 14, 158

Hansen, Georg 59, 86–87, 194
Harriman, Averell 44–45, 120, 138, 167
Harriman, Kathleen 138, 175
Havas, Laslo 113–114, 116, 126, 136, 193
Heydrich, Reinhard 18–19, 20, 23, 68, 123
Himmler, Heinrich 42, 63, 67, 73, 97–98
Hindenburg, Field Marshal Paul von 193
Hitler, Gefreiter, (later Führer) Adolf 4, 11–14, 17, 20–21, 23, 27, 33, 63, 85, 87, 95, 97, 102, 104, 123, 128, 132, 168, 188, 192
Holmes, Bob 158
Holten-Pflug, Rudolf 129, 131, 146, 150, 163–165, 174, 176, 180, 184, 186–187, 191, 193
Hopkins, Harry 3–4, 186
Horthy, Miklós 30
Howard, Leslie 26, 28, 66, 73
Hull, Cordell 100, 120

Imperial Kingdom of Iran 32
Iran 2–3, 32, 34–37, 57–66, 69, 71–76, 79–84, 86–89, 92–94, 100–102, 106–110, 113–114, 124–130, 137–138, 144, 146, 155, 163–165, 181, 186, 188, 192

Jenke, Albert 112

Kaganovich, Lazar 50
Kahn, David 42
Kaltenbrunner, Obergruppenführer Ernst 67–68, 86–87, 90, 99, 121, 179, 194
Kamenev, Lev 48
Kapler, Aleksei 139
Karimi (Iranian interpreter) 164
Katyn Massacre 6–8, 15
Kaverin, Nikolai 171–173
Kavtaradze, Sergey 138
Keitel, Field Marshal Wilhelm 15
Kennedy administration 193
Kesselring, Field Marshal Albert 85
Khan, Ismail 62
Khan, Nasr 62–63, 82–83
Khatib, Yousef 191
Khrushchev, Nikita 138, 144
King, William Mackenzie 91
King Boris III of Bulgaria 29
King Edward VIII 17
King George VI 169
King Simeon II of Bulgaria 30
Kleist, Ludwig von 108
Kleist, Peter 123
KLM (Dutch national air carrier) 42
Klop, Dirk 40
Knox, Frank 25
Komissarov, Daniel 63
Kordt, Erich 17
Kotkin, Stephen 51
Kovalska, Ida 62
Kramer, Karl-Heinz 91
Kubis, Jan 22
Kubizek, August 12
Kulikov, Anatoly 24
Kunt, Furkan 172–173
Kupferstein, Jakob 147–148
Kurmis, Martin 83–84, 86
Kursk (Russia) 8, 23, 79–80, 90, 128
Kuznetsov, Nikolai (Siebert) 108–109, 113, 121, 133, 140, 144

Lahousen-Viremont, Erwin 15, 114–115
Lakoba, Nestor 25
Lawrence, T.E. 82
League of German Girls 70
Leverkuehn, Paul 81
Lukin, Alexandr 147

Index

Manhattan Project 10
Manstein, Field Marshal Erich von 23–24, 80
Manure, Forest 177
Marcelle (code word) 108
Marshall, General George C. 181
Martin, John 3
Mayr, Franz 36–37, 57–58, 69, 74, 81, 89, 92–93, 122, 129
Melliyun-I-Iran 88
Merser, Ernst 58–62, 74, 81, 99, 107, 109, 111, 114, 116, 118, 122–124, 128, 130–131, 136, 140, 143, 146–152, 154, 156, 162–166, 172–174, 176–177, 180–182, 186, 190, 193
Metaxas, Ioannis 29
Mikhoels, Solomon 50, 140
Miklas, Wilhelm 75
Mikoyan, Anastas 138
Molotov, Vyacheslav 100, 111, 138, 157, 174, 186
Molotov, Polina 111
Montgomery, Field Marshal Bernard L. 7, 31, 61
Moran, Charles 169, 195
Morde, Theodore 157
Morrell, Theo 76
Mors, Harald 103
Moyzisch, Ludwig 112, 113, 119, 121, 125, 141
Mueller, Josef 43
Musa 92
Mussolini, Benito 84–86, 97–98, 103–104

Naujocks, Alfred 40
Nazmiyeh (Iranian law enforcement) 126, 132
NKVD (People's Commissariat of Internal Affairs) 21, 25, 50, 108–109, 127, 133, 136, 162, 173, 190–191
Nuremberg trials 4

Oberg, Winifred 59, 81, 99, 107, 116–119–122, 136–137, 140–141, 150, 152, 163, 183, 193
OGPU (United States Political Administration) Soviet state security agency 173
Ohnesorge, Wilhelm 21, 40–41
Operation Barbarossa 164, 168
Operation Bernhard 57
Operation Franz 82–84, 86, 88, 30
Operation Long Jump 96, 116, 118, 122, 125–128, 130, 135, 140–141, 150, 152, 164–165, 172–173, 179, 181, 184, 191, 193, 195
Operation Oak 104, 110
Operation Overlord 120–121, 167, 178, 181, 192–191

Operation Panzerfaust 30
Operation Pastorius 21
Operation Rosselsprung 17
Operation Salaam 41
Oster, Hans 42–43, 106

Pahlavi, Mohammad Reza (Shah of Iran) 32–35, 37, 62, 101, 126, 147, 153, 162, 179, 188, 194
Papen, Franz von 157
Parthian Kingdom 34
Pauker, Karl 48–51
Paulus, Field Marshal Friedrich 55, 139
Peacock Realm 126
Pearl Harbor (US) 6
Perkins, Frances 77
Persianate State 34
Pétain, Philippe 16
Pfuhlstein, Alexander von 41–42
Plettenberg, Graefin Elisabeth von 105
Pollack, Wanda 62
Pope Pius XII 27
Pourbaix, Paul 113–114
Pownall, Sir Henry 71
Prokofiev, Sergei 100

Qavam, Ahmad 128
Quadrant (code word) 92
Quandt, Harald 72
Quenzgut sabotage school 18, 36, 63, 65, 68–70, 81, 97, 99, 107, 129, 131, 135, 165

Rauff, Walter 88
Razaee, Bijan 88
Razaee, Farah 88
Reich Security Administration (RSHA) 37, 106
Reilly, Mike 53, 54–55, 77, 146, 154, 158, 166, 168, 172, 179–180, 194
Repubblica di Salo (Italian Socialist Republic) 104
Ribbentrop, Erwin 13, 17, 119
Riga operation 51
Ritter von Greim, Robert 65
Rohm, Ernst 59, 99
Rommel, Field Marshal Erwin 84–85
Roosevelt, Eleanor 53
Roosevelt, Elliott 168, 170
Roosevelt, Franklin Delano 1–2, 4–7, 9–11, 31, 44, 45, 54, 77–78, 92, 95–96, 100, 110, 115, 121, 124, 134, 147, 154–155, 157–160, 167–172, 174–175, 178, 181–182, 185, 188–189, 192, 195
Rosamund, John 28
Rose (code word) 55
Rosenman, Sam 7

Royal Scots Fusiliers 120
RSHA (Reich Security Administration) 37, 106
Russian 5th Shock Army 24
Ryutin, Martemyan 50

Sachsenhausen prison camp 84, 97, 130
Sadr, Muhsin 93
Safavid Empire 34
Sagi, Aragh 117
Sakht Sar 101
Salomon, Horst 60, 62, 81
Schellenberg, Walter 3–4, 17, 20–21, 23, 35–41, 51, 57–59, 63, 67–69, 73–76, 80–82, 85–87, 92, 94, 96–97, 99, 102, 105–107, 109–110, 112–113, 115, 119–121, 124–130, 132, 136, 140–142, 145–146, 154, 156, 165, 172, 176, 179, 187, 194
Schirach, Baldur von 90
Schirach, Henriette von 90
Schnabel, Joseph 18, 99, 117–118, 122, 132, 193
Schoellhorn, Lothar 143–144, 165, 174, 176, 180, 193
Schroeder, Christa 24
Schulenburg, Friedrich-Werner Graf von der 24
Schulze-Holthus, Julius 32, 35, 60, 62, 65, 69, 81, 83–84, 88–89, 130–131
Scots Fusiliers (Royal) 120
Shahrokh, Shah Bahram 107
Shkvarzev, Vladimir 126–127, 140, 174
Shostakovich, Dmitri 100
Siebert, Paul (aka Kuznetsov) 108, 121, 133, 135–136, 140, 142–143, 152, 164, 179, 184
Simeon II (King of Bulgaria) 30
Skorzeny, Obersturmbannführer Otto 30, 75–76, 81–82, 85, 93, 102–104, 107, 109, 114–115, 117, 127–128, 146, 194
Soames, Mary 44
Spitzy, Reinhard 81
Stalin, Chairman of the Council of Ministers of USSR Joseph 2, 6–7, 14–15, 20–21, 44–45, 48–49, 51, 78, 91–92, 95–97, 100, 111, 120, 123–124, 134, 138–140, 143, 152–153, 158–161, 167–172, 174–175, 177–178, 180–182, 185–186, 189, 192–193, 195
Stalin, Svetlana 25, 139, 195
Stalin, Vasily 138, 168, 174
Stauffenberg, Colonel Claus von 29, 81

Stevens, Richard 40
Suckley, Margaret "Daisy" 53
Sword of Honour (award) 170

Tehran *passim* 34, 113, 129–130, 140–141, 156
Thompson, Walter 45–48, 77–78, 115, 155, 166, 168, 172, 180, 192, 194
Tito, Josip Broz 17
Tresca, Carlo 53
Tresckow, General Henning von 28–29
Truman, Harry S. 31, 192, 195
Tshombe, Moise 193
Turkey (Türkiye) 105, 141

Ukraine 13, 23, 78, 88, 108, 140, 161
Umayyad Caliphate 34
Unternehmen Weitsprung 110, 179

Valkyrie affair 29
Vartanian, Gevork 162, 179, 184
Vatican 8
Venlo Incident 40
Vermehren, Erich 105–106
Vlasik, Nikolai 51–53, 79, 78, 123, 152, 166, 173–174, 191
Vlasov, Andrey 24
von Geldern-Crispendorf, Karl-Theodor Franz Heinz 60, 81
von Ortel, Hans 107–109, 113, 121–122, 129, 132, 135, 140, 142, 148, 150–151, 179, 193
von Pfuhlstein, Alexander 41–42
von Plettenberg, Graefin Elisabeth 105
Voroshilov, Kliment 167, 169–170
Vozhd 13

Wallace, Henry 195–196
Wegner, Gustav 139
Weinrich, Carl 39
Weygand, General Maxime 15
Wolff, Karl 27
Wollheim, Mervyn 177, 179, 184
Wulff, Hans 137

Yamamoto, Marshal Admiral Isoroku 25–26
Yusuf, Kel 130

Zeitzler, Kurt 56
Zeppelin (code word) 74
Zinoviev, Grigori 48

www.ingramcontent.com/pod-product-compliance
Lightning Source LLC
Chambersburg PA
CBHW032042300426
44117CB00009B/1154